Growing up and Getting old
in Ancient Egypt

Cover illustrations:
Front: A chief workman of the necropolis and his wife, accompanied by their three granddaughters and a small grandson, receive an offering. From the Theban tomb of Anherkhew the Younger (TT 359), Twentieth Dynasty (Photograph by Rosalind Janssen).
Back: The family of the workman Pashedu preceded by his white haired father and greying mother. From the Theban tomb of Pashedu (TT 3), Nineteenth Dynasty (Photograph courtesy of Dr. Alain-Pierre Zivie).

Dedicated to

Dr I.E.S. Edwards
(1909-1996)

The Nestor of British Egyptology

and to our friend Philip Wickens

in affection and esteem

Golden House Publications

© Rosalind M. & Jac. J. Janssen

Printed by
Biddles
24 Rollesby Road Hardwick Industrial Estate King's Lynn
Norfolk
PE30 4LS

London 2007
ISBN 978-0-9550256-9-3

Contents

viii

List of Illustrations

17. Children's jewellery: (a) electrum side-lock pendant. Unprovenanced, Middle Kingdom. Both sides, scale 1:1 (Fitzwilliam Museum Cambridge EGA 155.1947); (b) gold catfish hair ornament. From tomb 72 at Haraga, Twelfth Dynasty. Scale 1:1 (National Museums of Scotland, Edinburgh 1914.1079; drawing and © Christiane Müller-Hazenbos).

18. Nefer, with his pet dog, accompanied by his nude daughter who clutches a lapwing. From the mastaba of Nefer at Saqqara, Fifth Dynasty (After Moussa and Altenmüller, *The Tomb of Nefer and Ka-hay*, 1971, plate 2).

19. Children's toys: (above) left and right, painted reed and linen balls. Unprovenanced, Roman Period; (centre) blue faience tops. From the Faiyum, Roman Period; (below) wooden feline with crystal eyes and a moveable jaw fitted with bronze teeth. From Thebes, New Kingdom (EA 46709-10; 34920-21; 15671. Courtesy of the Trustees of the British Museum).

20. Painted wooden doll with moveable arms. She originally had a wig of mud beads. From tomb 58 at Hawara, Twelfth Dynasty (UC 16148. Courtesy of the Petrie Museum of Egyptian Archaeology, University College London).

21. In a kitchen hut one man is at work while his companion, who is eating, orders a boy to run an errand. The hieroglyphs give the lad's answer: "I'll do it". From the tomb of Pepiankh (A2) at Meir, Sixth Dynasty (After Blackman and Apted, *The Rock Tombs of Meir*, V, 1953, plate XXX).

22. A boy and a girl threatened by an irate doorkeeper while their nanny drinks from a jar. Part of a scene in which a lady is received by the Pharaoh Ay in the palace gardens. From the Theban tomb of Neferhotep (TT 49), Eighteenth Dynasty (After Davies, *The Tomb of Nefer-hotep at Thebes*, I, 1931, plate XIV).

23. Boys' games: (a) star game; (b) balancing act. From the mastaba of Ptah-hotep at Saqqara, Fifth Dynasty (After Touny and Wenig, *Der Sport im Alten Ägypten*, 1969, figure 32).

24. Boys' games: (a) *khazza lawizza*; (b) ?stampers. From the mastaba of Ptahhotep at Saqqara, Fifth Dynasty (After Touny and Wenig, *Der Sport im Alten Ägypten*, 1969, figure 34).

25. Painted limestone group statuette of a boy and a girl playing. From the tomb of Ny-kau-inpu at Giza, Fifth to Sixth Dynasty (OI 10639. Courtesy of the Oriental Institute of the University of Chicago).

26. Painted limestone ostracon showing a mouse juggling with two balls. From Deir el-Medina, New Kingdom (MM 14 048. Courtesy of the Medelhavsmuseet, Stockholm).

27. Painted limestone relief: (centre register) left, a fertility dance; right, the 'hut game'. From ?Giza, late Fifth to early Sixth Dynasty (After James, *Hieroglyphic Texts from Egyptian Stelae, etc.*, I, 2nd ed., 1961, plate XXV; now British Museum EA 994).

28. Black granite statue of an anonymous high official in the attitude of a scribe. From Saqqara, Fifth Dynasty (AST 31. Courtesy of the Rijksmuseum van Oudheden, Leiden).

29. Limestone block statue of the High Priest of Amun Bekenkhons inscribed with an autobiographical text. From Thebes, Nineteenth Dynasty (Gl. WAF 38. Courtesy of the Staatliches Museum Ägyptischer Kunst, Munich).

30. Pierced limestone schoolboy's writing board with six horizontal lines of hieratic text comprising a letter exchanged between two scribes exhorting the scribal profession. From Abydos, Twentieth Dynasty (E. 580. Courtesy of the Musées Royaux d'Art et d'Histoire, Brussels).

31. A high official followed by his apprentice son who carries a papyrus roll and a writing tablet. From the Theban tomb of Djeserkareseneb (TT 38), Eighteenth Dynasty (After Davies, *Scenes from Some Theban Tombs*, 1963, plate II).
32. The wife of a mayor of Thebes seated beside her husband, with a palette and a scribal kit bag below her chair. From the Theban tomb of Kenamun (TT 162), Eighteenth Dynasty (After Davies, *Scenes from Some Theban Tombs*, 1963, plate XVI).
33. Limestone ostracon with the names of Amenhotep I in cartouches, placed over the hieroglyphic sign for gold. (a) The recto written by the master; (b) the verso copied by a pupil. From Deir el-Medina, New Kingdom (MM 14 116. Courtesy of the Medelhavsmuseet, Stockholm).
34. Pottery ostracon inscribed in black ink with practice drawings of standard figures by a sculptor's pupil. From Deir el-Medina, New Kingdom (After Page, *Ancient Egyptian Figured Ostraca*, 1983, Cat. No. 81; now UC 33241).
35. Circumcision scene: right, the preparation; left, the operation itself. From the mastaba of Ankhmahor at Saqqara, Sixth Dynasty (After Badawy, *The Tomb of Nyhetep-Ptah at Giza and the Tomb of 'Ankh-m'ahor at Saqqara*, 1978, figure 27).
36. Circumcision of royal children. From the Horus chapel in the Mut Temple at Karnak, Eighteenth Dynasty (After Bailey, *Bulletin of the Australian Centre for Egyptology 7*, 1996, figure 3; drawing and © Amalthea Leung).
37. Wooden statue of Meryrehashtef as a young adult, clearly showing circumcision. From tomb 274 at Sedment, Sixth Dynasty (ÆIN 1560. Courtesy of the Ny Carlsberg Glyptotek, Copenhagen).
38. The conscription of recruits for the army. From the Theban tomb of Tjanuny (TT 74), Eighteenth Dynasty (After Champollion, *Monuments*, II, 1845, plate CLVII).
39. Painted limestone statue of Ra-maat wearing the gala-kilt with knotted band. From Giza, early Sixth Dynasty (PM 420. Courtesy of the Roemer- und Pelizaeus-Museum, Hildesheim).
40. A bride at her wedding celebrations. From Western Thebes, 1989 (Courtesy of Mr. John Mellors).
41. Limestone stela of Paneb who (above) adores a coiled serpent, doubtless Mertseger, the goddess of the Theban necropolis; (below) three of his descendants, including (right) his son Opakhte. From Deir el-Medina, Nineteenth Dynasty (EA 272. Courtesy of the Trustees of the British Museum).
42. Figure of Khaemwaset in its naos. Unprovenanced. Now lost, but in the early Eighteenth Century A.D. housed in a private collection in London (From Gordon, *An Essay Towards Explaining the Hieroglyphical Figures on the Coffin of the Ancient Mummy Belonging to Capt. William Lethieullier*, 1737, plate V).
43. Kenamun's mother nurses Amenhotep II. From the Theban tomb of Kenamun (TT 93), Eighteenth Dynasty (After Davies, *The Tomb of Ken-Amun at Thebes*, 1930, plate IX).
44. Paheri with his pupil Prince Wadzmose on his lap. From the tomb of Paheri at el-Kab, Eighteenth Dynasty (After Tylor and Griffith, *The Tomb of Paheri at El Kab*, 1894, plate IV).
45. Black granite statue of Senenmut holding the Princess Neferure. She wears a false beard equating her with the young Theban god Khonsu. From Thebes, Eighteenth Dynasty (EA 174. Courtesy of the Trustees of the British Museum).
46. Heqareshu with four princes on his lap. From Theban tomb 226, Eighteenth Dynasty (After Davies, *The Tombs of Menkheperrasonb, Amenmosĕ, and Another*, 1933, plate XXX).

47. The sportive king: (a) Min gives an archery lesson to Prince Amenhotep. From the Theban tomb of Min (TT 109), Eighteenth Dynasty (After Davies, *Bulletin of the Metropolitan Museum of Art*, Nov. 1935, figure 7); (b) Red granite block showing Amenhotep II shooting at a copper target. From Karnak, Eighteenth Dynasty (After Bothmer, *The Luxor Museum Catalogue*, 1979, figure 53; now Luxor Museum J. 129).

48. Wrestling and single-stick fighting: (a) From the First Court of the Medinet Habu Temple, Twentieth Dynasty (After *Medinet Habu* II = *Later Historical Records of Ramesses III*, 1932, plate 111); (b) At Abydos, A.D. 1901 (Photograph by Margaret Murray. Courtesy of the Petrie Museum of Egyptian Archaeology, University College London).

49. Ramesses III chucks his daughter under her chin. From the Eastern High Gate of the Medinet Habu Temple, Twentieth Dynasty (After *Medinet Habu* VIII = *The Eastern High Gate*, 1970, plate 639).

50. White sandstone stela of the Viceroy Usersatet. From the second cataract fortress of Semna, Eighteenth Dynasty (MFA 25.632. Courtesy of the Museum of Fine Arts, Boston).

51. Grey granite and limestone colossal statue of Ramesses II with the falcon god Hurun. From Tanis, Nineteenth Dynasty (JE 64735. Courtesy of the Egyptian Museum, Cairo).

52. Opaque red moulded glass inlay showing two young Amarna princesses. From el-Amarna, Eighteenth Dynasty (UC 2235. Courtesy of the Petrie Museum of Egyptian Archaeology, University College London).

53. Limestone ostracon depicting an out of breath elderly workman cutting into the rock. From Deir el-Medina, Ramesside Period (EGA.4324.1943. Reproduction by permission of the Syndics of the Fitzwilliam Museum, Cambridge).

54. The elderly Sennefer holding a stick. From the Theban tomb of Sennefer (TT 96), Eighteenth Dynasty (after Desroches Noblecourt *et al.*, *Sen-nefer. Die Grabkammer des Bürgermeisters von Theben*, 1986, p. 74).

55. An old man combing flax. From the tomb of Paheri at el-Kab, Eighteenth Dynasty (after Tylor and Griffith, *The Tomb of Paheri at El Kab*, 1894, plate III).

56. The Satirical-Erotic Papyrus: a girl attempts to seduce an exhausted man lying under her bed. From Deir el-Medina, New Kingdom (after Omlin, *Der Papyrus 55001 und seine Satirisch-erotischen Zeichnungen und Inschriften*, 1973, plate XIII; now Turin 55001).

57. Two figures of Khentika on both sides of the entrance doorway of his tomb. From the mastaba of Khentika at Saqqara, Sixth Dynasty (after James, *The Mastaba of Khentika called Ikhekhi*, 1953, plate VII).

58. A naked pot-bellied old man chats to a shipwright. From the tomb of Ukhhotep (B2) at Meir, Twelfth Dynasty (after Blackman, *The Rock Tombs of Meir*, II, 1915, plate IV).

59. Painted limestone relief of an anonymous aged official with a close-up of the face. From ?Saqqara, transitional Eighteenth/Nineteenth Dynasty (47.120.1, Charles Edwin Wilbour Fund. Courtesy of the Brooklyn Museum, New York).

60. A naked elderly labourer carrying a bundle of papyrus stems. From the Theban tomb of Puyemre (TT 39), Eighteenth Dynasty (after Davies, *The Tomb of Puyemrê at Thebes*, I, 1922, plate XIX).

61. Black granite head of an elderly man. From the Temple of Mut at Karnak, Twenty-Fifth Dynasty or ?Middle Kingdom (UC 16451. Courtesy of the Petrie Museum of Egyptian Archaeology, University College London).

62. The relatives of the workman Pashedu and his wife. First register: his family; second register: her family; third register: their children. From the Theban tomb of Pashedu (TT 3), Nineteenth Dynasty (Courtesy of Dr. Alain-Pierre Zivie).

63. Limestone statuette of an undernourished potter squatting at his wheel. From the mastaba of Nikauinpu at Giza, Fifth to Sixth Dynasty (OI 10628. Courtesy of the Oriental Institute of the University of Chicago).
64. Skeleton of Idu II lying in his cedar coffin. From the mastaba of Idu II at Giza, Sixth Dynasty (PM 2639/2511. Courtesy of the Roemer- und Pelizaeus-Museum, Hildesheim).
65. Skeletons of elderly women, each accompanied by a pot. From a Predynastic Cemetery at Naga ed-Deir: (a) Tomb N 7140; (b) Tomb N 7081 (after Lythgoe, *The Predynastic Cemetery N 7000: Naga-ed-Dêr*, IV, 1965, figures 17f and 33i).
66. The third entry of the houselist when Snefru was head of the family. From Kahun, Thirteenth Dynasty (UC 32163. Courtesy of the Petrie Museum of Egyptian Archaeology, University College London).
67. Two clusters of houses in the Southern zone of el-Amarna. Nos. N 49.9 and N 50.29 (after Borchardt and Ricke, *Die Wohnhäuser in Tell el-Amarna*, 1980, plan 73).
68. Group of old men sitting in the shade. West Bank of Luxor, 1996 (Photograph by Rosalind Janssen).
69. The lower half of the Second Kamose stela depicting the overseer of the seal Neshi, the ancestor of Mose. From Karnak, late Seventeenth Dynasty (Photograph courtesy of the late Dr. Labib Habachi; now Luxor Museum J.43).
70 Limestone *akh iqer en Re* stela of Dhutimose. From Deir el-Medina, Twentieth Dynasty (UC 14228. Courtesy of the Petrie Museum of Egyptian Archaeology, University College London).
71. Wooden anthropoid busts: (a) with short hair. From tomb 136 at Sedment, Eighteenth Dynasty (UC 16554. Courtesy of the Petrie Museum of Egyptian Archaeology, University College London); (b) with tripartite wig. Unprovenanced, New Kingdom (UC 16550. Courtesy of the Petrie Museum of Egyptian Archaeology, University College London).
72. Funerary procession: four men carry a canopic shrine on a sledge (right), two men with anthropoid busts (centre), followed by a man with a mummy mask and a necklace (left). From the Theban tomb of Haremhab (TT 78), Eighteenth Dynasty (after Brack and Brack, *Das Grab des Haremheb. Theben Nr. 78*, 1980, plate 61c).
73. Pottery dish inscribed on the interior with a Letter to the Dead. From tomb Y84 at Hu, First Intermediate Period (UC 16244. Courtesy of the Petrie Museum of Egyptian Archaeology, University College London).
74. Painted wooden statuette of Ankhiry against the Letter to the Dead. From Saqqara, Nineteenth Dynasty (AH 115 and AMS 64. Courtesy of the Rijksmuseum van Oudheden, Leiden).
75. Blind harper. From the Theban tomb of Neferhotep (TT 50), late Eighteenth Dynasty (after Hari, *La tombe thébaine du père divin Neferhotep (TT 50)*, 1985, plate IV).
76. Head of a limestone block statue of the High Priest of Amun Bekenkhons. From Thebes, Nineteenth Dynasty (G1.WAF 38. Courtesy of the Staatliches Museum Ägyptischer Kunst, Munich).
77. Limestone statue of the chamberlain Antef. H. 65 cm. From Abydos, Twelfth Dynasty (EA 461. Courtesy of the Trustees of the British Museum).
78. Wooden cubit-rod of Amenemope. From Saqqara, late Eighteenth Dynasty (Turin Inv. Cat. 6347. Courtesy of the Museo Egizio, Turin).
79. Limestone stela of Amenysonb. From Abydos, Thirteenth Dynasty (Louvre C 11. Photo Chuzeville. Courtesy of the Musée du Louvre/DAE, Paris).

80. Hieroglyphic signs: (a) for elderly and old age, clearly distinguished from (b) that for an upright dignitary (after Gardiner's Sign List); (c) picture of an old woman once used in writing the feminine word for old age. From the mastaba of Ti at Saqqara, Fifth Dynasty (after Steindorff, *Das Grab des Ti*, 1913, plate 51).

81. Women bringing the revenue of Nubia to the Viceroy Huy. One of them, with white hair, is leaning on a stick. From the Theban tomb of Huy (TT 40), Eighteenth Dynasty (after Davies and Gardiner, *The Tomb of Huy, Viceroy of Nubia in the Reign of Tut'ankhamun (No. 40)*, 1927, plate XVI).

82. Wooden figure of a standing man holding a *medu*-staff. From Saqqara, Sixth Dynasty (PM 1106. Courtesy of the Roemer- und Pelizaeus-Museum, Hildesheim).

83. Wooden staves of Senebtisi. From the tomb of Senebtisi at el-Lisht, Thirteenth Dynasty (after Hayes, *The Scepter of Egypt*, I, 1953, figure 187).

84. Representation of Hetepherakhet on the right side of the entrance to his mastaba-chapel. His eldest son, pictured as a boy, is clinging to his staff. From Saqqara, Fifth Dynasty (F 1904/3.1. Courtesy of the Rijksmuseum van Oudheden, Leiden).

85. Rock relief of Montuhotep II and his mother Ioh faced by the "god's father" King Antef and the chancellor Khety. From Wadi Shatt er-Rigal, Eleventh Dynasty (after Petrie, *Ten Years Digging in Egypt*, 1893, figure 56).

86. Diorite statue of Senenmut carrying the Princess Neferure. From Karnak, Eighteenth Dynasty (Inv. Nr. 173800. Courtesy of the Field Museum of Natural History, Chicago).

87. Heqareshu with Tuthmosis IV in full regalia on his lap. From Theban tomb 226, Eighteenth Dynasty (after Newberry, *Journal of Egyptian Archaeology* 14, 1928, plate XII).

88. Ay shows off his new red gloves, a reward from Akhenaten and Nefertiti. From the tomb of Ay at el-Amarna, Eighteenth Dynasty (after Davies, *The Rock Tombs of El Amarna*, VI, 1908, plate XXX).

89. Relief of Hesysunebef with a pet monkey, on the side of a fragmentary seated statue of Neferhotep and his wife Ubekht. From the Theban tomb of Neferhotep (TT 216), Nineteenth Dynasty (after Bruyère, *Rapport sur les fouilles de Deir el Médineh (1923-1924)*, 1925, figure 1 on p. 41).

90. Mery-aa and his wives: (above) Mery-aa himself with his ?first wife Isi; (below) his five other wives. From the tomb of Mery-aa at el-Hagarseh, Ninth Dynasty (after Petrie, *Athribis*, 1908, plate VII).

91. Djau stands face-to-face with his father Djau/Shemay, who holds a *medu*-staff. From the tomb of Djau at Deir el-Gebrawi, Sixth Dynasty (after Davies, *The Rock Tombs of Deir El Gebrâwi*, II, 1902, plate X).

92. Limestone ostracon relating the charity shown by a man to a divorced woman. From Deir el-Medina, Twentieth Dynasty (UC 19614. Courtesy of the Petrie Museum of Egyptian Archaeology, University College London).

93. Limestone statue of Maya wearing the 'gold of honour'. From ?Akhmim, Eighteenth Dynasty (Inv. Nr. 19286. Courtesy of the Ägyptisches Museum und Papyrussammlung, Berlin).

94. Anhermose dressed as High Priest. From the tomb of Anhermose at el-Mashayikh, Nineteenth Dynasty (after Ockinga and al-Masri, *Two Ramesside Tombs at El Mashayikh*, I, 1988, plate 53).

95. Nebamun (left) receives his appointment to police chief from the royal scribe Iuny. From the Theban tomb of Nebamun (TT 90), Eighteenth Dynasty (after Davies, *The Tombs of Two Officials of Tuthmosis the Fourth (Nos. 75 and 90)*, 1923, plate XXVI).

96. King Neuserre carried in the Upper Egyptian palanquin. From the Sun-Temple of Neuserre at Abu Ghurab, Fifth Dynasty (after Von Bissing and Kees, *Das Re-Heiligtum des Königs Ne-Woser-Re*, II, *Die kleine Festdarstellung*, 1923, plate II).

97. Limestone lintel depicting the Sed Festival of Sesostris III. From the Temple of Montu at Medamud, Twelfth Dynasty (after Lange and Hirmer, *Egypt*, 1956, plates 102-103; now Egyptian Museum, Cairo JE 56497).

98. Limestone block depicting Amenhotep III running the ceremonial course before Amen-Re. From the Open Air Museum at Karnak, Eighteenth Dynasty (Photograph by Rosalind Janssen).

99 Travertine ('Egyptian alabaster') statuette of Pepy I. From Saqqara, Sixth Dynasty (39.120. Courtesy of the Brooklyn Museum, New York).

100. Limestone statue of Montuhotep II Nebhetepre in his *Heb-sed* garb. From the causeway of the Montuhotep Temple at Deir el-Bahri, Eleventh Dynasty (Photograph by Rosalind Janssen).

101. Limestone unfinished triad identified in the 1990's as Amenhotep III, Teye, and Beketaten. From el-Amarna, Eighteenth Dynasty (UC 004. Courtesy of the Petrie Museum of Egyptian Archaeology, University College London).

102. Ramesses III: (a) face of granite standard-bearing statue. From the Karnak cachette, Twentieth Dynasty (CG 42150. Courtesy of the Egyptian Museum, Cairo); (b) head of his mummy. From the Deir el-Bahri cache, Twentieth Dynasty. (CG 61083. After Elliot Smith, *The Royal Mummies*, 1912, plate LI; photograph courtesy of Mr. Robert Partridge).

103. Limestone statue of the elderly Vizier Hemiunu. From the mastaba of Hemiunu at Giza, Fourth Dynasty (PM 1962. Courtesy of the Roemer- und Pelizaeus-Museum, Hildesheim).

104. Diagram of a reconstructed chapel. Abydos, Middle Kingdom (after a line drawing by David O'Connor in Simpson, *The Terrace of the Great God at Abydos*, 1974, figure 2 on p. 7).

105. Limestone stela of Ikhernofret framed by a raised border. From the tomb-chapel of Ikhernofret at Abydos, Twelfth Dynasty (Inv. Nr. 1204. Courtesy of the Ägyptisches Museum und Papyrussammlung, Berlin).

106. Khaemwaset: (a) upper part of a yellow limestone statuette ?of this prince. Unprovenanced, Nineteenth Dynasty (MFA 72.716. Courtesy of the Museum of Fine Arts, Boston. Hay Collection, Gift of C. Granville Way, 1872); (b) black steatite headless shabti. ?From the tomb of Khaemwaset at Saqqara, Nineteenth Dynasty (UC 2311. Courtesy of the Petrie Museum of Egyptian Archaeology, University College London).

107. Limestone headrest decorated with fabulous creatures. From the tomb of Qenhikhopshef at Deir el-Medina, Nineteenth Dynasty (EA 63783. Courtesy of the Trustees of the British Museum).

108. Green basalt naophorous statue of Udjahorresnet. H. 69 cm. Head and hands modern. From Sais, Twenty-Seventh Dynasty (Inv. nr. 196. Courtesy of the Museo Gregoriano Egizio).

109. Margaret Murray, aged sixty-eight, wearing her doctoral robes of 1931 (Courtesy of Miss Margaret Drower).

110. Margaret Murray, aged ninety-seven, on the steps of the portico at University College London, 1960 (Courtesy of the Petrie Museum of Egyptian Archaeology, University College London).

111. Margaret Murray reading her citation at her hundredth birthday celebration at University College London, July 1963 (Courtesy of The Times Newspapers Ltd.).

112. Map of Egypt and the Fayum, showing the sites mentioned in the text and the captions.

113. Detailed map of Thebes and Nubia, showing the sites mentioned in the text and the captions.

Acknowledgements

We wish to express our gratitude to the many museum curators and the one private individual who have provided photographs, in many cases gratis, and permission for their publication. Each institution is fully credited in the List of Illustrations. Mr. Peter Harrison and his staff of the Central Photographic Unit, University College London, deserve the highest praise for the habitual skill with which they have produced our other photographs. The line drawings are the painstaking work of Juanita Homan.

Visits to the Museum of Childhood at Bethnal Green, London, were a source of joy and inspiration to us.

To Anthea Page and Juanita Homan, the Editors of The Rubicon Press, we express our sincere thanks for their ever willing help, lively interest, and continuous encouragement.

Finally, it is not usual to thank one's co-author, especially when that person happens to be a spouse, for stimulation and support. But in view of the fact that this book came to be written during our first year of marriage, perhaps it is not so very surprising that we should wish to do so!

The present revision of Part I has taken place in our sixteenth year of married life. We owe an enormous debt to our friend Philip Wickens, Honorary Secretary of the Thames Valley Ancient Egypt Society (TVAES), who has scanned the original text. Katherine Griffis also helped with the scanning of Part I, and Amalthea Leung drew our new figure 36. Wolfram Grajetzki of Golden House Publications has seen the entire volume through to its appearance under the title: *Growing up and Getting old in Ancient Egypt*.

Preface

The title of Part I of this book is borrowed from Hamed Ammar's classic study *Growing up in an Egyptian Village* (London, 1954). Whereas he, however, originated from the village which he describes (namely Silwa, midway between Kom Ombo and Edfu) and could base his account on his own memories as well as on lengthy discussions with his informants from that community, we were wholly dependent upon written sources and objects that have by chance survived. Moreover, whereas his aim was sociological and educational, ours was purely historical. We did not search for general theories, instead we wanted to understand one individual case: the Ancient Egyptian civilization from a particular aspect, that of the child and childhood. Suffice it to say that the pages that follow totally refute the thesis promoted by Philipe Ariès in his classic account: *Centuries of Childhood* (1960). He argues that a period of childhood did not occur as a separate entity until the Sixteenth Century A.D.!

So far as we are aware, this was in its earlier edition of 1990 the first book on the subject. It is conspicuous in this respect that still in 1998 an Egyptologist could write: "how little our archaeological and textual sources tell us about childhood in Ancient Egypt". Of course there exist many articles, and even some more extensive studies, on specific features of the younger generation in the Nile Valley, but only one larger and fundamental publication has as yet appeared. That is Professor Erika Feucht's book *Das Kind im Alten Ägypten. Die Stellung des Kindes in Familie und Gesellschaft nach altägyptischen Texten und Darstellungen* (Frankfurt/New York, 1995), which is an updated and enlarged edition of the author's Habilitationsschrift of 1981. It is a highly scientific work of over 600 pages, mainly intended for professional Egyptologists. The last chapter, for instance, deals extensively with fifteen Ancient Egyptian words for child, a valuable philological study presenting much interesting evidence, but too technical for the general reader. The present volume, however, is written for the general public, although it is based on scientific studies, several of which are quoted in the bibliography.

In a review of the first impression in the *Journal of Egyptian Archaeology* (vol. 80, 1994) Gay Robins uttered some mild criticism of a few details. Some of them induced us either to small corrections or minor additions in the present edition. Her main complaint, that we did not present notes with references to the scientific works on which our book was based, did not convince us. As we wrote in the original Preface to the volume on Old Age (Part II below):

xvii

"Our colleagues should not need them; they are capable of recognizing our sources themselves, while lay people would hardly enjoy them, even if they could ever track down these studies". Although the bibliography is here slightly enlarged, mainly with the titles of books and articles which have appeared after the first impression was published, we still adhere to our former opinion.

As regards the translations from Egyptian texts, scholars will immediately see that many are taken from those three invaluable volumes of Miriam Lichtheim, *Ancient Egyptian Literature* (Berkeley, 1973-1980), although with slight alterations where they seemed necessary for our purpose. The sources for other quotations are generally familiar to every Egyptologist. We have throughout adapted them to the style of our book, avoiding as far as possible the specific 'translator's language' found in scientific studies.

In our choice of illustrations we have attempted to steer clear of pictures and objects that are common in popular works on Ancient Egypt. In some chapters that was easy, the material being abundant; in others we could not completely escape from the well-known. Yet, all our photographs and line drawings were chosen because they illustrate some part of the text, even where the objects or representations were in themselves far from aesthetically pleasing.

Of course, we hope that the reader will enjoy this not so common study on particular aspects of Egyptian civilization, and that he or she will thereby broaden his/her knowledge. We suspect that no one, however, will learn as much from it as we ourselves have. This means that writing this book, although 'work' to us, at no time threatened to become a chore, and was mostly a pastime of the utmost satisfaction.

Composing this second edition was a particular pleasure to the authors. If, as we hope will be the case, the reader also enjoys the volume, then we have succeeded in our aim. That writing together as a married couple sometimes causes minor frictions in daily life will be readily understood, but our paramount feeling now that the second impression is completed is still one of happiness and mutual affection.

February 1990   Rosalind and Jac. Janssen
Revised July 2005

Part I: Growing up

1 Pregnancy and Birth

Both myths and stories from Ancient Egypt reveal some bizarre ideas about conception. The sky goddess Nut, for instance, was believed to swallow the sun every evening at dusk in order to give birth to it anew every dawn morning. In the New Kingdom *Story of the Two Brothers* the hero Bata is transformed into a tree. When this tree is felled at the request of the Queen, Bata's ex-wife, a splinter flies into her mouth. She immediately becomes pregnant and, many days later, she gives birth to a son. Yet, such miraculous narratives do not reflect the everyday notions of the Egyptians, no more than that the Greeks really believed a child could be born from its father's head, as Athena was from Zeus.

More realistic remarks are contained in other stories. For example, in the New Kingdom composition *Truth and Falsehood* a lady espies a blind tramp who had been found under a thicket, and she desires him since he is handsome. "He slept with her that night, and knew her with the knowledge of a man, and she conceived a son that night". In the contemporary *Tale of the Doomed Prince* there occurs a king who has no son. He begs one from the gods, and they decree that an heir should be born to him. "That night he slept with his wife, and she [became] pregnant. When she had completed the months of childbearing, a son was born".

That rational beliefs regarding conception were in vogue appears evident from medical papyri (fig. 1). Written in hieratic (cursive) script, these contain advice on ways to stimulate it, as well as indicating methods of birth control, albeit without using any kind of contraceptive aid. Unwanted pregnancy was obviously not unknown, for there are prescriptions to stimulate an abortion, together with those designed to prevent the occurrence of a miscarriage, which include the use of a tampon as occasionally depicted on the oil vessels described below. To modern eyes some of these procedures are hardly practical, and great reliance is placed on purely magical spells, but the texts do show that the physical process was known, although not of course in all biological details.

These papyri also indicate the means to establish whether a woman is pregnant, some of which are indeed quite sound. For instance, taking her pulse, observing the colour of both her skin and eyes, and testing her propensity to vomit are just three logical signs. However, much more irrational, but obviously typical, magical practices were adopted in order to discern pregnancy and the sex of the unborn child:

1

You shall put wheat and barley into purses of cloth.
The woman shall pass her water on it, every day.
If both sprout, she will bear.
If the wheat sprouts, she will bear a boy.
If the barley sprouts, she will bear a girl.
If neither sprouts, she will not bear at all.

A second similar example reads: "A crushed plant is mixed with milk of a woman who has given birth to a boy. If another woman drinks it and vomits, she will give birth; if she emits wind, she will never give birth".

Fig. 1 Gynaecological papyrus containing prescriptions for women. From Kahun, Twelfth Dynasty

How pregnancy became news is told in the Demotic *Story of Setne*, of the Graeco-Roman era. A woman who, after conceiving, reached her appointed time of cleaning, underwent no purification. When women purified themselves

2

after menstruation, it was evidently publicly known, so that "it was reported to the Pharaoh and his heart was very happy".

Pregnant women, as is still the case today, were accustomed to massage themselves with oil in order to prevent stretch marks and to ease the birth itself, if they could afford it with a valuable perfumed brand. In the Eighteenth Dynasty this liquid was sometimes stored in special anthropomorphous containers taking the form of a naked, childbearing figure, either standing or squatting (fig. 2). She rubs her abdomen with both hands and exhibits a distinct lack of genitalia; occasionally with a prominent tampon to prevent either miscarriage or to check the escape of blood at the birth. Her grotesque face and pendulous breasts show obvious affinities to Thoeris the pregnant hippopotamus goddess (fig. 6b). In one instance she holds an oil-horn, illustrating the intended contents of these vessels. The particular shape of the small vases, normally made of travertine ('Egyptian alabaster'), was believed to possess an additional magical force. Examples were even exported to Crete and Syro-Palestine.

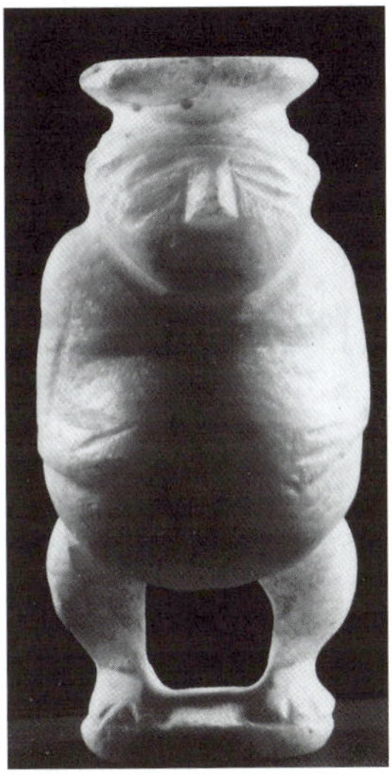

Fig. 2 Travertine ('Egyptian alabaster') oil vessel in the shape of a standing pregnant woman with grotesque features. H. 8.5 cm. Unprovenanced, Eighteenth Dynasty

The duration of pregnancy was of course roughly familiar from experience, as evidenced by the phrase "when she had completed the months of childbearing", already quoted above from the *Tale of the Doomed Prince*. However, nowhere are the nine months explicitly mentioned, the nearest proof being the sentence in the New Kingdom *Instruction of Ani*: "when you were born after *your* months". In a folktale from the Middle Kingdom composition known

3

as the *Tales of Wonder* (Papyrus Westcar) the king asks a magician, Djedi, when a woman will give birth. The answer is: on the fifteenth day of the fifth month of the year. However, although Djedi was old, wise and respected, we must remember that this is a fairy tale!

Delivery took place in special surroundings, namely in a distinctive structure known as the confinement pavilion, or else in a particular room of the house. The former is depicted in New Kingdom wall paintings in the houses of the artisans of Deir el-Medina at Western Thebes, and in those of the workmen's village East of el-Amarna. The documentation is necessarily scanty since hardly any houses of commoners have been preserved elsewhere, and most murals have anyway been largely destroyed.

However, figured ostraca (potsherds or flakes of limestone) from Deir el-Medina, clearly copies of and/or models for these paintings represent a fairly reliable picture. They show (fig. 3) a pavilion with papyrus stalks forming the columns which are decorated with tendrils of the convolvulus or grapevine. Sometimes garlands are hung on the walls. Clearly specifically erected, immediately prior to the confinement, in the garden or on the roof, its walls consist of plants and its roof is a mat.

Such a structure seems to be pictured in one of the rooms of the royal tomb at el-Amarna, which is situated deep in the desert, in a wadi East of the city. However, Princess Meketaten is here represented standing in the pavilion, while Akhenaten and Nefertiti, and three of the princesses, are depicted in the habitual attitude of mourning. Clearly the Pharaoh's second daughter had died in childbirth, as is confirmed by another scene in the same room. There she is lying on a bier; her parents are again portrayed in the posture of mourning, while a nurse carries an evidently living baby from the room. That this was a royal child is indicated by the women following the nurse, for they bear fans, the sign of royalty. The death-room of Meketaten is badly mutilated, but seems to have been unadorned, hence it is not a representation of the birth chamber.

In daily life, so far as less wealthy people were concerned, confinement would have taken place in a normal room in the house, the decoration being the wall paintings mentioned above. These particularly depict two divinities: the dwarf god Bes (fig. 6a), connected with sexuality and fertility, and Thoeris, the patroness of pregnant women, once called "she who removes the (birth) waters". At Deir el-Medina the low walls of a kind of platform can still be seen in the front room, on which the birth took place, as the remaining decoration corroborates.

Particular furniture is shown in the pavilion, comprising a bed with a mattress, a headrest, a mat and a cushion, and a stool fashioned from a palm-tree stump. Toilet equipment, such as a mirror, is also illustrated. Apotropaeic wands (see below) and the special confinement stool of today, with its wide opening in

Fig. 3 Painted limestone ostracon depicting the confinement pavilion. A servant girl offers a mirror and a kohl tube to a lying-in woman suckling her child. From Deir el-Medina, New Kingdom

the seat, are not depicted. On most occasions, as is still the practice in primitive societies, birth would have taken place when the woman was squatting on four bricks. Recent excavations in a house of a Middle Kingdom mayor of Abydos has for the first time brought to light such a birth-brick, decorated with scenes which show, for instance, a mother with her newborn son. When such bricks were

5

depicted in copies of the *Book of the Dead* they are presented as a rectangle with a female head on one corner. We also know a spell which was spoken over such confinement bricks. Actually it is a hymn to Meskhenet (fig. 6d), the personification of the confinement chair, portrayed in human guise with the uterus of a cow on her head. The spell derives from a hymn to the goddess of heaven.

The woman was assisted during her labour by some elderly female relatives grasping her from behind, one kneeling before her. It is doubtful that trained midwives existed. In the *Tales of Wonder*, as we shall see, the function is performed by itinerant dancing girls. It has been suggested that the profession was 'impure' and hence not highly esteemed. In the texts from Deir el-Medina 'wise women' feature, but, so far as we know, they merely practised divination. There is no indication that the husband was present at the birth, and the special pavilion indeed points to separation. On the other hand, a front room, through which everyone had to enter or leave the house, made isolation problematic.

In all representations of either this confinement pavilion or of the birth chamber the mother is shown practically naked, sitting on the bed or the stool while suckling her baby. She wears only a collar and a girdle, and her headdress is conspicuous. It consists of bunches of hair standing out on both sides of the head, and a cone bound by a piece of cord on its crown. It has been surmised that the hair of a woman in labour was initially tightly bound and later loosened in order, by sympathetic magic, to accelerate birth. It is from this hair-style that we can recognize the lying-in woman and the young mother.

This type of hair-style also occurs on the so-called 'concubine' figures of the New Kingdom, although the majority exhibit a full festal wig (fig. 4). The objects, made of terracotta or limestone, portray a naked woman lying either on a bed or on a plank, sometimes with a child, usually male, beside her thigh or being suckled. They have been interpreted as 'erotic' (which they certainly are), bed mates of a deceased man. In fact, they were intended to stimulate fertility in all aspects, with the precise aim also of projecting the image of mother and child. The fact that they occur in burials points to the continuation of these functions in the netherworld. This interpretation is reinforced by a particular Middle Kingdom female figure in Berlin. The free-standing form carries a child on her left hip and exhibits an inscription on the opposite leg, which reads: "May there be given birth to your daughter Sah". The model was put into the tomb of the father. To prevent escape from this funerary context, the birds among the hieroglyphs miss their legs, as does the woman herself. Although not lying on a bed, this object too – not the only example of this type – clearly belongs to the category of fertility figures.

In the pictures of the birth pavilion the mother is attended by girls who are as naked as she and sport the same hair-style. In a few instances a Nubian boy is shown with equally conspicuous hair: shaved and with a prominent tuft on the crown (see p. 34). These servants assist the lady at her toilet and wait upon her with food and drink. Perhaps the representation depicts the ritual and accompanying feast at the end of the isolation period (of fourteen days; see the *Tales of Wonder* below). Based on this scene there are also satirical drawings on ostraca where the mother is a mouse and the servants cats. In both cases the attendants are clearly dressing their mistress for her re-entrance into the world.

Fig. 4 Painted limestone concubine figure lying on a bed. Convolvulus decoration at each side and infant at bottom right. From Gurob, Nineteenth Dynasty

Birth is a dangerous event, and was nowhere more so regarded than in the ancient world. Therefore, it was surrounded by an aura of magical superstition. In one spell a dwarf (clearly Bes) is summoned, who is sent by the sun-god Re. The recitation runs:

7

Come down, placenta, come down, come down! I am Horus who conjures in order that she who is giving birth becomes better than she was, as if she was already delivered ...... Look, Hathor will lay her hand on her with an amulet of health! I am Horus who saves her!

This has to be recited four times, probably by the 'midwife', over a dwarf of clay (an amulet in the form of Bes) placed on the brow of a woman who is undergoing a difficult labour.

A particular magical artefact connected with pregnancy and the baby, and already mentioned in passing above, is the so-called apotropaeic wand (fig. 5). It was formerly referred to as a magical knife, although it possesses no sharp edge. In appearance it looks like a boomerang, the sickle-shape being due to the fact that it is made of hippopotamus teeth. However, some of these objects are made of travertine, faience, or ebony. A total of about a hundred and fifty surviving examples are known, all dating from the Middle Kingdom and the Second Intermediate Period.

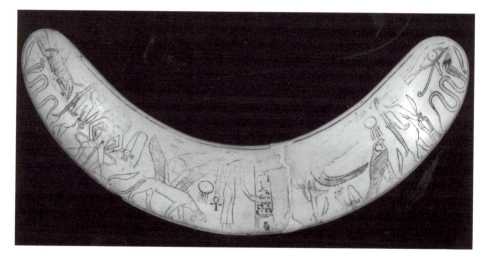

Fig. 5 Hippopotamus ivory apotropaeic wand inscribed for the "Lady of the House Seneb". L. 37 cm. From Thebes, Twelfth Dynasty

They have a flat and a convex face, on both of which are incised rows of demons: griffins, snake-headed cheetahs, the divinities Bes and Thoeris, and figures referring to the sun-god such as a seated cat or a double lion. In several instances the flat side also bears an inscription, for example the phrase: "protection by night and day", or a more extensive formula: "words spoken by these protective figures: we have come to spread protection over this child". Then follows the name of the juvenile, always a boy, or that of a woman, who is evidently the mother.

These items would have been used in a ritual, and were probably laid either on the stomach of a pregnant woman or on the body of the baby. Their function was to identify the infant with the sun-god Re, who was threatened in his youth by such monsters. As he survived, so by inference will the new-born child be safe. In one instance, namely in the tomb of the nomarch (provincial governor) Dhutihotep at el-Bersheh in Middle Egypt, the wand occurs in the hand of what seems to be a nanny or wet-nurse, confirming that it was used around the event of the birth of a child.

Another proof that magical practices were customary is the discovery, in a cupboard beneath the stairs of a house at el-Amarna, of four objects. They comprised a small painted limestone stela (upright slab) depicting a woman and a girl adoring Thoeris; a terracotta figure of a naked female with the typical hair-style of the lying-in woman and very prominent breasts; and two painted pottery beds. It can be suggested that these items were used at the the confinement and subsequently stored safely away, perhaps for future occasions. All four clearly refer to fertility and childbirth.

Finally, there are more than a hundred and seventy-five small faience figurines known which obviously acted as talismans for protection at birth and during nursing. They are blue or green, many with dark painted dots, and they represent mostly the figure of the god Bes nursing a baby. Others represent a female ape or a cat, or also a naked woman. They have mainly been found in the Eastern Delta, and date from the Libyan Period.

Above we cited the *Tales of Wonder*, a compilation of folk stories. In one of them the Pharaoh, the famous Khufu (Cheops) of the Fourth Dynasty, hears about an old and wise magician named Djedi. This sage is brought to the court by a prince, for the king hopes that he can reveal to him the place where a secret is hidden. Indeed Djedi says he does know it, but it would only be found by "the eldest of the three children who are in the womb of Ruddedet". Then Djedi tells the king, as quoted above, when the triplets will be born.

In the continuation of the story the delivery of the woman is recounted: "On one of these days Ruddedet felt the pangs and her labour was difficult. Then the Majesty of Re, Lord of Sabkhu (a Delta town), said to Isis, Nephthys, Meskhenet, Heqet (a frog-headed goddess of birth; fig. 6c), and Khnum (the ram-headed god of Elephantine): 'Please go and deliver Ruddedet of the three children who are in her womb, who will assume this beneficent office in the land'"; that is, who in future will become Pharaohs.

The four goddesses go, with Khnum as their porter, disguised as dancing girls. When they reach the house they find Ruddedet's husband, the priest

Ranofer, standing before it in distress, for the throes are painful. The ladies claim to have the knowledge of midwives and are requested to enter. Isis places herself before the woman, Nephthys behind her (as described above), while Heqet hastens the birth. When the child appears Isis pronounces the name of the boy, and he "slid into her arms, one cubit long, strong in bones, his limbs overlaid with gold, his headdress of true lapis lazuli". Clearly he shows all the markings of a royal child. The goddesses wash the baby after first having cut the umbilical cord, and lay it on a pillow of cloth. The same happens with the two other boys.

Afterwards the ladies with their servant vacate the house, leaving behind in a sealed room the sack of barley they had received as their recompense. Secretly they had placed three crowns of gold in the sack. Then "Ruddedet cleansed herself in a cleansing of fourteen days", the time the young mother had to spend in isolation in the confinement chamber or pavilion. The miracles that follow concerning the crowns are of no importance to us here.

Although a tale and full of supernatural events, the narrative evidently contains references to daily life, and is, therefore, the only written source we possess about birth. Some elements are missing, especially the confinement stool; others are only clear from this particular text, such as the role of the 'midwives' and their lowly status in society. But undoubtedly the story presents a picture of reality.

One further subject merits discussion. In the tale just related triplets are born, a relatively rare matter, mentioned nowhere else in Egyptian sources. Twins, however, were certainly less unusual. Approximately one per cent of all births must have resulted in twins, over half of them like-sexed. In view of the high mortality rate only a total of 0.3 per cent would have survived. Yet during the millennia of Egyptian history this presupposes a considerable number.

Curiously enough, only three pairs are at present known. One of them, the brothers Niankhkhnum and Khnumhotep, of the Fifth Dynasty, shared an impressive tomb at Saqqara. On its walls they are represented holding hands and even embracing – which is generally only seen in couples – expressing their close relationship. Niankhkhnum as the eldest twin is accorded a slight superiority in his position in the scenes. They occupied the same post, that of manicurist to the king, which means that they belonged to the inner court circles. Moreover, they were administrators of the royal properties, which explains the wealth of their burial.

The second pair are the architects of the Amun Temple under Amenhotep III, Suti and Hor, well-known from their grey granite stela inscribed with a hymn to Aten (the god of the 'heretic' Pharaoh Akhenaten), now in the British Museum. That they were indeed twins is evident from a sentence in this text: "He (my brother) went forth with me from the womb on the same day". They were named after the gods Seth and Horus who, according to the myths, were uncle and nephew. However, the Egyptian word for 'brother' encompasses the relationships of brother, cousin, nephew and uncle.

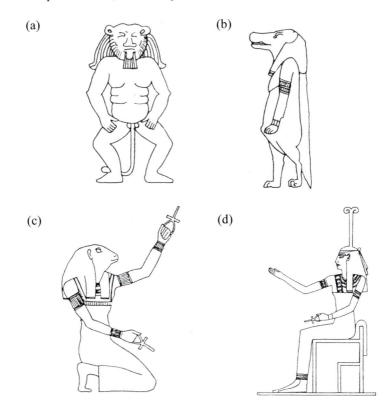

Fig. 6 Four divinities connected with birth: (a) Bes; (b) Thoeris; (c) Heqet; (d) Meskhenet. From the birth scenes of the Divine King at Deir el-Bahri, Eighteenth Dynasty

A third pair may be the two sisters represented on a Twelfth Dynasty stela, now in Paris. They are also shown embracing, and both are called "his (the owner of the stela) beloved daughter Sitamun".

Three instances are certainly not very many, but in later times there is more evidence. We then find a special word for twins, and 'twin' even developed into a common name (in Greek: 'Didymos'). Yet, the documentation for the flowering epochs of Egyptian history is conspicuously meagre. There is, for instance, no evidence for unlike-sexed twins.

11

One explanation could be that, as in other cultures, twins were killed, either one of them or both; but it must be emphasized that there is not a shred of proof for this. It has also been suggested that multiple births, regarded as weird, an accident or even a misfortune, excluded the children from public life; or that it was ignored in the texts so that we never hear about them. On the other hand, Niankhkhnum and Khnumhotep were closely connected to the king, and Suty and Hor received divine names. That suggests that twins were rather conceived of as an anomaly in the world-order, honoured but requiring symbolic correction in order to be acceptable. They seem to have been regarded as an incompletely formed unity, or an excess of unity, in either case contradicting concord.

Obviously this particular facet of Egyptian civilization requires further study, as indeed do other aspects of the fascinating sphere of pregnancy and birth.

2 The Baby

As we have already seen from the *Tales of Wonder*, the child received its name at birth, not, as in Moslem Egypt, at a special ceremony held a week or a fortnight later. Usually it was the mother who decided upon it, as evidenced by a New Kingdom hymn to the great state-god Amun which states: "…... his mother who made his name".

Names of various types occur. Some, like Amenhotep, "Amun has proved to be gracious", are unconnected with the bearer, whereas others, such as Wersu, "Big is he", have attributive indications. However, in the latter case it is possible that an unmentioned god may be implied, so that we should rather translate "Great is he". Names may point to physical qualities, for instance, Pakamen, "The blind one"; or occupations: Pakapu, "The birdcatcher". Still others denote a foreign origin: Pakharu, "The Syrian" or Panehsy, "The Nubian", the latter occurring in the Old Testament as Pinehas, a son of the priest Eli, mentioned in I Samuel 1, verse 3. However, as names were inherited by children and grandchildren, they quickly lost all connection with their source. Thus not every Panehsy was a Nubian, as our surnames have similarly lost their original meaning, for how many by the name of Smith or Baker can now claim to exercise that particular profession?

Many Ancient Egyptian names are statements, wishes, or even cries uttered by the mother at the precise moment of birth. So Dhutimose (Greek: Tuthmosis), "Thoth lives", is comparable with the joyful Christian shout at Easter: "Christ has risen". Other examples of wishes and exclamations are Mersure, "May Re love him" and Aneksi, "She belongs to me". 'In the latter case the 'me' evidently refers to the mother. Some names, such as Yotesankh, "Her father lives", show that the baby reminded the mother of a deceased person, in this case her own husband. That other persons, for instance the 'midwives' or perhaps the father, may have been present at the confinement and are responsible for giving the name, is obvious. Even a group of onlookers may do so, as the name Senetenpu, "It is our sister", proves.

An exceptional but illuminating case is contained in a New Kingdom papyrus now in Cairo. The text is the record of a lawsuit centring around the purchase of a female Syrian slave called Gemnihiamente. This means "I found her on the West Bank" (of Thebes). It was clearly given at the moment her mistress obtained her, perhaps because the girl's original Syrian name was unpronounceable for the lady.

One specific category of names points to the actual day of birth. For instance, the appellation Mutemwia, "Mut is in the bark", that is, she makes her procession. It refers to a particular festival day when the statue of this deity was carried around by the priests, and it may be that the mother wanted in this way to keep the special occasion in memory.

It is unknown whether the Egyptians before the Late Period generally knew their day of birth. In Graeco-Roman times they certainly did, and a Twenty-first Dynasty stela already contains an indication, for it records the exact age, in years, months and days, of a man and his daughter at the moment of their decease.

Fig. 7 Painted limestone group statuette of a woman nursing her child, while a maid dresses her hair. From el-Lisht, Twelfth Dynasty

From Deir el-Medina we possess several references in lists of absences to a personal feast of one of the artisans, noted down as "his feast". It was recorded since these men were then absent from their work of building the royal tomb in the Valley of the Kings. It remains uncertain, however, whether this was the celebration of a birthday. In some cases it is additionally called "his feast of Hathor", or another divinity, which seems to suggest a different reason. Once we find "his feast of his daughter", which could indeed mean her birthday. A wedding day is less plausible here, since the Egyptians never seem to have marked the beginning of a marriage relationship (see p. 91).

Normally, of course, the baby was nursed by its mother. There are in total almost forty known representations of a breastfeeding mother, statues as well as reliefs and stelae (fig. 7). Nursing may have lasted for a long period, as a sentence from the *Instruction of Ani* suggests:

> When you were born after your months, (your mother) was still yoked to you, her breast was in your mouth for three years.

It may be that weaning was sometimes postponed since breastfeeding was even at that time believed to be an effective form of birth control. Whether a child did generally suckle for so long is uncertain.

Breastfeeding was, quite naturally, regarded by the mother as a pleasure. In a New Kingdom description of the joys of the scribal profession its satisfaction is compared with that of a mother who:

> has given birth and whose heart felt no distaste; she is constantly nursing her son, and her breast is in his mouth every day.

Yet, there still existed wet-nurses who took over this motherly duty, either out of necessity or to provide the puerperal woman with more rest. They occurred especially in upper class households, but not exclusively, for they are also mentioned among the inhabitants of Deir el-Medina at the end of the Ramesside Period. A scribe of this community, admittedly one of its more well-to-do members, once wrote in a letter to his son that the addressee should look well after a woman, her little daughter, and her nurse. Now in Turin is an account from the same village (also written on a papyrus), in which the recompenses a workman paid, following his wife's confinement, to a doctor and a wet-nurse are recorded. All are in tangible objects since money was not yet in existence. The payment to the woman comprised three necklaces of jasper, an ivory comb (both typical feminine items), one pair of sandals, one basket, one block of wood, and half a litre of fat. Amounting to 30½ *deben* (1 *deben* equals 90 grammes of copper), it is even higher than the value of 22 *deben* paid to the physician, who received a bronze vessel, two pairs of sandals, various baskets, one mat, and one litre of oil. Perhaps this was because she had suckled all three children of the family, which would necessitate a far longer service than that of an attendant doctor.

Wet-nurses of leading officials were highly esteemed. They were sometimes portrayed in tombs and on stelae among the daughters. Although drawn at the same scale, they are usually relegated to the very end of the row. In the early Eighteenth Dynasty tomb of the mayor Paheri at el-Kab no less than three nurses are depicted on a par with his children. Probably there was one for

15

each daughter, since there are three girls with them. In a Middle Kingdom tomb a wet-nurse (her figure is now destroyed) is shown, together with one, or perhaps two, nannies, one of whom is holding an apotropaeic wand (see p. 9). Their names and occupations are rendered in hieroglyphic captions beside them. All this proves the close ties which existed between wet-nurses and the family. That the word for the function was the same as that for 'milchcow' may strike us as unpleasant, but this was clearly not so regarded by the rational Egyptians.

Wet-nurses of the royal children performed a particularly vital rôle (see chapter 10). For example, the career of their husbands was likely to be enhanced because of their close relationship to the royal family. A famous instance is that of Teye (see fig. 13), the wet-nurse of Nefertiti and the wife of the chariotry commander Ay, who was one of the leading figures behind the throne during the Amarna Period, and later on one of Akhenaten's successors.

Above we mentioned in passing a nanny, a related function, though less highly valued. In the *Story of the Two Brothers*, after the Queen has borne a son, it is stated that a wet-nurse and nannies were assigned to him. The word here rendered as 'nanny' is usually translated as 'attendant' or 'servant', once even 'day-nurse'. It was clearly a special female position.

The word for wet-nurse is also used for male nurses/tutors, which seems strange to modern eyes. A Middle Kingdom chamberlain, for instance, calls himself "nurse of the god (i.e. the King) in the private apartments", while a contemporary army general states that he "was indeed a support for old people, a wet-nurse of children". As the word is written with the sign of a woman suckling a baby, it is surely 'wet-nurse' that is intended. In our language, a wider meaning to the noun 'nurse' is also common.

Although a wet-nurse had her own child, and will have been chosen because of her capacity to feed two babies (unless her own had died), we nevertheless find prescriptions to stimulate her milk flow. One states that her back should be rubbed with "fish cooked in oil", which probably means: with the oil in which a fish was cooked. Other medical treatises reveal how good milk can be distinguished from bad: bad milk stinks like fish, whereas good milk smells like crushed aromatic plants. Among the advice for mother and child one text suggests grinding tips of the papyrus plant and tubers, and mixing them into the milk of a woman who has given birth to a son. The resulting concoction should be administered daily to the infant, so that it will pass day and night in a healthy slumber. Evidently this was one of the numerous popular remedies to keep a baby quiet; perhaps it did indeed work!

Mother's milk also occurs-elsewhere in the pharmacopoeia as a cure for various ailments. As such it was still widely used in Coptic times. The milk of a woman who had given birth to a boy was considered to be particularly effective.

A medical text designates it "the curing liquid that is in my breast", the speaker being the great mother-goddess Isis.

How was this milk stored? Over a dozen examples survive of a feminoform vessel which are all dated from the Eighteenth to Nineteenth Dynasties (fig. 8). Standing from eleven to seventeen centimetres high, they are all made of reddish-brown baked clay with the details painted black, apart from a solitary exception in steatite. Their cubic capacity at over a tenth of a litre is roughly the amount that one breast produces at one feed.

Fig. 8 Painted pottery vessel in the shape of a woman with a child sitting on her lap. She possibly wears a moon amulet. H. 11 cm. Unprovenanced, Eighteenth Dynasty

Although comparable to the anthropomorphous vases discussed in chapter 1 that contain massaging oil for the pregnant woman, the two types display completely different external characteristics. In most, but not all, of these milk containers a female holds a child, which is never represented suckling, although it sometimes reaches towards a breast which the woman may be holding and squeezing. The infant either sits on the lap or lies drawn upon it, or else it is carried on the back in a sling.

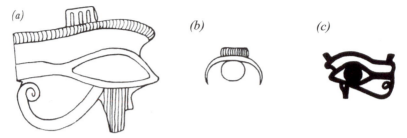

Fig. 9 A rising moon amulet flanked by two Horus-eyes. Scale 1:1

The woman herself is shown squatting, the habitual attitude during breastfeeding (fig. 7), as the hieroglyphic determinative employed in related words proves. She is dressed in a skirt with a fringed shawl draped over her upper torso: suitable attire for the situation, and one which is still used in modern Egypt. Around her neck is an amulet shaped as a rising moon (figs. 8 and 9b), referring to and stimulating the milk supply. Her hair-style is conspicuously different from that of both the pregnant and the lying-in woman. The hair hangs down her back, either loosely or in a ponytail, and two equally long tresses reach to her lap in front.

Fig. 10 Transporting babies (a) Nubian woman employing a basket. From the Theban tomb of Huy (TT 40), Eighteenth Dynasty; (b) Egyptian women using slings. From the Theban tomb of Neferhotep (TT 49), Eighteenth Dynasty

Probably this female represents a professional wet-nurse rather than the mother. On three vessels she holds an oil-horn in one hand and is dripping the contents on to her other palm. The oil would have been used to massage her back

18

in order to stimulate the flow of milk, as in the prescription cited above. It seems likely that these objects belonged to the dispensary of a doctor, who from their shape and features could easily discern their contents, and make the distinction from the oil held in the pregnant-shaped containers.

In one instance the woman carries the baby on her back. The same position can be seen in reliefs and paintings, usually for foreigners, Nubians, Libyans, and Syrians (fig. 10a). They often transport the infant in a basket, whereas Egyptians were accustomed to place the child either on the arm or on the hip. When on the back, it was supported in a linen sling (fig. 10b). Nursing mothers hold the baby on the lap (fig. 7), or else they kneel or squat with it resting on their upper thigh. Representations of a woman breastfeeding while standing occur only in connection with toddlers, but are mostly confined to religious images of goddesses suckling the Pharaoh.

A baby's life in those days was threatened by many infections and maladies, infant mortality being high. Numerous instances of child burials can, of course, be cited, but we will mention only two here. Sir W.M. Flinders Petrie, the pioneer of scientific archaeology in Egypt and Palestine, noted in his Journal of the 1889 Kahun excavations that he had found "many new-born infants ...... buried in the floors of the rooms". Clearly the inhabitants of this pyramid builders' town in the Faiyum had interred their dead babies, sometimes two or three to a box, under their house floors, usually in chests made for other purposes such as clothes or toilet equipment. Some of these boxed baby burials survive in Manchester. At Deir el-Medina, above the village on the western slope of the Qurnet Murai, is a cemetery where more than a hundred children were buried, in common domestic pottery jars or amphorae, in baskets, even fish baskets, in boxes and chests, or in proper coffins. The poorest graves were those of still-born infants, containing no amulets or jewellery, only one or two small vessels filled with food for the netherworld. A sad case is that of a boy called Iryky, who was born so badly deformed that one wonders how he could have lived even one day. He had an abnormally large torso and head, but stunted limbs.

The precarious nature of the young life is made abundantly clear in the following passage from the *Instruction of Ani*:

> Do not say: 'I am too young to be taken away',
> for you do not know your death.
> When death comes he steals the infant
> from the arms of his mother,
> just like him who has reached old age.

In order to guard the vulnerable child, amuletic charms were placed around its neck. Numerous types are known and can be found in every collection of Egyptian antiquities, although it is uncertain which ones were particularly worn by new-born sucklings. A likely candidate may be the Horus-eye amulet (fig. 9a and c), safeguarding its bearer against the evil eye, a risk believed to endanger the existence of the young all over the world. The charm played a rôle comparable with that of a cross in Christian communities, especially around the Mediterranean.

Noticeable protection was also expected from small fresh papyrus rolls inscribed in cursive hieratic script. They were tightly folded and rolled into tiny packets, bound with flax and inserted into miniature cylindrical cases of wood, metal, or even gold. Worn as a pendant suspended around the child's neck on a cord, they are frequent during the centuries after the New Kingdom. As some have been discovered still bound, the texts were probably never seen by their bearers.

An early example derives from Deir el-Medina. It contains a spell against catching a common cold, the form, as is usual in these texts, being a decree by a god. In this case the Lord of the Netherworld Osiris is stated to have spoken to his vizier, the earth god Geb, in the following words:

> Erect your mast, unfold the sail, depart for the
> Iaru-fields! (the Fields of Rushes, an ideal resort in the
> hereafter). Take with you the male and the female possessor,
> the male and the female dead, who are before the face of
> Anynakhte, son of Ubekht (the boy's mother), together with
> the fever and the cold and all bad and evil things,
> when they have come to him for three days.

Later texts contain guarantees to keep a boy or a girl, who is individually named, safe from all kinds of mishaps and disasters, of which an extensive list is presented. These may be diseases, some like leprosy, blindness, snake and scorpion bites, being specifically mentioned. Also cited are miseries caused by humans, such as accusations and sneers. In between these common evils, misfortunes suffered from the hands of deities and demons are listed, all mixed up together, without an attempt at any logical order. The oracle god undertakes to guard the child day and night, wherever it will go, on every kind of journey, either abroad in a ship or riding along the desert edge in a chariot. He will prevent death and give his protégé a happy infancy, he may even promise a girl that she will conceive many children of both sexes. Protection is assured against the magic of an Egyptian, a Nubian or a Libyan (foreigners appear to have been especially feared), or even of a physician! Security is also provided against spirits connected with water and watery places: canals, lakes, pools left after the recession of the inundation, swamps, etc. These spirits seem to be similar to the European elves.

The oracular amuletic decrees, as these papyri are called, present us not only with a catalogue of dangers threatening the infant's life, they also permit us insights into normal daily life. Some are rather long, despite being compressed to a small volume, and all are different, although containing passages that recur in others.

Fig. 11 Gold over copper core cylindrical amulet case. Scale 2:1. From tomb 211 at Haraga, Twelfth Dynasty

From the Middle Kingdom too, cylindrical charm cases have survived. These are either solid or hollow, and generally contain no papyri but loose garnets and perhaps amulets. A spectacular example in sheet gold over a copper alloy core, now in the Petrie Museum, is illustrated here (fig. 11). It had been stated, ever since its discovery in 1913 at Haraga, to be solid. However, neutron

21

radiography, carried out by the National Non-destructive Testing Centre, Harwell Laboratory, was undertaken for us in 1989 and indicated a hollow case with contents. The subsequent scientific removal of one of the caps revealed three balls of copper wire and decayed organic material, perhaps papyrus. The contents are reminiscent of a particular spell on a Berlin papyrus full of protective suggestions for mother and child, from which we have frequently quoted above. The pertinent sentences run:

> Spell for a knot for a baby: 'Are you warm in the nest?
> Are you hot in the bush? Is your mother with you?
> Is there no sister to fan you? Is there no nurse to afford protection?'

The first lines allude to the young god Horus who, according to the myth, passed his boyhood in the marshes of the Delta. After these questions the text continues:

> Let there be brought to me pellets of gold, balls of garnet,
> a seal with a crocodile(-figure) and a hand to slay and to
> dispel the 'Sweet One' (a female demon), to warm the body,
> to slay his male or female enemy of the West (the netherworld).
> You will break out! This is a protection!

The spell is to be recited over the various items mentioned. It is then "to be made into an amulet and put to the throat of the child. Good!"

As throughout, such spells – some intended to promote a successful delivery, others to safeguard against children's diseases – refer to demons. One of them, male or female, is said to enter the house stealthily, "his nose backwards, his face averted", in order to escape recognition. Asked whether he or she has come to kiss the infant, to hush it, to harm it, or to take it away, the answer to each question is the guarantee that the questioner will not permit this to happen. Its protection is stated to be ensured additionally with clover, garlic, honey, a fish-tail, the jawbone of a cow, and the dorsal part of a Nile perch! Yet another spell is actually a prayer to the sun-god Re at dawn and dusk, which has to be spoken over the child to keep the dead away from its mother, for they wish to snatch the babe from her breast.

All this clearly reveals just how dangerous a new-born life was conceived to be. Fearful of all manner of evil, its mother, its wet-nurse, and others try to conjure up the goodwill of the propitious gods, at the same time controlling and eliminating the perils by charms. Thus pious and magic practice go very much hand-in-hand, as indeed they still do in present day society.

3 The Infant Dressed and Groomed

How were children dressed in Ancient Egypt? Our information derives mainly from reliefs, paintings and statues, but, for two reasons, these sources are not reliable. Firstly, the concept of status is all pervasive, so the actual age of the youngsters was by no means important, simply their stage in life. This implies that reality was disregarded. For example, in the Fifth Dynasty tomb of Seshemnefer III from Giza, now in Tubingen, the owner is once depicted as a naked boy with a side-lock, for there he is shown together with his deceased mother.

Secondly, these mediums are dominated by strict artistic conventions. Egyptian art was designed mainly for temples and tombs, hence it was by its very nature conservative. Thus until the New Kingdom men were mostly depicted with their upper torsos exposed. This is neither plausible for daily life, since in the winter at least it is distinctly cold in the early mornings and late evenings; nor is it confirmed by real garments that have survived. We therefore need to be suspicious when infants are represented naked.

That is in fact how they are everywhere seen during the Old Kingdom, with only a few exceptions (see fig. 27), nudity being a state which lasts right up until puberty. For instance, on a Fifth Dynasty limestone statue group, now in Hildesheim, of a woman with her son, twice represented, one of the boys standing beside his mother reaches up to her breasts. He therefore appears to be about ten years of age, and yet he is completely naked.

By contrast, in the Middle Kingdom the children are more often dressed than not, wearing the same types of clothes as their elders. Yet, this may be due to a reform in the artistic canon rather than the reflection of a change in daily habits. A clear illustration is that the boys and girls playing games (see chapter 5) are now shown clothed, whereas in the same activities on Old Kingdom tomb walls they appear nude (see figs. 23, 24, 27). It may be that the draughtsman indiscriminately considered them as infants and adolescents, but it seems more the effect of a difference in official style.

During the New Kingdom both nude and dressed children occur. In an Eighteenth Dynasty Theban grave a metal statuette was discovered of a naked boy, together with a far larger wooden statue of his clothed elder brother. Both pieces had been dedicated by the boys' father, and placed in their mother's coffin. It seems evident that these beloved sons had died prematurely. At what age we cannot know, but the fact that only the younger one was nude does not necessarily imply that his elder sibling was already fully adult.

Fig. 12 Painted limestone statue group of a seated couple and their daughter.
Unprovenanced, New Kingdom

In this era, as in the Old Kingdom, girls were also sometimes represented as undressed, even when they reached puberty. A painted limestone

24

statue group of a father, mother and their daughter, now in Toulouse, shows the girl standing between her parents (fig. 12). A wide mop of hair falls down the right side of her face, and she carries a duck on her left arm (see p. 36). Although she already exhibits slight breasts, she is still naked. That girls of this age really went around exposed is doubtful. Thus the nudity may here merely indicate her status as a child.

The six daughters of the remarkable Pharaoh Akhenaten and his co-regent Queen Nefertiti are mostly shown in diaphanous dresses, exact copies of those of their mother. However, there are some exceptions among the reliefs from the royal capital at el-Amarna, in which particularly the youngest one represented is nude. In this case it can be inferred that she was indeed still a baby.

This leads us to the question of whether babies were always completely naked. It can certainly be doubted. One text concerning Sesostris I, the second ruler of the Twelfth Dynasty, states that he already became Lord of the Two Lands before his swaddling clothes were removed. However, the word here rendered as 'swaddling-clothes' (modern: nappies) may simply be an error of the scribe who copied the text during the Eighteenth Dynasty. His original may have run: "before the foreskin was removed", i.e., before he was circumcised (see p. 78). Yet, such a mistake is understandable if there was indeed a word for 'nappies'.

The monuments do not help us to solve the problem, for they always show babies as naked. Actual pieces of cloth in the form of linen bands have been found in large numbers, and are frequently designated by the Egyptians themselves, for example in laundry lists. However, we do not know for what purpose they were used. Although it is pure hypothesis to suggest that, in order to keep their limbs straight, Egyptian mothers wrapped their babies in swaddling-clothes, it is likely that they indeed did the same as Mary for the new-born Jesus in the stable at Bethlehem.

Returning to the Amarna princesses, there are some cases in which even the older ones among them are shown naked. A famous example is the painted plaster fragment found by Petrie on the wall of a small palace in the capital and which is now in Oxford. Part of a family scene, it shows two bald girls of different sizes sitting on cushions beside their parents, of whom only the lower limbs are preserved. The figures of three more sisters were also heavily damaged; whether they too were naked is uncertain.

Similarly, on a limestone altar slab now in Berlin, the royal couple occurs with three of the daughters. The middle one is fondled and kissed by the father, the eldest sits on her mother's knee and looks up to her, while the youngest rests against her breast in a somewhat unnatural posture. The eldest sister wears an earring, but apart from that all three are entirely nude. In this particular case it is the difference in hair-style which provides an indication of the ages, as will be demonstrated below. That in the intimate domestic circle even older princesses went around without clothes would be an unwarranted conclusion.

Fig. 13 Ay and his wife Teye rewarded by the royal family. From the tomb of Ay at el-Amarna, Eighteenth Dynasty

This is clear from another Amarna scene, a relief on the wall of the rock-tomb of the later Pharaoh Ay (fig. 13). Akhenaten and Nefertiti here reward the faithful servant and his wife, the royal wet-nurse Teye (see p. 16) by dispensing golden goblets, collars, and other precious items, from a balcony. Three princesses accompany their parents, the elder two assisting them by also dropping necklaces at the feet of the honoured couple. Once more the girls are individually distinguished by the length of their hair. All three are nude – but so seem to be the King and the Queen, although the entire court is present, everyone being exceptionally well attired.

The scholar who published this tomb scene in 1908 suggested that the surprising lack of modesty was due to Akhenaten's admiration of the human body. Perhaps we have to look further. Although, as we shall argue below, nudity was not considered to be shameful in Ancient Egypt, it is highly uncommon in depictions of the King. The Queen and other ladies in the Amarna Period may seem to be hardly dressed since, through their fine linen garments, the body contours are clearly visible. This is mere artistic style rather than reality. So too is the undress of the royal family in this relief. It has to do with the belief, promulgated by Akhenaten, in the concept of "Living from Truth", and not with daily practice. This should warn us not to take the nakedness of the princesses at face value.

In the numerous representations from both tomb walls and stelae of the workmen's village at Deir el-Medina nudity is again encountered as the normal 'dress' of children. An obvious case is our front cover illustration, from the Twentieth Dynasty tomb of Anherkhew the Younger (TT 359), one of the chief workmen of the gang of the necropolis. The owner and his wife Wabe are pictured with their four grandchildren: two older girls and a younger, and a very young boy, still a toddler. All are naked, but the lasses wear jewellery: earrings, collars, bracelets, and even armlets and anklets, the boy nothing. The only means to roughly determine their ages, apart from their height, are the differences in hair-style (see below).

In the Nineteenth Dynasty tomb from the same group, that of Sennedjem (TT 1), a banquet scene is depicted. Two girls are shown standing beside their mother, one nude, the other dressed in the flared pleated robe fashionable at that time. The first one is the smallest, but both wear their hair in exactly the same way. A couple more daughters are seen under the chairs of two female guests, obviously their mothers. They too are fully clothed in festive attire.

From these and other instances from this community we would be inclined to conclude that nudity was here permissible for girls until they reached puberty. After that, perhaps immediately after the first menstruation, it was no longer thought to be decent. It can also be suggested, on the basis of drawings on ostraca, that nakedness for boys was even more common.

Even adults, in special circumstances – such as young mothers in the confinement pavilion (see p. 4 ff.), or men engaged in particular activities, for example, fishing and fowling in the marshes – are shown without dress. This is never the case with the tomb-owners, however. It implies that in real life the Egyptians were less afraid of nakedness than we are – or perhaps one should say, used to be. Of course, the hot climate makes this understandable.

The Theban banquet scenes of the Eighteenth Dynasty, from the reign of Amenhotep II onward, show nude dancers and serving wenches. It is worth noting, for the sake of comparison, that in a similar situation in the Twelfth Dynasty tomb of Antefoker and his wife Senet (TT 60) the lasses wear loincloths, although in the register below a naked lad appears. In the tomb of Rekhmire (TT 100), the vizier of Tuthmosis III, the waitresses are fully clad in long tunics. It is only immediately after this reign that nude feminine beauty becomes the norm for personnel at feasts.

For example, the lute player in the tomb of Nakht (TT 52) is dressed only in a scanty girdle, a wide collar and earrings, whereas her co-musicians, playing a harp and a double oboe, are well covered. One case of a Theban tomb (TT 45) is particularly interesting in this respect. It was usurped after less than a century by an official from the time of Ramesses II, who ordered his painter to transform the figures of the nude girls (according to their skin colour evidently foreigners), covering them with white paint as if they were clothed. This has been interpreted as a case of prudish behaviour. However, several other alterations were made which had nothing to do with nudity but were intended to bring the scenes into accordance with the religious concepts of the tomb in that later period. Therefore to see nakedness as having been regarded as indecent is just not correct.

In view of all this it cannot surprise us that youngsters were more frequently rendered nude than dressed. Indeed, toddlers as well as young servants, some of them slave-boys and -girls, may have walked around without garments, at least at special occasions. That does not mean, however, that they did not possess them or wear them when it was cold. The same is true for older infants as the few surviving items of children's clothing amply demonstrate.

Of these, four are particularly interesting. The first one is a partially pleated linen dress for an older child, which can claim to be the oldest surviving garment in the world and is certainly the earliest from the Nile Valley (fig. 14). It was discovered in 1977 in a batch of dirty rags belonging to the Petrie Museum. As the cloth derived from the large mastaba 2050 at Tarkhan in the Faiyum district, the dress can be precisely dated to the reign of King Djet in the First Dynasty, about 2800 B.C. Although Petrie had not recognized it when excavating the tomb in 1912, he nevertheless fully appreciated the potential of such evidence by retaining the rags.

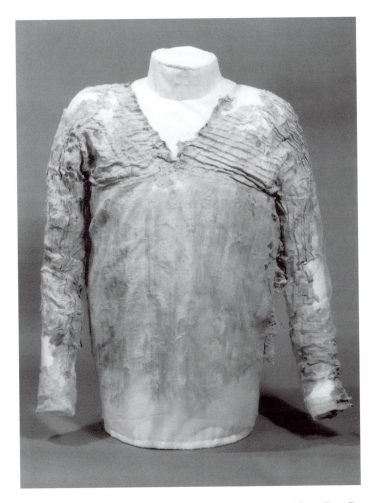

Fig. 14 Child's pleated linen dress. From mastaba 2050 at Tarkhan, First Dynasty

Splendidly conserved and mounted at the Victoria and Albert Museum, London, this garment consists of a main skirt joined selvedge to selvedge down its left-hand side with an ornamental weft fringe; no part of the hem remains. A stubbed yarn imparts an irregular grey stripe in the warp, deliberately used for decorative effect. The sleeves and yoke, cut from two pieces of material, are seamed to the top of the skirt, meeting at centre front and back to form a V-shaped neckline, edged with selvedge. Both areas display knife pleating

29

following the line of shoulder and arm. The direction of the whipping stitches shows that the 'tailor' was right-handed. The measurements, especially of the sleeves, are those for a child of about ten years of age.

Creasing, particularly round the armpits and elbows, proves that the dress was worn in life. It had been pulled off over the head, the sleeves with their very narrow wrists following in an inverted manner, and was so discovered inside-out. Following conservation and the application of a silk crêpeline support, the entire garment was intricately turned right-side out. Each pleat having been re-ironed, the elbow crease marks were studied to determine its front and back before mounting on a frame body shaped to fit. So despite the Old Kingdom representations which would lead us to believe in the universal nakedness of infants we have here a dress which was actually part of the wardrobe of an older child.

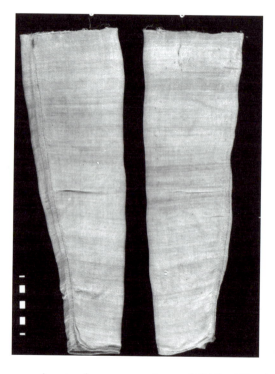

Fig. 15 A pair of child's linen sleeves. From tomb 25 at Gurob, late Eighteenth to early Nineteenth Dynasty

As we have seen above, Middle Kingdom depictions often show children fully clothed and aping their elders in fashion styles. This is confirmed by our second piece, albeit a 'false' dress consisting of the front half only. It was discovered in 1982 by a joint Hanover/Berlin expedition in the Eleventh Dynasty tomb of a young girl called Niuty at Saqqara. The cut with its skirt and separate V-shaped bodice simulates the sheath dress which was the typical garb of adult females from the Old Kingdom until the mid-Eighteenth Dynasty. Niuty's garment for the netherworld has fine tie-cords at the neck and intricate overall horizontal pleating, so no effort was spared to produce an exact model of a costume for life itself.

A pair of child's linen sleeves now in the Petrie Museum constitutes our third example (fig. 15). These pristine and beautifully made items derive from tomb 25 at New Kingdom Gurob. They are new, possibly even unworn, but were not designed as funerary equipment. Each is approximately 41 cm. in length and displays the remains of stitching at the top, indicating that they were once sewn into the armholes of a sleeveless tunic. This is proved by one of two children's sleeves now in Manchester, which still bears an attached shoulder fragment from a jacket. All four have run and fell seams, particularly suited to children's clothes subject to frequent wear and washing. Indeed sleeves are listed as separate items in laundry lists on Deir el-Medina ostraca. Evidently they were made separately and attached to garments only when required at times of adverse cold. Detachable sleeves are therefore by no means a new vogue of the fashion industry!

Fourthly, we have a beautiful baby's robe which belonged to Tutankhamun. Together with a shawl and a scarf, it covered the famous jackal shrine in his tomb. All three items are now in the Victoria and Albert Museum. The robe bore a hieratic docket at its bottom left-hand side which gives the date, the seventh regnal year of Akhenaten, possibly the very year of Tutankhamun's birth. This would be about 1343 B.C. We can therefore speculate that it may have been worn for a presentation ceremony at the court, and constitutes the equivalent of a modern christening robe. It does show signs of usage, the evidence of which was skilfully retained in 1986 when it underwent conservation. The linen, which is exceptionally finely spun and evenly woven, was originally bleached a pure white. It has been scientifically estimated that it would have taken three thousand hours to make or nine months of eleven-hour days. Evidently it was fit for a new-born royal prince!

In design it is a typical 'bag-tunic', one of the simplest types of garment, formed by doubling over a long length of rectangular linen with knotted fringes at each end. It is stitched up the sides, the fine over-sewing joining the two selvedges edge-to-edge, but leaving a slit for the arms. Its measurements at 1.64 metres in length by 1 metre wide mean that it is clearly a full-sized garment of adult proportions.

However, the neck-opening is only large enough to accommodate the head of a new-born baby. Conspicuously, this hole has been cut down from the fold at the shoulder, which enables it to sit well, for it would have fallen closed at the top when worn, but at the same time have parted slightly over the breastbone.

The small circle has a further keyhole shaped cut ending in a point, which would have allowed it to be pulled over the head. The entire neckline is finished with a rolled hem of the most exquisite workmanship.

It is interesting here to note in passing that excavations conducted in the early 1980's at the workmen's village East of el-Amarna yielded a number of small ovals of cloth which correspond in shape to neck-openings of short-sleeved tunics. Their size suggests that they came from children's rather than adults' clothing.

Altogether Tutankhamun's wardrobe, discovered by Howard Carter in his tomb, comprised nearly fifty child's garments and so-called 'shawls', plus belts, scarves, caps, headdresses, nearly thirty gloves and gauntlets, several pairs of socks, and even a fingerstall and a sling bandage. His underwear took the form of shirts, similar in design to the robe described above and also exhibiting such delicately hemmed necklines, and nearly a hundred and fifty triangular loincloths. The measurements of the latter reveal Tutankhamun's 'vital statistics': he had a narrow waist (70 cm.) and very wide hips (110 cm.). These undergarments were sometimes found in sets with the basic and universally popular over-kilt. By contrast, the boy-king's cumbersome state robes show absolutely no indication of ever having been worn. This suggests that even the extant garments have to be viewed with caution, for not all present us with normal daily dress.

The most typical hair-style of Egyptian children, boys as well as girls, was a braided plait with the end rolled up in an outward facing curl. It was worn at the right side, with the rest of the skull either shaved completely, or the hair kept very short. This haircut is found at all periods, but in the Old Kingdom it seems the most common.

An example from the late Fourth to early Fifth Dynasty is the painted limestone group statue of the disabled Seneb and his wife with their two offspring, now in Cairo, where the boy wears this plaited side-lock. The man, with his atrophied legs crossed, sits on a seat beside his wife. The sculptor has skilfully disguised the deformity by placing the chubby youngsters where, in a normal case, the legs of the man would be. Both the boy and the girl are naked, each with a finger to their mouth in accordance with the iconographic rules for infants. From this statue it appears that the side-lock was not the only possibility for children's hair, for the daughter wears hers close-cropped, like a cap over the skull. In other representations one finds girls with a pigtail hanging down their back (see fig. 18).

During the Middle Kingdom the same styles occur, but with more variants such as a wide plait falling from the crown down onto the back, or more than one pigtail. The New Kingdom fashion was for a wide mop of hair at the right side, a variation of the smaller side-lock. This is, for instance, shown in several representations of the Amarna princesses (fig. 13). Such a thick, braided mass was secured by a hair-slide, as is clearly visible in the case of the Twentieth Dynasty princes. In the tomb of Anherkhew the Younger, however, the boy and the girls all wear one, or in the case of the elder girls two, small side-locks (see front cover illustration).

That such locks were indeed worn, and not a mere artistic devise, appears evident from the few well-preserved mummies of boys. A young prince, probably from the Twentieth Dynasty, and conceivably a son of Ramesses III, was found in his coffin in the Valley of Deir el-Medina. He had been abandoned there during a removal of mummies from a tomb in the Valley of the Queens to a cache, in order to escape the ever active tomb robbers. The prince still wears the wide side-lock, as does another mummy of a royal child (see p. 80), this one from the Eighteenth Dynasty. Perhaps he was a son of Amenhotep II, in whose tomb his mortal remains were discovered. The first prince was, according to his body, about five years old when he died, the latter was approximately eleven.

This conspicuous hair-style was not totally restricted to children. It occurs likewise on representations of the high-priest of Ptah at Memphis, the administrative capital. It was also *en vogue* among some members of the clergy of the mortuary cults for deceased rulers at the religious capital Thebes during the New Kingdom. These are the so-called *sem*-priests who looked after the offerings for the Pharaohs, a duty that was performed for private persons by the eldest son. Hence, these priests also played that rôle, which explains why they were groomed like 'sons'.

In a Middle Kingdom tomb at Meir in Middle Egypt the daughter of the local nomarch Ukhhotep is seen with a fish-shaped piece of jewellery dangling from her side-lock (fig. 16). Several of these hair ornaments have survived from that period, executed in gold or silver with inlays of carnelian, turquoise or lapis lazuli (fig. 17b). The fish they represent is the Catfish, *Synodontis batensoda*.

The *Tales of Wonder* (see p. 4) tells a story about King Snefru. He went for a pleasure trip on a lake, his boat being manned by twenty beautiful maidens, scantily clad in see-through net-dresses. "They rowed up and down, and His Majesty's heart was happy when he saw them rowing. Then one who was at the stroke oar fingered her side-lock, and a pendant of turquoise fell into the water". The attractive crew stopped rowing, and the Pharaoh offered to replace her ornament, but the girl was adamant that she wanted her own back. A scholar was summoned, and he "placed one side of the lake's water upon the other, and found the pendant lying on a sherd".

The story admirably confirms that such jewellery was worn in the hair-lock. However, miniature fish pendants also exist that seem too small for this purpose and may have been suspended from a necklace instead. Another type of charm was even shaped like the side-lock itself (fig. 17a). They are very rare, for

Fig. 16 Girl wearing a fish-shaped pendant. From the tomb of Ukhhotep (Cl) at Meir, Twelfth Dynasty

only eight examples are known, and how they were worn is a matter of doubt. Probably they too were attached to the bottom of the plait.

In a few instances we encounter a very peculiar hair-style consisting of three tufts on the sides and the top of the head. One of the granddaughters of Pashedu, a Deir el-Medina workman of the Nineteenth Dynasty, is so groomed in one of his tomb scenes (TT 3). A grandson in the same painting wears the wide mop of hair common in that period, while both children are naked except for an earring. The unusual hair-cut of the girl is that of Nubian children (see fig. 10a). It seems to have been adopted by some Egyptian families.

Until what age was the side-lock worn? In the circumcision scene in the Sixth Dynasty tomb of Ankhmahor (see fig. 35), the boy – who from his height seems to be about twelve years old – does not wear it. Yet, other lads such as those playing the 'hut-game' in the contemporary Giza mastaba of Idu (see p. 54), are also depicted without one. It could be surmised that the lock was shaved off at the beginning of puberty, just before circumcision, as is the hair in the modern Moslem ceremony (see p. 80), but there is no proof for this theory as far as Ancient Egypt is concerned.

Above we discussed the Toulouse statue-group (fig. 12), where the girl, although already showing a feminine form, still wears the lock and is nude. A painted limestone bust of an Amarna princess, now in Paris, also displays the beginning of breasts as well as a wide side-lock, but here the child is dressed. It seems that there was no general rule for when girls were too old to go undressed *and* had to cut off their children's hair. Perhaps the latter occurred when she became nubile (see chapter 9).

(a) *(b)*

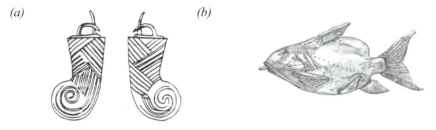

Fig. 17 Children's jewellery: (a) electrum side-lock pendant. Both sides, scale 1:1. Unprovenanced, Middle Kingdom (b) gold catfish hair ornament. Scale 1:1. From tomb 72 at Haraga, Twelfth Dynasty.

In a few instances the length of the side-lock does offer an indication as to the age of the infant. On the Berlin altar slab of the Amarna Period mentioned above, where the royal family is seen intimately together, the eldest princess wears a full, wide mop; the middle one a definitely shorter one, whereas the youngest still appears to be bald. Note, however, that the Oxford painting, also described above, shows two bald princesses, the one who is definitely larger being probably not anymore a baby. For a similar instance see figure 52.

In the recompense scene in Ay's tomb (fig. 13), there is also a clear distinction between the very short lock of the youngest daughter, evidently still a toddler, the wider one of her elder sister, and the full version of the eldest. In these cases the length of the hair, based on its natural growth, is a clue for estimating their respective ages. But this is only possible when several children appear in the same representation. Moreover, as we stressed in the introduction to this chapter, it is not their actual age which is depicted, but rather the stage of life they are suggested to have reached. With the Amarna princesses this seems to be in accordance with reality, since, fortunately, we do have a rough idea of their ages, but in other cases it can be purely conventional.

Evidently, Egyptian infants wore their hair in many ways, which changed during the course of time according to the dictates of fashion. There were also various styles present at the same time. As with dress, many questions still remain unanswered, and may regrettably always be so due to the strict artistic rules which screen reality. The tangible objects: dress, human hair, and jewellery, can provide solutions, but unfortunately they have rarely survived.

4 The Realm of Childhood

An insight into the upbringing of children in Ancient Egypt can be afforded by a study of the tomb scenes, surviving artefacts, and textual evidence. These sources reveal that youngsters kept pets, owned toys, participated in games (chapter 5), and were gradually introduced into the adult world by rôle play. Although earlier at work alongside their parents, they could still, on occasions, be as badly behaved as their modern counterparts.

The Ancient Egyptians are renowned for their love of animals. Dogs were man's faithful companions, cats are often depicted under the chair of their mistresses, while monkeys with their clownish antics and capacity for imitation amused their owners.

Therefore, it does not surprise us that children are frequently represented with their pets. Some New Kingdom wooden and ivory mirror handles are carved in the form of young girls who hold animals on their arms. Kittens are depicted on examples in Berlin and Bolton, and on a handle, now in Bologna, a small duck nestles in the child's left hand which rests in front of her breast. A bird is similarly nursed by the girl on the Toulouse statue (see fig. 12).

Indeed, birds are fairly commonly represented as children's pets. In the Fifth Dynasty tomb of Nefer and Kahay at Saqqara, for instance, a naked girl with a pigtail (see for this hair-style p. 32) holds a lapwing by its wing (fig. 18). In the Middle Kingdom tomb of Ukhhotep at Meir, the owner's daughter, mentioned above in connection with the fish-ornament dangling from her side-lock (see p. 33), stretches out her left hand. In this she grasps a lotus-flower on which a pigeon is perched (see fig. 16).

Boys are often shown clutching a hoopoe in one hand, a bird that becomes tame in captivity and attracts the attention of youngsters by its gaily coloured plumage. Pigeons were also kept by boys, as attested by reliefs in the famous Fifth Dynasty mastaba of Ti at Saqqara. They are held by the two elder girls in the family scene in the Twentieth Dynasty tomb of Anherkhew the Younger (TT 359) (see front cover illustration). The Nineteenth Dynasty tomb of Sennedjem (TT 1), also from Deir el-Medina, depicts a girl in a flared robe who has what appears to be the Egyptian or Nile goose in her grip. The same bird occurs in children's hands on some stelae from this site. Whether in such New Kingdom instances these animals, which could be aggressive towards humans, were indeed pets, or rather offerings, is not quite clear. This is especially so in view of another painting in Sennedjem's tomb where adults are carrying geese, which in this case are probably intended for sacrificial purposes.

Fig. 18 Nefer, with his pet dog, accompanied by his nude daughter who clutches a lapwing. From the mastaba of Nefer at Saqqara, Fifth Dynasty

An unusual scene is found in the tomb of the courtier Meryre II at el-Amarna. Six royal princesses are here depicted standing in two rows in a kiosk behind their parents' throne. Of the younger ones, in the bottom row, both the first and the second each carry a young gazelle, while the last girl tickles the animal held by her sister. The representation is conspicuous since gazelles in general cannot be domesticated, although other equally untameable animals such as antelopes and ibexes are known to have been kept in the North Palace at el-Amarna. These wild beasts do not usually return signs of affection, as kittens, for example, are accustomed to do.

Egyptian children played with toys, as do infants all over the world. Not with the sophisticated kinds as are presented to them in modern society, although, as we shall see, some were of principally the same type as in our age. Excavations have brought to light objects which were certainly, and in some instances probably, made to amuse the youngsters.

Particularly in the Middle Kingdom town of Kahun several toys have been found. For instance, there are balls, made either of wood or segments of leather sewn together, and stuffed with dried grass or barley husks. One of the latter type, now in Manchester, had obviously cracked and subsequently been carefully re-stitched, demonstrating that it was a valued possession. Painted reed and linen balls are known from other sites (fig. 19). For the various games that especially girls played with them, see chapter 5.

Kahun has also yielded whip tops, ranging from 2.5 to over 7 centimetres in height. They are circular pieces of wood flattened at one end and pointed at the other. Examples in blue faience (a glazed composition) have been found elsewhere (fig. 19). A special type of toy from Kahun consists of long wooden sticks, measuring up to 16 centimetres, which are pointed at both ends. These were tipcats, which were thrown into the air and hit with a stick or a club before they fell on the ground. The child who managed to hit the 'cat' the furthest was the winner. This game is still played in the United Kingdom in Lancashire where it is called 'Piggy', while a different version, with complicated rules, occurs in modern Egypt.

Already from Prehistory we find proof for another pastime. In a child's grave, number 100 at Naqada, Petrie found a complete set of nine travertine and breccia skittles, with four porphyry balls and a small gate made up of three marble bars through which the balls had to be rolled. This group is now in Oxford. Parts of a similar game, from another tomb at Naqada, are in the Petrie Museum. It consists of sixteen balls (ten being of limestone, four of porphyry, and two of breccia) and one porphyry bar from a similar gate, but no skittles.

From many sites small animal figures, roughly modelled from Nile mud, are known. They comprise hippopotami, crocodiles, cattle, sheep, pigs, monkeys and apes, etc. A particularly fine example is the pack donkey now in New York.

It was discovered by the Earl of Carnarvon's expedition in the area of Deir el-Bahri, and dates from the Second Intermediate Period. The nine clay sacks which the animal carries are supported by four vine-leaf stalks thrust into the body of the beast. Although this is indeed most probably a children's toy, not all clay figures were made for or by youngsters. Some were plainly votive offerings.

The exact nature of numerous doll figures is equally uncertain. Very probably most rag dolls were the possessions of girls, perhaps also of boys. Some even have their own accompanying wardrobes, comprising several changes of outfit. A clear indication that the human figure was indeed a toy is when it was found in a child's grave. An example is the wooden doll with moveable arms from the Twelfth Dynasty tomb of the girl Sitrennut at Hawara (fig. 20). A carefully made wooden model bed was also discovered in this burial, perhaps for the same doll. The entire tomb group is now in the Petrie Museum.

Other specific female figures, however, are the so-called 'concubines' (see p. 6), magical representations intended to stimulate fertility, and therefore placed in a funerary context. In these the genitalia are mostly emphasized, which clearly distinguishes them from girls' dolls.

Fig. 19 Children's toys: (above) left and right, painted reed and linen balls. Unprovenanced, Roman Period; (centre) blue faience tops. From the Faiyum, Roman Period; (below) wooden feline with crystal eyes and a moveable jaw fitted with bronze teeth. From Thebes, New Kingdom

In Kahun too some painted wooden puppets with moveable limbs were found, like that belonging to Sitrennut. Moreover, Petrie discovered in one house a large stock of doll's hair, consisting of fine flax threads, about 15 centimetres in length, placed together and rolled with mud, which would have been inserted into holes in the figure's head. (Sitrennut's doll was found with such a wig, which was unfortunately lost soon after discovery.) Hence this building at Kahun has been dubbed 'the toy-maker's shop'.

More intricate still than dolls with loose limbs are some jumping jacks. In Berlin there is a wooden crocodile with a moveable lower jaw, and in the British Museum are similar figures of both a mouse and a feline (fig. 19). Leiden has a crude wooden human figure with outstretched arms which, when a cord is pulled, moves up and down on a board as if grinding corn.

Somewhat doubtful is the purpose of a New Kingdom wooden model boat on wheels, discovered by Petrie in a tomb at the town of Gurob in the Faiyum, and now in the Petrie Museum. A very fragile object, it was found in pieces and subsequently reconstructed. On the bow is what seems to be a ramming device, in the centre on relatively long poles a light awning, and at starboard a steering oar. It has been suggested that it was originally a funerary boat, intended for a grave, and was later adapted for use as a toy by adding the wheels. Ships on wheels are very rarely depicted, just as generally vehicles on four wheels seldom occur. Tuthmosis III mentions in the report on his Syrian campaigns at Karnak that his transport-ships were placed on wagons pulled by oxen, and a few representations of two- and four-wheeled carts do exist, proving that they were not quite unknown. So it may indeed be that someone put a funerary boat on an under-carriage for the amusement of a child. The delicate object was perhaps rather more ornamental than an actual plaything.

One exceptional and splendid toy deserves a more extensive description. It was excavated in the Middle Kingdom tomb of a girl called Hapy at el-Lisht, in the Faiyum district, and consists of four small ivory figures, about 6 centimetres high. One is a loose piece, now in New York, and three, now in Cairo, are together placed on a rectangular base. All four stand on round, 'spoon'-shaped, pierced bases. They represent naked dancing pygmies. The loose one puts his hands together in a gesture of clapping; the three others hold them with their palms outwards at shoulder level. All four have bowed legs. Their bases were placed in boxes which are also pierced. When strings were attached to the figures and threaded through the holes, they caused, when pulled, jerking movements of the dancers, even to the sophistication of full pirouettes.

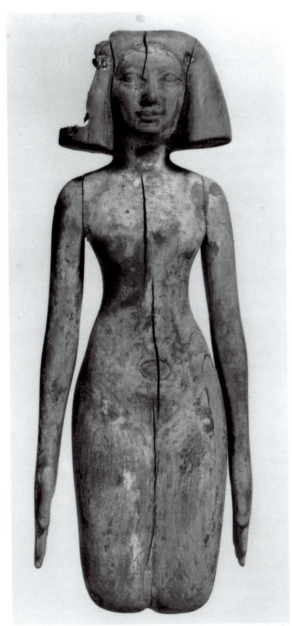

Fig. 20 Painted wooden doll with moveable arms. She originally had a wig of mud beads. From tomb 58 at Hawara, Twelfth Dynasty

41

Pygmies were famed in Ancient Egypt for their special dances. In the *Pyramid Texts* (spells for the deceased king) a sentence occurs stating: "He is a pygmy of the divine dances, who diverts the god in front of the Great Throne". During the Sixth Dynasty an expedition leader named Harkhuf brought back from Nubia such a pygmy, as had been done earlier by another traveller for King Isesi of the Fifth Dynasty. When Harkhuf sent a message about his journey to the Pharaoh, Pepi II, who was still a boy, the youthful ruler was so enthusiastic at the prospect of possessing the dwarf that he wrote by his own hand a letter to his emissary. He urged him to bring the African quickly and safely to the court at Memphis, for "My Majesty desires to see this pygmy more than the gifts of Sinai and Punt". This private letter was evidently considered a high honour by its recipient, who had a copy inscribed on the outer wall of his tomb at Qubbet el-Hawa, opposite Aswan. So we still know the story.

Against this background it is clear why the ivory dancing pygmies with their expressive faces constituted not only a sophisticated, but also a highly prized toy. So treasured in fact, that already in antiquity it was painstakingly repaired with tiny dowels. Whether, however, its child owner even played with it looks doubtful. Its material, ingenious construction, and fairly fragile structure, all rather suggest an object for grown-ups.

A child's life, in those times, was not completely filled by playing. It also contained a gradual introduction into work as an adult, a process which began at an earlier stage than in our society. This is understandable, for the majority of the youngsters, and virtually all girls, never attended a school. So they had all the opportunity, first as a natural matter for fun by rôle play, and progressively more seriously, of taking part in their parents' activities, at home, in the fields, and in the workshops.

That is still the case in the rural areas of modern Egypt where, already from the age of three onward, boys run errands and feed animals. As the Egyptians say, this period in life is for them "to be moistened with earth". From about seven years of age on their help becomes more important, and at twelve they fulfil essential duties in the tilling of the fields. Girls are also sent out at an early age on errands, and get to perform small chores in the house, in the preparation of food, for instance, or attending to poultry or sheep. Later on, after reaching approximately their seventh birthday, they help in baking bread and collecting fuel for the oven. At all ages, children, particularly girls, but boys as well, are supposed to look after their younger siblings. Doubtless the same would have held true in Pharaonic times.

In the representations on the tomb walls we encounter, for instance, juveniles when they bring offerings to the gods and the deceased in the company of their parents. On some New Kingdom stelae from Abydos a boy or a girl is depicted adoring Osiris, together with adults. Similarly they appear in the tomb chapels of Deir el-Medina in adoration scenes.

According to their nature children are accustomed to imitate their elders. So we see girls among the female mourners at funerals, in the same attitudes as their mothers and elder sisters, doubtlessly uttering the same shrill wailing cries. A famous instance occurs in the Theban tomb of the vizier Ramose (TT 55), of the Eighteenth Dynasty, where in the painted scene of the funeral cortège a naked girl is depicted with her hands in the same typical gesture as the elder women. A similar representation occurs in the roughly contemporaneous Theban tomb of Neferhotep (TT 49) (see fig. 10b).

Boys too imitated their elders, as can be seen on a New Kingdom stela now in Turin. Two sisters are kneeling before an offering stand, at the other side of which the deceased housewife, very probably their mother, is seated. Behind them squats their younger brother, who holds his arms in an attitude of mourning similar to that of one of his sisters. The youngest sibling, still an infant for she is rendered naked, brings up the rear and apes her seniors.

At an early age children started to help their parents. A New Kingdom proverbial expression states: "You shall not spare your body when you are young; food comes about by the hands, provision by the feet". The representations show girls looking after their younger brothers and sisters, and, like their mothers, carrying them in a sling (see fig. 10b). A sentence from a spell quoted above (see p. 22): "Is there no sister to fan you?" is also of relevance here.

Boys, but also girls, are depicted in agricultural scenes engaged, for instance, in gleaning. This is shown in the Eighteenth Dynasty Theban tomb of Djeserkareseneb (TT 38), where a boy and a girl are seen, beside each other (but drawn, according to the Egyptian artistic conventions, above each other), picking up the ears amidst high standing corn. They put the gleanings in a basket which they carry on their arm.

In Old Kingdom tomb scenes we find particularly boys watching flocks or tending cattle, thereby assisting the herdsmen. In the Fifth Dynasty mastaba of Hetepherakhet, now in Leiden, a naked boy hands up a vessel to an adult for the latter to drink from. A similar gesture occurs in another relief from the same tomb, but in this case the action takes place on a cargo-boat on the river. In the Old Kingdom tomb of Pepiankh at Meir a kitchen hut is represented (fig. 21). On the right a man is busy roasting a duck on a spit over a brazier, fanning the glowing charcoal with his other hand. Above him, joints of meat and a duck are hanging on a line. His companion to the left, who is also squatting, tucks into a piece of meat. Between them a boy is standing who carries a pot in his right hand and in his left an unidentified object. The fellow on the left orders him: "Get to work, that you may summon the lads to eat", whereupon he answers: "I'll do it".

Fig. 21 In a kitchen hut one man is at work while his companion, who is eating, orders a boy to run an errand. The hieroglyphs give the lad's answer: "I'll do it". From the tomb of Pepiankh (A2) at Meir, Sixth Dynasty

Evidently the boy had his own duties in the kitchen, apart from running errands. From a New Kingdom 'schoolbook' we learn that the baker, in the act of placing bread on the fire, puts his head into the oven, while his son holds his feet. "In the event of slipping from his son's hand, he thereby falls down into the oven's bottom". Such a child bore a heavy responsibility!

In the Nineteenth Dynasty tomb of Ipuy (TT 217) at Deir el-Medina we find a boy chasing birds from a heap of grain, also a type of simple 'work'. Other scenes of that period depict youngsters assisting at ploughing, or themselves sowing, and a text describes the personnel of a vineyard as consisting of seven men, four adolescents, four old men, and six children, totalling twenty-one.

All this demonstrates that the economic importance of even fairly young children was not negligible for the households of the poor. In the case of the upper classes, however, it would have been the slaves or servants who performed the minor duties. In the Eighteenth Dynasty Theban tomb of a certain User (TT 260) there is a scene of a nude girl arranging cushions on a chair, under the supervision of an elder servant. In the register above another lass is smoothing down the linen on a bed. A similar representation, but badly damaged, occurs in the contemporary Theban tomb of Amenemhat (TT 82); enough has been preserved to allow us to surmise that she is also making the bed.

As in these cases, the girls assisting their mistress at the toilet may also have been slaves and the same holds true for those nude beauties serving at banquets in many Eighteenth Dynasty tombs. In one instance such a 'waitress' even washes her hands before handing out food and drink. Whether the dancing girls or those in the orchestra at the festival meals (see p. 28) were free citizens or not is uncertain.

Boys are rarely represented as dancers, but one at least occurs, accompanied by an all female orchestra, in the tomb of Neferhotep (TT 49), while another infant, perhaps still very young, waves a branch. On the same wall are seen two nude Nubian boys, recognizable from their striking hair-style, and wearing earrings. They walk among the ladies accompanying Neferhotep's wife when she leaves the palace after an audience. Although these tiny boys were probably indeed slaves, they seem to have been kept almost as pets.

In the Deir el-Medina tomb of the sculptor Ken (TT 4), dating from the Nineteenth Dynasty, a girl, carrying a baby in a sling, is depicted in a funeral procession, conspicuously wearing the 'Nubian' hair with tufts. As such a cut did indeed occur in some Egyptian families among the necropolis workmen (see p. 34), it remains uncertain whether she was a young member of the family or a slave.

Since such servants, whether free or not, appear to have been fairly young, their performance can hardly have been impressive. That this was felt to be so according to the Egyptians themselves is amply demonstrated by an early Eighteenth Dynasty letter. The author asks a high official why his female servant, who was with him, has been taken away, for "she is a child and cannot work".

All these instances of more or less serious activities does not mean that children did not play, as appears evident from their toys; nor that they were invariably well-behaved and helpful. In the famous Eighteenth Dynasty Theban tomb of Menna (TT 69) we see two girls in a corn-field who are quarrelling and trying to tear out each other's hair. In the register below this others are depicted in a more friendly pursuit. One sits, leaning back and stretching out her bare foot, while her companion examines it, probably attempting to pull out a thorn.

The much cited tomb of Neferhotep (TT 49) gives us a delightful picture of naughtiness (fig. 22). While the wife of the official is received by King Ay in his garden house, she is followed by a train of well-dressed female servants. The last figure in the row, very probably a nanny, lags somewhat behind. Obviously the day had been hot and the children had worn her out, so she is happy to be able to gulp down a draught of beer from a jar. Meanwhile her charges, a boy and a girl, both of whom are naked, have teased a doorkeeper, who appears from a gate brandishing a stick.

Fig. 22 A boy and a girl threatened by an irate doorkeeper while their nanny drinks from a jar. Part of a scene in which a lady is received by the Pharaoh Ay in the palace gardens. From the Theban tomb of Neferhotep (TT 49), Eighteenth Dynasty

If all the representations of infants seriously occupied seem to render a stern picture of their life, these last scenes show that the realm of childhood was, as might be expected, the same in Ancient Egypt as in all other times and cultures.

In a small number of Old and Middle Kingdom tombs several representations occur of different games, played by boys and girls. With a few notable exceptions (see below) the two sexes are never portrayed together. In this connection it is interesting to note that neither are there any mixed groups of players in Upper Egypt at the present time. In the Old Kingdom scenes it is clearly lads and lasses who are shown, the boys being sometimes, although not always, distinguished by their side-locks, and in all cases naked. In the Middle Kingdom the age is less evident; perhaps children as well as adolescents are here depicted (see p. 23).

Some of the games we would term 'acrobatics' or even 'dancing'; most, at least, were 'athletics'. Yet, there is nothing like the physical education of the Greeks or of modern times. Genuine sports are only for specific groups, especially for soldiers as a requisite part of their drill, and in this category New Kingdom princes and their companions should also be reckoned (see chapter 10). Exercises are also characteristic in the training of professional dancers.

It is not always clear why the games were featured on tomb walls, and what the deeper meaning was that motivated their portrayal. They are certainly not simply pictures of daily life, but rather connected with religion and the afterlife. In addition, the games have been generally supposed to possess didactic contents as a preparation for adult life, and a psychological aspect concerned with the repression of sexuality.

Acrobatics, closely connected with dancing, played a role in the cult. An example is the scenes of girls turning back flips or somersaults. A group of four such lasses, resting on both their hands and feet with either their backs or fronts bowed upwards in an arch, occurs on the Red Chapel of Hatshepsut now reconstructed in the Open Air Musuem of the Karnak Temple. On the same walls is another group of six, and in the Luxor Temple even twelve are shown. Each time they are accompanied by musicians, playing harps and sistra (Egyptian rattles), and they clearly form part of a procession.

It may be that the girls are not children any more, but young professional dancers. Such acrobatics, however, had to be gradually learnt. In the Middle Kingdom tombs of the nomarchs Baqt and Kheti at Beni Hasan these exercises are represented, in which girls help each other to turn head over heels in a somersault. One picture shows two stages, another three.

Although only girls seem to have 'danced' at religious occasions, boys also mastered the skill, though they never turn somersaults. The tomb of Amenemhat at Beni Hasan shows them engaged, during the transport of a statue, in a pirouette, several stages being depicted beside each other in the form of a strip cartoon. In another scene in the same register a boy turns cartwheels, ending up standing upon the back of a crouching friend.

Other types of physical exercises include balancing acts. For instance, a boy is standing on his head, his arms crossed over his chest. Elsewhere three lads carry a fourth on their shoulders (fig. 23b). The 'donkey-game' appears in an Old

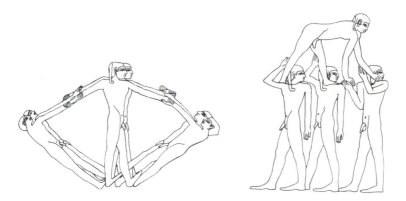

Fig. 23 Boys' games: (a) star game; (b) balancing act. From the mastaba of Ptahhotep at Saqqara, Fifth Dynasty

Kingdom scene where an older boy on all fours carries two small children on his back. They are poised one at each side, precariously hanging like sacks on a donkey, so that they have to clutch each other firmly in order to keep balance. This would require considerable strength for a toddler.

(a)   *(b)*

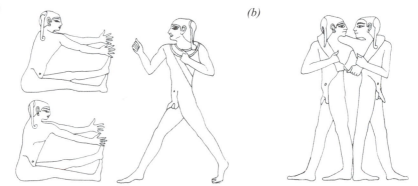

Fig. 24 Boys' games: (a) 'khazza lawizza'; (b) ?stampers. From the mastaba of Ptahhotep at Saqqara, Fifth Dynasty

A conspicuous counterpoising activity, represented in Old and Middle Kingdom tombs, has been dubbed by scholars the 'star-game' (fig. 23a). Its Ancient Egyptian name is 'erecting the wine-arbour'. Two boys are standing in the middle, holding with outstretched arms two, or even four others, who lean back balancing on their heels. They are spun around as quickly as possible. This is one case in which, in a single representation, boys and girls play together, for four lasses are rotated by two standing lads.

Equally obvious is the game known under its modern Arabic name *khazza lawizza* or 'jumping over the goose' (fig. 24a). It is still played in Egypt and in the Near East. Two boys are sitting, face to face, each putting his feet and his hands with outstretched fingers in a tier upon each other. So they form a living hurdle over which a third lad has to leap. In modern times the seated boys keep their feet wide apart; the trick here is therefore not only to jump high but also far enough. That may likewise be the case in the Sixth Dynasty mastaba (free-standing tomb) of Ptahhotep at Saqqara, where the seated boys are shown side by side, and a third during his run (fig. 24a). He has to spring over the hands and the feet of both friends in a single bound, or, after alighting midway between the two, he must leap again.

The Middle Kingdom representations of wrestling are famous. They occur in three different tombs at Beni Hasan, namely those of Amenemhat, Baqt III, and Kheti, where each time a large part of a wall is covered with figures in various stances. In order to easily distinguish the contestants one is coloured a darker reddish-brown than the other. They grasp each other around the waist, lift each other bodily from the ground, and even hold one another upside-down, until one lies prone on the floor.

That wrestling was popular appears evident from various small three-dimensional groups of the Middle Kingdom. The sport is also pictured on a New Kingdom Deir el-Medina ostracon, now in Cairo. In this case, however, it is soldiers who are exercising, not children. On the other hand, the scenes in the Old Kingdom tomb of Ptahhotep clearly represent young boys, as their side-locks prove.

The unique Fifth-Sixth Dynasty limestone group now in Chicago and illustrated here (fig. 25) has been called a wrestling scene, but this is not quite certain. In a most unusual mixture of the sexes a naked boy stands astride the neck and shoulders of a clothed girl. His knees are slightly bent and he leans a little forward. His hands, which lie on her back, grasp an unknown object, and he gazes straight ahead. The girl is kneeling beneath him resting on her hands, knees and toes. Very exceptionally in Egyptian art, her head is turned aside and upward, looking at the boy's back. A similar attitude is seen in the Fifth Dynasty mastaba of Hetepherakhet, now in Leiden, but there a man is beating a boy, perhaps in fun, which is clearly not the case in the Chicago group. It could be a version of leap-frog, that all time favourite pastime, which is here depicted.

Fig. 25 Painted limestone group statuette of a boy and a girl playing. From the tomb of Ny-kau-inpu at Giza, Fifth to Sixth Dynasty

Another contest, and one that is also still universally played, was that of tug-of-war. It is represented in the Sixth Dynasty mastaba of Mereruka at Saqqara, albeit without a rope, and is one of the very rare team games. Two lines of three boys stand facing each other. The captains grasp each other by the wrists, each placing one foot resting on its heel against that of his opponent, while their upper bodies lean backwards. Behind them the other two are standing, each holding the one in front with both hands around his waist, so forming a human chain. At a given command they begin to pull. The shouts of the team members are rendered in hieroglyphic captions above each group as: "Your arm is much stronger than he. Don't give in to him", to which the opposing party retorts: "My side is stronger than yours. Hold them firmly, my friend".

A game that is still popular in Britain is that of 'elbows'. The two contestants, sitting face to face, put their right elbows on a table and clasp each other's right hand so that their forearms are vertically aligned against each other. The aim is to force the partner's forearm back onto the table by brute strength. In Ancient Egypt what looks to be a variant was played standing up. The boys interlock their hands behind their necks, averting their faces. They try to hit each other's elbow so as to knock the opponent off balance.

In certain Middle Kingdom tombs girls' games with balls (see fig. 19) are represented. So we see them juggling with three balls, trying to keep them in the air by quickly throwing each one up, while the other two are still in momentum. A more difficult version is played with the arms crossed. On a satirical ostracon from Deir el-Medina, now in Stockholm, a mouse performs the same feat, but with only two balls (fig. 26). Perhaps she took them from the chest in front of her. At any rate, she looks well-pleased with her achievement!

Another trick involves passing balls to each other while riding piggy-back on a partner. Yet another is rhythmic throwing, performed in a group with four girls who stand around clapping their hands, while two others toss and catch three balls in rotation.

It may be that these amusements were partly exercises for cult games. We can even doubt whether the players were indeed young children, for they exhibit a special hair-style, that of pigtails with a tassel at the ends, which seems to belong to the official costume of dancers.

A ritual ball game is indeed known from the monuments where it is played by the Pharaoh in the presence of a female deity. He hits the ball with a stick or club, not unlike the batsman at cricket, while two priests attempt to make a catch. The goddesses, such as Hathor, are all connected with the concept of 'love', and the caption speaks of enjoyment. Moreover, this scene, as far as the Luxor Temple is concerned, is located in the Birth Chamber. It seems that a rite alluding to the sacred marriage of the Pharaoh and a goddess is here depicted.

This is far removed from our dexterous girls. Yet, they too may be involved in, or exercising for, a ritual performance. Already in the Old Kingdom *Pyramid Texts* mention is made of a ball game for the entertainment of the deceased.

Apart from athletic activities, there are also some pursuits of a much more sedentary nature. Surprisingly, they are never board-games, although these were widely indulged in by adults. Instead we have guessing games. For instance, a boy kneels on all fours with his eyes closed, while one of his two companions pokes him in the back. He has each time to guess which one has hit him. A similar version has been popular in Britain for centuries and is known under many names, such as 'Stroking the baby' or 'Hot cockles'. It is the same diversion that the guards used to taunt the blindfolded Jesus with when in the house of the high priest on the night before the Crucifixion.

Fig. 26 Painted limestone ostracon showing a mouse juggling with two balls. From Deir el-Medina, New Kingdom

Another gambling contest may have been played with four pots upside-down, the two competitors sitting at opposite sides. One of them secretes an object, perhaps a stone, under one of the vessels, and the other has to guess under which it is hidden. However, it must be admitted that this interpretation of the

52

scene is somewhat hypothetical. As the explanatory caption is a completely unknown word, there is some doubt as to whether this was indeed the purpose.

Easily recognizable are games such as 'territories' and 'flashing figures'. In the former two boys throw pointed sticks in sequence. They land upright in what appears to be a square sandpit. In the modern version the aim is to draw a line through the place where the dart fell in order to cut off a segment from the other's territory. Whether something similar is intended here is unclear. In the latter game one player calls out, according to the caption, "say it", i.e., 'guess', whereupon he opens his hand. The number of extended fingers decides who wins. If the guess is correct the two change places. Several variations occur in present day Britain, for instance that of 'Finger and Thumb'. It is also similar to the Italian 'Mora', which is especially used in deciding who will be 'he' or 'it', i.e., the odd man out.

Most of the activities discussed so far involve two participants, others being solely spectators. They are of the duelling, the exerting, or the guessing types. Games of chasing, such as 'Touch' or 'Tag'; of catching, like 'Farmer, Farmer, may we cross your golden river?', or seeking, notably 'Hide-and-seek', with all their possible variations, are simply not recognized on the tomb walls. Nevertheless, this does not mean that they were not played in real life.

At least one pretending game occurs: a variety of 'Cops and Robbers'. In the Old Kingdom mastabas of Ptahhotep, Mereruka, and Khentika/Ikhekhi at Saqqara, a bound captive, his elbows tied behind his back, is led away on a cord by a group of other naked boys. The caption runs: "Come, vagabond, who has followed his desire. If another one sees this, he is afraid".

Also of a make-believe character is the 'hut-game', a name coined by Egyptologists. It is clearly shown on a limestone block from an Old Kingdom tomb, probably at Giza, which is now in the British Museum (fig. 27). On the right of the central register are five boys, all with side-locks and naked, apart from the middle figure who is clad in a loin-cloth. Four of them are enclosed by a double line with rounded corners, which may represent a structure such as a hut, but may also depict, in plan, a cord or a narrow ditch. The two youngsters at the right are standing, with one hand raised. A third one, the principal figure, is stretched out on the ground and puts one hand through or over the enclosure, while a fourth is bending over him and seems to pin him down. The fifth stands outside the enclosure, and appears to be touching it with one hand. The caption over the scene runs: "Rescue you alone from it, my friend", meaning "you should attempt to escape from the enclosure alone".

A second instance of this game occurs in the Sixth Dynasty Giza mastaba of Idu. It is almost identical, except for small variations such as the absence of the side-locks and the loin-cloth of the bending figure. Above the head of the boy outside the enclosure are the additional words: "I shall rescue you". So despite what the others within say, this lad offers help to his companion.

The third example is a more vigorous interpretation found in the Middle Kingdom tomb of Baqt III at Beni Hasan. Here, however, there are several deviations from the earlier two: no enclosure, no side-locks, and all the participants are clothed in short kilts. The one 'outside' is held back by two others who grasp his arm while the prostrate youth seems to be pinned down by force. The figures at the right-hand side are missing. That it is nonetheless a rendering of the same scene is apparent from the caption, which is practically identical.

The absence of an enclosure raises the question of how essential this detail was to the 'game', the exact rules of which are unknown. It was, however, particularly on account of this feature, which was interpreted as a 'hut' that a suggestion has been made that the activity was derived from puberty rituals, for huts and enclosures are a facet of such ceremonies among several African peoples. However, the argument is very weak, and the lack of this particular detail in the later tomb could simply be an indication of variations that children's games are apt to show at different times and places.

In the mastaba of Idu the activity seems connected with what two girls right of the 'hut' are doing, for the pigtail of one of them is hanging over the double line of the enclosure. Note that this can also be seen in the British Museum relief, although the child herself is lost (fig. 27). The lasses in Idu's tomb are standing, each with one arm on the other's shoulder. The caption above runs: "Linking the linkers", but what this means is obscure. An almost identical representation occurs in Ptahhotep's tomb of two boys (fig. 24b). Unfortunately the inscription here is equally cryptic, but a kind of 'scuffle' appears to be pictured, in which one lad attempts to knock the other down. Perhaps it is a version of the modern 'Stampers', where two contestants place their hands on each other's shoulders and stamp as hard and as many times as possible on the other's feet.

A final instance of a boys' game may actually be a ritual, although it is executed by youngsters and is juxtaposed to the 'hut' scene. It is a unique instance, showing dancing around a fertility figure, and occurs on the left-hand side of the central register of our, by now familiar, British Museum block (fig. 27).

Five naked boys, with side-locks, hold a staff in their right and what may be a reed-stalk or ear of grain in their left hands. They are running or cavorting around a central motionless figure. This also seems to be a lad, although the three strips of cloth hanging from his girdle veil his sex. In his right palm he holds a stick terminating in a hand, a sign of (low) authority. Most conspicuous is his head, which is covered by a mask. That it is indeed a disguise appears evident from the youth's lack of a neck, for it rests directly on his shoulders. The large tripartite wig is surmounted by two pointed, triangular ears. The human face, seen of course in profile, features a prominent nose, an enormous eye, and two horizontal grooves above the eyebrows. It is significant that, whereas all the figures in this scene, as well as in the 'hut-game', still show clear traces of reddish-brown pigment, the masked one is uncoloured. Possibly it was originally painted white.

Fig. 27 Painted limestone relief: (centre register) left, a fertility dance; right, the 'hut game'. From ?Giza, late Fifth to early Sixth Dynasty

Although suggestions have been made that the disguise represents the lion-eared god Bes (see fig. 6a), a more convincing argument is to see in the erect ears a genet rather than a lion or a leopard. The costume is one that connects the figure with lower rank fertility divinities, possibly a specific vintage deity. Therefore, the masked boy alludes to fertility, and the dance around him may depict a fecundity or harvest ritual, in connection, perhaps, with the reaping scene in the lower register. This would be more likely if the youngsters did indeed carry ears of corn. The accompanying caption, which probably reads: "Dancing by a group of children", sheds no light on the interpretation of the scene.

Some of these games clearly had the function of preparing the participants for adult life, either physically or, albeit seldom, mentally. So 'Cops and Robbers', as described above, evidently has the task of teaching the children that the law and order of the community should be maintained. This aspect may explain why the scene was depicted on the walls of three Old Kingdom tombs; clearly it had here a deeper significance than simply that of youngsters having fun. Such is also clear from the fertility dance, but in other cases, like the 'hut-game', the reason for its representation is just not explicit. Yet, there must have been a more profound meaning than that which meets the eye on the level of everyday activities. At least this will have been so in the conception of the artists and the tomb-owners who chose to have them represented. But what that implication may be is pure hypothesis. In the meantime, such scenes present us with tantalising glimpses into the secret world of childhood.

6 The Schoolboy

The ruling class in Ancient Egypt were called 'scribes', that is, literates, those who could read and write. This group comprised not only the state officials, but also the higher levels of the clergy, who administered the extensive properties of the temples, as well as a part of the officers' corps.

During the Old and Middle Kingdoms most of the army leaders were civil servants, but when, at the beginning of the Eighteenth Dynasty, Egypt set about conquering her Near Eastern and Southern neighbours and founded an illustrious Empire, the army became the third power in the land, on a par with the bureaucracy and the priests. Among its members the officers of the chariotry were destined to play particularly important rôles. To what extent they were literate is uncertain. The administrative staff, however, who looked after transport and supplies during the campaigns, and the levying and organization of the troops, clearly had to be able to read and write. They also needed some knowledge of arithmetic and mathematics. This category of officers began their career as military 'scribes'. Some of them rose to high positions in the state.

A famous example is Amenhotep, the son of Hapu, under the mid-Eighteenth Dynasty Pharaoh Amenhotep III. Originating from the Delta town of Athribis, possibly from a simple family, he became the King's favourite, even replacing his lord at the celebration of the Royal Jubilee in the temple of Soleb in Nubia, and supervising the extensive building activities of this reign. In this capacity he was responsible for the erection of the Colossi of Memnon, in front of his master's funerary temple at Western Thebes, huge statues, over 18 metres high, which dominate the landscape to this day.

So highly valued was the position of literates in society that even the most important officials had statues made of themselves as scribes, squatting on the ground and writing on a papyrus roll stretched on their legs over their kilts (fig. 28). The edge of the roll is held in their left hand, the brush in the right. More than one figure of this type of Amenhotep, son of Hapu has survived. On the other hand, in the reliefs actual writing is always delegated to subordinates, scribes of lower rank, whereas the leading civil servants are merely represented as supervisors.

Some of these even became venerated in later ages, attaining the fame of saints, almost of deities. Best known are Imhotep, the architect of the Step Pyramid at Saqqara, built for his employer King Djoser of the Third Dynasty, and, from the New Kingdom, the Amenhotep just mentioned. Whereas deification in other societies is mainly restricted to warriors and priests, in Egypt the 'wise men', that is, literate bureaucrats attained this position. It clearly shows the exceptionally high appreciation of the Pharaonic culture for writing.

Fig. 28 Black granite statue of an anonymous high official in the attitude of a scribe.
From Saqqara, Fifth Dynasty

There was yet another category of people for whom literacy was essential, namely the artists, draughtsmen and sculptors. Theirs was the task of converting hieratic texts, written on papyri and ostraca, into hieroglyphs on tomb and temple walls, as well as inscribing them on statues. This would obviously have required a thorough knowledge of both scripts. Although less honoured than the administrators, artists too attained a status above the mass of the population, roughly equal to that of goldsmiths and physicians.

For all these professions a formal schooling was required. Yet, important as they were, we know surprisingly little about the organization of schools and their methods of teaching. The Egyptians in general do not record the means leading to an end, for instance, how they built the pyramids. So they never tell us in detail how boys were educated, nor are there any pictures of schools. The reason for this frustrating paucity of information should be sought in a trait of the Pharaonic civilization. One was interested in what lasted, what was permanent, rather than in the transitory; not in the way something was achieved, but in the end result. To be a scribe was essential, how one became one was hardly worth noting down. Still, as will appear, it is possible, from various sources, to compose a rough picture of schools in Ancient Egypt.

During the Old Kingdom no regular schools seem to have existed, except at the court. On a stela from his Fifth Dynasty tomb at Saqqara, now in the British Museum, a certain Ptahshepses relates that after he had "knotted the band" (for this expression, see pp. 90-91), he was educated among the royal children in the palace, where "the king valued him above all children". Perhaps he attended a school there. Later on he even married a princess.

Schoolmasters are unknown from this period. Usually the boys will have been trained by their fathers, although some elderly men took sons of others as their pupils. In that case they were respectfully called 'father', a custom that persisted through all Egyptian history, so that a man could have two different 'fathers'. The *Instruction of Ptahhotep*, probably from the Fifth Dynasty, distinguishes between "a son by the grace of god" and an actual "offspring who can make trouble" and disobeys his parent. Such an adopted pupil was also called, as a real son, "a staff of old age", one who looked after his elder mentor. Having been instructed "in the sayings of the past", the young man was supposed to be devoted to him who taught him how to behave, for "no one is born wise".

Some wise men took several 'sons'. In the Middle Kingdom *Tales of Wonder* (see p. 4) the magician Djedi had so many students that they had to be transported, together with his 'books', on a special ship. Among fellow pupils of one master a relationship could spring up. Pharaoh Merikare, from the First Intermediate Period, is exhorted by his father in his *Instruction* to be merciful to defeated rebels, particularly: "Do not kill a man whose virtues you know, with whom you have chanted the writings"; that is, with whom you have been at school. In chapter 10 we shall deal with such classmates of the Royal Princes.

It is in the Middle Kingdom that we first come across the Egyptian word for school, literally "house of instruction". It occurs in a text in the tomb of Kheti, a nomarch at Asyut. He urges "every scribe and every scholar ... who has been to school", when passing his monument, to behave properly and to speak an offering formula for the deceased. Although the text is lacunary, it is possible to deduce from it that scribes were at that time formally educated.

It is not difficult to guess at the reason for the creation of educational institutions in the Middle Kingdom. The state, following the reunification of Egypt under a single, strong ruler, required capable administrators. During the troubles at the end of the Old Kingdom such skills had been largely lost, so that it was impossible to rely any more on the few trained in an informal way by their fathers. It was the needs of the new bureaucracy that occasioned the foundation of schools.

The most important was certainly that in the Residence, which during the Twelfth Dynasty was situated near el-Lisht. It was to that central training institution that the author of the contemporary text known as the *Satire of the Trades* brought his son. The composition has recently been characterized a "treatise on the joys and benefits of education using both negative examples and positive encouragement". The first sentence of this text runs: "Beginning of the Instruction made by a man of Sile, whose name was Khety, son of Duauf, for his son called Pepi, as he journeyed south to the Residence, to place him in the school for scribes, among the children of the magistrates, with the élite of the Residence".

It is noteworthy that Khety, who came from the provincial town of Sile at the north-eastern tip of the Delta, bears no title. Probably he was a simple citizen, yet he succeeded in finding a place for his son at the esteemed school for the children of the topmost class, which of course offered excellent opportunities for the pursuit of a successful future career.

Perhaps there still existed a particular educational establishment at the court, specifically for princes and the sons of courtiers. Pepi's school, on the other hand, seems rather intended for the future functionaries in the central government, and evidently accepted boys of lowly birth too. Whether such institutions also occurred in provincial centres is not clear; at least, there seems to have been none near Sile. But it was at the academy in the Residence that the top civil servants were trained, and this may well be the reason why Khety preferred it for his son.

Concerning the age of the schoolboy, the numbers to a class, the curriculum and the didactics, and all related matters, nothing at all is known until the New Kingdom. It is only in that period that our sources begin to flow more abundantly.

As regards the age, education seems normally to have commenced at the same time as in our society. Of course, this was not regulated by law; it will have depended very much upon the physical and mental ripeness of the individual boy, so could have been anything from five to ten years of age. In one case we are at least able to make a reasonable guess as to when the Egyptians first went to school.

The High Priest of Amun at Karnak, Bekenkhons, from the reign of Ramesses II, presents us, on one of his block statues, with detailed information concerning his career. This limestone statue, which is now in Munich (fig. 29), probably provenances from a sanctuary at the back of the Karnak Temple which was dedicated to the deity Amun-Re-Harakhti 'who-hears-petitions', and was built by Bekenkhons himself. The sculpture, as well as its counterpart, now in Cairo, is an unfinished product from the post-Amarna Period, but the inscriptions are due to the later owner. He tells how he passed four years in the primary school, which was situated, according to the text on the Cairo piece, in the Mut Temple at Karnak. Then followed eleven years of apprenticeship in the royal stables, a time during which he learnt the basic ropes of the administration.

Only after those fifteen years of education did his real career in the temple begin. His first four years were spent as a simple priest, still under the supervision of his father who was also connected with the Amun Temple. There followed a progressive rise up the hierarchical ladder, until, after thirty-nine years, he reached the top and served another twenty-seven as High Priest. Altogether, from his earliest schooldays, this represents a time span of eighty-five years. When exactly he first went to school he does not tell us, but he can hardly have been older than five or six. The long-lived Bekenkhons must therefore have been at least ninety when he died.

Other evidence seems to confirm this picture. A Middle Kingdom high official, Ikhernofret, who presents on his stela, now in Berlin, a report on his management of the Osiris Mysteries at Abydos, states that he became a courtier when he was twenty-six after having been educated as a foster-child of the king. A certain Antef, from the same period, boasts on his stela, now in Paris, that he received his first office while still a child, that is, shortly after his formal education. Although his age is not mentioned, and we should not rule out the possibility that he may have been a precocious boy, this too suggests an early commencement for schooling.

A final indication can be found in the *Instruction of Ani*, from the Eighteenth Dynasty (see p. 15). There we are informed that it is the mother who sends a boy to school, where he is taught to write, hence a primary school. "She kept watching over you daily, with bread and beer in her house". Clearly, the lad still lives at home since she feeds him. Note that, in contrast to Pepi in the *Satire of the Trades* who was brought to school by his father, it is here the mother who takes care of her son's education. "Pay attention to your offspring", says Ani, "bring him up as your mother did you".

We also gain from this text the impression that, in the New Kingdom, children generally continued to reside at home during the first part of their

Fig. 29 Limestone block statue of the High Priest of Amun Bekenkhons inscribed with an autobiographical text. From Thebes, Nineteenth Dynasty

studies. Of course this was not applicable when they attended the court school, for then they dwelt in the palace. Nor will Kheti's son have lived with his parents, for Sile is far away from the Residence. In such cases the boys were probably placed in boarding houses, but whether these were attached to the schools we do not know. Hence we should not make the analogy with boarding schools in the modern sense.

One text conveys the impression that it was not the sturdiest lads who pursued an administrative career. It occurs in one of the so-called *Miscellanies*, anthologies composed by teachers and used as schoolbooks. These comprised various types of short texts such as model letters, hymns to certain gods, praises of the Pharaoh or the Residence, didactic treatises describing the misery of all professions other than that of scribe, etc. The relevant passage contains the following description of a schoolboy:

> Be a scribe! Your body will be sleek,
> your hand will be soft.
> You will not flicker like a flame,
> like one whose body is feeble.
> For there is no bone of a man in you.
> You are tall and thin.
> If you lifted a load to carry it, you would stagger,
> your feet would drag terribly.
> You are lacking in strength;
> you are weak in all your limbs, poor in body.

Therefore, "set your sights on being a scribe, a fine profession that suits you".

Although this is written from the viewpoint of the attraction which a military career was apt to exercise on the minds of adventurous young people, about which more will be stated below (see p. 68), these lines show us the delicately-built, less sportive and more scholarly type of boy as the future 'scribe'.

Concerning the school-hours very little is known. In the *Satire of the Trades* we come across the sentence: "If you leave the school when midday is called and go roaming in the streets ......" (the rest of the sentence is lost), which seems to indicate that, in the Middle Kingdom, the classes were held during the morning. As this text was used as a schoolbook in the New Kingdom, we would expect that the situation had not changed. It may be, however, that there was only a break at midday, and that in the later afternoon, after a siesta during the hottest hours, lessons were resumed.

One of the chapters of a *Miscellany* presents a picture of the everyday goings-on in the classroom. Unfortunately, the papyrus on which it is written is lacunary, but sufficient remains for us to be able to understand what happened. Evidently it is the father who is speaking:

I have placed you at school with the children of the magistrates
– a free quotation from Khety (see p. 60) –
in order to instruct and teach you in this profession with promotion
prospects. I will tell you how it goes with a student, when they call him:
'Awake! At your place! Your chums already have their books before
them. Lay your hand at your clothes, put your sandals right!'
You have to bring your exercises daily. Be not idle! They say: 'three
plus three ......'
On another happy occasion you grasp the meaning of a papyrus roll
......You begin to read a book, you quickly make calculations. Let no
sound of your mouth be heard; write with your hand, read with your
mouth. Ask from those who know more than you, and don't be weary.
Spend no day in idleness, or woe to your body. Try to understand what
your teacher wants, listen to his instructions. Be a scribe! 'Here I am',
you will say, every time he calls you.

From this lively description it is possible to deduce certain facts. Firstly, the boys
are not only taught reading and writing, but also arithmetic. Reckoning was done
silently ("Let no sound of your mouth be heard"), but the Egyptians read aloud.
Therefore, the word for 'to read' actually means 'to chant' or 'to recite', as can
also be seen from our quotation from the *Instruction of Merikare* (see p. 59).
Moreover, we get the impression of a strict discipline, which fits remarks in
other *Miscellanies*. In one a pupil states: "I grew up beside you (his master), you
smote my back, and so your teaching entered my ear". An almost proverbial
expression runs: "A boy's ear is upon his back; he hears when he is beaten". At a
later age, when he became an apprentice, even harsher punishments were applied
(see pp. 69-70).

We do not know how widely spread the school system was during the
New Kingdom. At Thebes there were at least two of these institutions, probably
more; one in the Mut Temple, where Bekenkhons received his education, and
one at the back of the Ramesseum. It has been suggested that there was also a
school in or near the Valley of Deir el-Medina, run for the children of the
necropolis workmen, several of whom were literate. However, the place where
the boys were taught has not yet been discovered. After the abandonment of the
village they were perhaps educated at the Temple of Medinet Habu. It may also
be that they went to the school at the Ramesseum.

Their time of apprenticeship they would have passed with an elderly
workman, their father, uncle, neighbour, or whoever. In that period they were
introduced into the secrets of drawing and sculpture, but they also continued to
extend their knowledge of writing and literature. The ostraca bearing such texts
have been found all over the area, in the Valley of the Kings, in the workmen's
village itself, and elsewhere. Therefore it seems that this part of the instruction

was not bound to a particular place; they simply wrote their exercises wherever they by chance happened to be.

Recent French excavations at the Rameseum have revealed the administrative buildings of a school: small offices and storage rooms complete with school texts, but no larger classrooms. That classes ever assembled within such a building is unlikely, even though the word for 'school' is written with the determinative sign for 'house'. Most Egyptian life took place in the open air, as will have been the case with the classes, the pupils sitting cross-legged on the ground around the master or one of his assistants. The phrase 'house of instruction', the equivalent of our 'school', therefore rather indicates the institution.

Perhaps the young children began by writing on wooden tablets covered on both sides with gesso, which played the rôle of the school-slates previously used in our era. A text written with brush and ink on such a medium could easily be wiped out. Several of these tablets have been found, but none with beginners' attempts.

Fig. 30 Pierced limestone schoolboy's writing board with six horizontal lines of hieratic text comprising a letter exchanged between two scribes exhorting the scribal profession. From Abydos, Twentieth Dynasty

A Twentieth Dynasty piece of limestone, in the shape of a tablet, provenances from Abydos and is now in Brussels (fig. 30). It bears a letter of six lines, in black and red ink, from one priest to another, who was probably his apprentice. The text deals with the manner in which a scribe should behave. It may in fact be a model letter, copied out on the stone after a former text had been erased, although this was done slightly carelessly, as its traces are still visible. Therefore, it may be a school exercise, and, to judge from its contents, not from the primary stage but the product of an advanced pupil.

The tablets have a hole in their upper side, as has this limestone example, through which a cord was passed so that they could easily be carried. Wooden types were also used in the administration, as is demonstrated by a scene from the Eighteenth Dynasty tomb of Djeserkareseneb (TT 38), an official of the Amun Temple at Karnak (fig. 31). He is measuring the corn in a field, which is why he is wearing protective leggings against the prickly ears, and is followed by his son who is also his assistant. As an apprentice, the latter carries a papyrus and a tablet, while the father holds his palette in his hand.

Another writing material used in schools was ostraca. Not papyrus, for that was, although probably not expensive, hard to obtain. It was only delivered by the ateliers to the administration, and even when a palimpsest, used and subsequently cleaned from its initial text, papyrus was too scarce to entrust to young pupils.

The training in writing began with hieratic (see fig. 1). Not, as we do, with single signs, but with words or even sentences. Very few examples of such early exercises survive. We do indeed possess a handful on which single words are written or even paradigmata, such as: "I am – he is – you are", etc., but the script is probably that of a fully fledged scribe, not a beginner. Although these exercises may reflect some insight into grammar, that did not in fact belong to the curriculum.

Instead, the procedure involved the chanting, on a single monotone, of short pericopes from venerated compositions to the boys, who in return would chant them parrot fashion until they knew them by heart. This method is still followed in Egyptian schools, particularly in learning the Koran. When they were familiar with the text, they wrote it down, either from a model supplied by the master, or later, when they had passed the first stages, from memory. Formerly Egyptologists believed that writing was also produced by taking dictation from the teacher, but a thorough investigation into the nature of the errors has proved that this was not the case, for none appears to be the result of a mishearing.

The order in which the texts were learnt seems to us incredible. One started with the only real schoolbook we know of, the book *Kemit*. This title means something like 'Compendium' or 'Summary'. It is a compilation of polite introductory formulae to letters; a story about the return of a traveller, at the request of his wife, as a model of the narrative style; and short sentences such as frequently occur in ideal autobiographies. All these are in the language and manner of the period when the *Kemit* was composed, that is, the early Middle Kingdom. Therefore in a language the poor students of the New Kingdom scarcely understood, written in old-fashioned hieratic and in vertical columns, an archaism that had, already in the Twelfth Dynasty, been exchanged for horizontal lines (see fig. 1). The pupil's difficulties are comparable to those which the copying of a medieval English manuscript would present to six year olds now! That this was indeed the first exercise that was tackled appears evident from the numerous surviving ostraca with sections of the *Kemit*, several of which are written in an untrained hand. Obviously, it was not the intention that the children should understand what they wrote; they merely learnt a venerated technique.

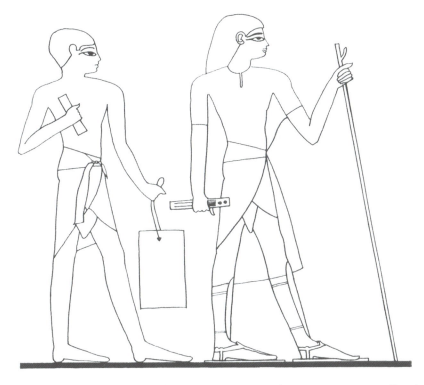

Fig. 31 A high official followed by his apprentice son who carries a papyrus roll and a writing tablet. From the Theban tomb of Djeserkareseneb (TT 38), Eighteenth Dynasty

So it continued. After the *Kemit* the boys memorized and wrote down passages from classical, Middle Egyptian texts, either Instructions or well-known literary compositions such as the *Story of Sinuhe*. Only subsequently did they turn to Late Egyptian texts, from their own period, of which at least the grammar as well as the words were familiar to them. It may be that these subjects were only reached when they were apprentices, and not at primary school any more. All ostraca, and certainly the papyri that bear them, show a well-trained hand.

As we have seen above, the boys not only learnt reading and writing, but also arithmetic. Perhaps singing also belonged to the curriculum. In one

Miscellany the teacher says to a schoolboy: "You have been taught to sing to the reed-pipe, to chant to the flute, to recite to the lyre". The pupil in this case is certainly beyond the primary school, for he is scolded because he now sits in a brothel among the girls. Therefore, singing seems to have belonged to the secondary stage of his education and perhaps to those courses geared to future members of the clergy – although most vocalists in the temple-choir were in fact women.

Whatever, during the years of apprenticeship the broader education necessary for a particular profession took place: medicine for physicians, cult practices for priests, art for draughtsmen and sculptors, metalwork for jewellers and goldsmiths, etc. We even know of an assistant of a musician and one of an actor, but it is uncertain whether these were actually trainees. It is to this stage that most chapters in the *Miscellanies* refer, particularly to the training of future administrators. Formal higher education as we know it at universities did not exist, and for creative thought there were no opportunities within the bureaucratic system.

Life at school must have appeared dull to many a boy, good only for weaklings (see p. 63). A career in the army, the romance of campaigning in foreign lands, the possibility of drawing the attention of Pharaoh himself by one's gallant deeds, all seemed far more alluring. Therefore, many a chapter in the *Miscellanies* points to the hardships of a soldier's life. There was clearly avid competition between the army and the bureaucracy to recruit the ablest youngsters.

Even in the religious texts included in the schoolbooks we discover a reflection of this tension, for instance in a prayer to Thoth, the god of wisdom and writing:

> Suffer me to relate thy feats in whatever land I may be.
> Then the multitude of men shall say:
> 'How great are the things that Thoth has done!'
> They shall come with their children in order to brand them
>   for thy calling,
> a calling good for the Lord of Victory (i.e., the Pharaoh).
> Happy is he who exercises it.

So, even in a prayer, propaganda is made for the scribal profession. This is also a convenient place to note that there was no regular 'school-god', unlike Nisaba in Sumer. The Ancient Egyptians first promoted Seshat, the goddess of writing, but later Thoth was felt to be sufficient.

Another approach in advertising a scribal career was the painting in deterrent colours of life in other occupations, as we find in the *Satire of the Trades*. It is not for nothing that this became one of the most quoted textbooks.

Yet another theme was the picture of a boy, or rather an adolescent, who neglects his studies.

> I am told that you have abandoned writing
> and whirl around in pleasures;
> that you go from street to street,
> and it reeks of beer wherever you quit.
> Drink drives the people away,
> it causes your soul to wander.

Is not this as if we hear complaints about young people in modern society, although today we expect drugs rather than beer?

> You are like a crooked steering-oar in a boat,
> that obeys on neither side,
> like a shrine without its god, like a house without bread.
> You have been caught out while scrambling over a wall,
> after you broke the stocks.
> People are running away before you,
> for you inflicted wounds upon them ......
> You are sitting in public houses, surrounded by whores;
> you sit in front of the girl, drenched in ointment,
> a wreath of flowers around your neck,
> drumming on your belly.
> You stumble and fall flat on your face, smeared with dirt.

Certainly a vivid picture of the tearaway the young man had become. Did it indeed hold them back from following their yearnings? Schoolmasters of all times seem to believe so: "Are you an ass? One will master you. There is no sense in your body".

Evidently, such words had not always an effect, even when the culprit was put in the stocks. On the other hand, these measures do sometimes appear to have brought the lad to his senses, as when a teacher reminisces about his own schooldays, during which he admits to having been full of mischief:

> When I was of your age, I spent my time in the stocks;
> it was they that tamed my limbs.
> They stayed with me three months.
> I was imprisoned in the temple,
> whilst my parents were in the fields,
> and my brothers and sisters as well.

The stocks here mentioned were wooden blocks around the feet, used to hold criminals in prison. Unruly apprentices were therefore treated as lawbreakers. But some succeeded in escaping: the young man of whom we told above, and also another one:

> You set fire to the stocks at night
> that you may climb over a high wall
> in the place where you are.

The last incident was a particularly serious case since the pupil was already thirty years of age, far too old to be indulging in such childish pranks!

On the other hand, the texts teem with remarks about how wonderful a position in the administration could be:

> The scribe is ahead of all work in this world.
> Be a scribe, for he is controller of everyone.
> He who works in writing is not taxed,
> nor has he any dues to pay.

> As for writing, it is profitable to him who knows it,
> more than any other office,
> pleasanter than bread and beer, clothing and ointment.
> It is more precious than a heritage in Egypt,
> than a tomb in the West.

Hence:

> Spend the day writing with your fingers,
> whilst reading by night.
> Befriend the papyrus roll and the palette.
> It pleases more than wine.

The teachers did not shrink from depicting the material advantages of a career in the bureaucracy. One did not have to pay taxes! One chapter in a *Miscellany* describes the beautiful villa and estate that a certain scribe Raia, who was a fairly high official, built for himself. The text enumerates its halls, doors and portals, its granaries, stables, and fish-ponds, all making it pleasurable to live there. At the end it is duly called "the sustenance of Amun", but that does not sound really convincing.

In the preceding chapter of the same papyrus a pupil promises to construct such an estate for his master, which in a schoolbook seems to us to border on an appalling flattery. Of course, such texts offered an ideal opportunity to teach the pupils, who learnt them by heart, several words and phrases concerning objects and products found at an estate. This was certainly one of the reasons why they were included in the syllabus. That they really stimulated the young man's perseverance in his studies we may doubt. As in the Nineteenth Century A.D., the Ancient Egyptian schoolmasters firmly believed in the results of moralistic texts. When we fail to do so any more, is it because we have become too cynical?

Not one word has yet been said about physical education. Sports do not seem to have belonged to the normal curriculum (see p. 47) – in contrast to the instruction of Royal Princes and their companions. The description of a pupil as a weakling with soft hands (see p. 63) confirms this. We read in the New Kingdom story of *Truth and Falsehood* that the boy (for his birth, see p. 1) was "sent to school and learnt to write well. He practised all the arts of war and surpassed his older companions who were at school with him". From those "arts of war" it is clear that he was educated at the court, not among ordinary future administrators.

Were girls also taught to read and write? In the bureaucracy there was no place for them, nor among the clergy, except for a few special posts. Where the feminine form for the word 'scribe' seems, very rarely, to occur, it may in most cases indicate a woman who 'painted', i.e. made-up, her lady.

Yet, there is circumstantial evidence that some women were literate. In a late Twentieth Dynasty letter, written by a man travelling far from home to his son, we read: "You shall see that daughter of Khonsumose and let her make a letter, and send it to me". That the girl's name is not mentioned suggests that she was still young. Although the use of the verb 'make', instead of 'write', seems to mean that she should dictate the message, it does in fact rather point to the opposite.

It has been stated that the palette of Akhenaten's eldest daughter Meritaten, found in Tutankhamun's tomb, shows that she could write. The same would then hold true for a miniature example, of unknown provenance, belonging to her younger sister Meketaten. However, these items bear pigment blocks in several colours, whereas scribes used only black or red ink. They were therefore painting equipment, and as such suitable for the education of Royal Princesses. Tutankhamun's own palette, also found in his tomb, shows signs of having been used. It is indeed proof that he could write, but that was never doubted.

More reliable evidence for female literacy comes from Deir el-Medina. Among the thousands of ostraca there are several which bear letters, mostly concerning trivialities. Some of them are addressed to, or sent by women, a handful even by one woman to another. They deal with feminine matters, for instance, a request for underwear to be made. Therefore, it seems unlikely that both sender and recipient, being illiterate, had to turn to a 'scribe' in order to produce and read the message. Evidently, at least some women in the workmen's families had been to school. In view of the exceptionally high cultural level in the village this does not come as a surprise.

Certainly there existed educated women among the upper classes. In tomb scenes we occasionally see under their chairs, instead of the usual toilet articles such as mirrors, or animals like cats and monkeys, scribal artefacts: a palette, the leather scribal kit bag in which the equipment was kept, and once even a papyrus roll (fig. 32). There is no proof that the lady indeed used these objects, but why else should they be depicted?

Fig. 32 The wife of a mayor of Thebes seated beside her husband, with a palette and a scribal kit bag below her chair. From the Theban tomb of Kenamun (TT 162), Eighteenth Dynasty

For what purpose did such high-born ladies receive a school education? Certainly it was not in order to obtain a post in the administration. Perhaps it was rather to be able to serve in a temple. More probably, however, it was a matter of culture, as in the Middle Ages when noblewomen were sometimes literate, whereas their warrior husbands were not.

Some of the love poems of the New Kingdom, written in a highly artificial language, were put into the mouth of an enamoured girl and may very well have been composed by young ladies. Despite obvious differences, they are

72

reminiscent of the medieval *chansons d'amour*. It would fit our picture of the courtly life style of the period when they were written and were enjoyed not only by women of high society.

As stated above (pp. 58-59), sculptors and draughtsmen were by necessity also literate. Apart from being trained in their artistic profession, they received a formal school education. This is the reason why the necropolis workmen who decorated the royal tombs, show such a high level of culture as evidenced by the numerous ostraca with literary texts found in the surroundings.

(a)

(b)

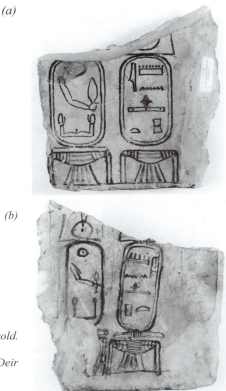

Fig. 33 Limestone ostracon with the names of Amenhotep I in cartouches, placed over the hieroglyphic sign for gold. (a) The recto written by the master; (b) the verso copied by a pupil. From Deir el-Medina, New Kingdom

For the ability of the draughtsmen to write we possess a proof from as early as the Fifth Dynasty. In the pit of a mastaba at Giza a wooden tablet was found, of which, it is true, the board itself was destroyed, but the white plaster coating, with writing in black, red and green pigment, was preserved. The cartouches of King Neferirkare and some names of deities were written in vertical columns, each being repeated four times, except the last one is written

73

only in triplicate. The pupil seems to have become weary of the repetition! On the reverse are, among other signs, drawings of various species of fish and geese. Since the latter do not function as hieroglyphs, it is evident that the board was the product of a trainee draughtsman.

A different proof occurs on a Deir el-Medina ostracon now in Stockholm (fig. 33). On one side of the limestone flake the master carefully drew, in black and red, the names of King Amenhotep I, within cartouches and over gold signs. On the reverse the pupil copied them, in a shaky and uncertain style. He was clearly still a beginner. Note that in the right-hand cartouche the signs drawn by the pupil have been turned in a different direction, i.e., from right to left.

Fig. 34 Pottery ostracon inscribed in black ink with practice drawings of standard figures by a sculptor's pupil. From Deir el-Medina, New Kingdom

Other such exercises on ostraca consist of figures, not hieroglyphs, and each is on an individual piece of limestone. A fine drawing of a Pharaoh on his throne, his pet lion beside him, finds its counterpart in a less successful piece by a novice. It is in itself not a bad copy, hence probably from the hand of a slightly advanced apprentice. Both pieces are now in Berlin.

To work from the very outset of a career belong ostraca with a series of simple signs, for instance the semi-circular ⌣, a basket. To draw and incise a straight half circle was evidently a problem for a boy. Less elementary are pictures of heads and incised hands, or even various hieroglyphic signs such as occur on a piece of sandstone from el-Amarna, now in Oxford. A similar ostracon from Deir el-Medina in the Petrie Museum bears the signs of a human face, a baby, an ibis, a so-called anthropoid bust, and a hardly identifiable squatting human wearing a large wig (fig. 34). Since some of these are not hieroglyphs, this will also be the exercise of a sculptor's disciple.

There is also proof that young draughtsmen copied literary texts when training. A Nineteenth Dynasty ostracon from Deir el-Medina bears a few lines of a literary composition, and concludes with the words: "By the draughtsman Merysakhmet, his beloved apprentice, to the scribe Nefersenut". The 'homework' was dedicated to the master by an advanced pupil.

Although many details still remain obscure, it appears evident from this long chapter that school education is perhaps the best known aspect of growing up in Ancient Egypt. This is quite in accordance with the high appreciation of literacy and the scribal profession.

In many primitive societies there exist mandatory public rituals which mark the transition between childhood and adult life. One possible component, the 'hut-game', is described under the general heading of boys' games (see pp. 53-54). Another element of such a puberty ritual could be circumcision, occurring still in modern Moslem Egypt as will be shown at the end of this chapter.

There is no proof that clitoridectomy was performed on girls in Pharaonic Egypt, which is not the same as stating that it did not occur. How would it be shown if it was indeed practiced? Circumcision of boys, on the other hand, did certainly exist, as several statues demonstrate. However, we possess only one rather clear representation of the operation itself. This is the famous depiction in the Sixth Dynasty tomb of the vizier and "royal architect" Ankhmahor at Saqqara (fig. 35). Admittedly, the scene has recently been interpreted as representing a ritual purification, namely depilation, but that seems to us not quite convincing. In the doorway to room VI there are two adjacent scenes. At the right-hand side, a boy is standing at his ease, with his left hand on the head of a man squatting before him. This man applies something to the boy's penis in order to make the procedure less painful, as is apparent from the accompanying hieroglyphic caption: "I will make it comfortable".

At the left-hand side the boy is firmly grasped by a third person standing behind him, while a *ka*-priest performs the operation. It has been stressed that it was a priest who acts as surgeon, suggesting that circumcision was a religious rite. In fact the title was borne by various members of the personnel of high officials, who were not professional clerics. Therefore, the *ka*-priest could be, for instance, the butcher or the barber of the household.

This 'priest' urges his assistant to "Hold him firmly. Don't let him swoon". In passing it is worth noting that, so far as is visible, the relief indicates that the foreskin was not removed but merely incised with a V-shaped cut, known as a dorsal slit. This is confirmed by Old Kingdom statuary. After that period it seems not anymore to have been done. It is of far more significance, however, that in so far as Egyptian wall scenes show particular ages (see p. 23), the boy seems to be from ten to twelve years old, that is, indeed a puber. It is very probably Ankhmahor who is depicted here, the boy who subsequently became a high state official.

There is perhaps one later representation, which occurs in the Horus chapel in the Temple of Mut at Karnak (fig. 36). However, the scene is heavily damaged, only the lower part being preserved. Clearly, someone is kneeling, holding two boys from behind, while a man is squatting before them and operating upon the foremost one. From the location of the representation in a sanctuary it seems certain that these boys are royal children. Yet, because the upper part is lost, the scene is not fully clear. Since this is all the evidence, it is not even certain that circumcision was still practiced during the New Kingdom.

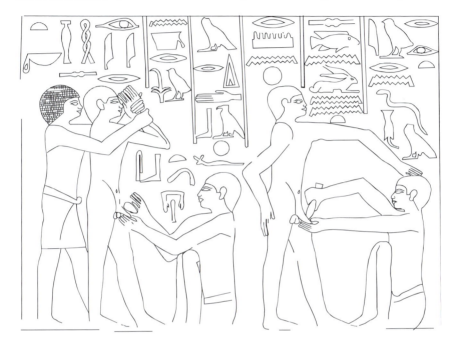

Fig. 35 Circumcision scene: right, the preparation; left, the operation itself. From the mastaba of Ankhmahor at Saqqara, Sixth Dynasty

Some texts mention circumcision, although it must be admitted that the medical papyri nowhere describe the procedure. Could it be that the operation was not conceived to be a medical action, or is it simply due to the paucity of the surviving sources? Two inscriptions from the First Intermediate Period do seem to indicate that it was still widely practised. In one, on a stela from Naga ed-Deir, a man states: "(when) I was circumcised together with 120 men". This total seems to suggest that an entire age group was operated upon, at one single ceremony, although of course the object of the ritual was each candidate individually, not the group as a unity. This is on a par with baptism and confirmation in the Christian church which may be celebrated for several individuals at the same time. At least, the text indicates that the operation was still very common. In the other inscription, on a block from the tomb of Mereri at Dendera, the tomb-owner relates how he "[buried] its (i.e., the town's or the nome's) old men, I circumcised its youths". It is clear that Mereri is boasting how well he looked after his people, and the sentence suggests that circumcision was a custom undergone by every boy, as every old man should be buried. If our interpretation is correct, the operation appears to have been an element, or perhaps the only rite, of a puberty ritual, constituting the transition from infancy to adulthood.

Fig. 36 Circumcision of royal children. From the Horus chapel in the Mut Temple at Karnak, Eighteenth Dynasty

From the succeeding Middle Kingdom there are three texts which mention circumcision, all of which involve only one boy with no data for his age. Nor is it evident from these instances that many boys, let alone all, had their foreskin removed. As this is a far better documented period, it would suggest that circumcision became less common. The phrase used is: "when I was a boy, before the foreskin was removed for me". It is interesting to note that once, in a New Kingdom copy of an older text, this phrase is written in such a way that one would be inclined to translate it as "before the nappies were removed for me" (see p. 25). The words were not understood any more, possibly because the custom was no longer in vogue.

The Second Intermediate Period has not (yet?) presented us with a single piece of evidence, and from the New Kingdom the operation is recorded in only one instance. Unfortunately, this is a fragmentary papyrus, of which neither the general meaning nor the exact translation is certain. It concerns the later vizier Useramun, uncle and direct predecessor of the well-known vizier Rekhmire. He is described as being received in audience by the boy-king Tuthmosis III, possibly for his promotion to vizier, the highest position in the state. On this occasion, the king asks him: "How many years ago the foreskin [was removed for you]?" to which Useramun replies: "Thirty years ago, oh

Pharaoh, my Good Lord". If he had been circumcised as a boy of approximately twelve years, he would be in his early forties, a suitable age for such an exalted office. The Egyptians died younger than in our times, but were also considered adult at an earlier age. Yet, it remains uncertain whether our restoration of the text is indeed correct, and whether, as suggested, the papyrus really deals with Useramun's promotion.

After this Eighteenth Dynasty text there is no written data, except for a remark on the stela of the Twenty-Fifth Dynasty Nubian Pharaoh Piankhy, which is now in Cairo. Four local rulers from the Delta failed to gain audience to the king because they were "uncircumcised and did eat fish". Another ruler, namely Nimlot, that erstwhile vanquished prince of Hermopolis in Middle Egypt, was received, however, because he was "pure and did not eat fish". It is evident that to be circumcised was equated with being pure. This is confirmed by the Greek historian Herodotus who states in his *Histories* of *circa* 450 B.C. that the Egyptians underwent the surgery since they "preferred purity above fresh air". This may be what Herodotus learnt from his Egyptian sources and it seems to have been the common belief in the later ages of Egyptian history.

In the Graeco-Roman Period the priests at least were circumcised, which is in accordance with this concept of purity. However, that cannot be the origin of the custom. Everywhere in the world, and still in the Moslem Egypt of today, circumcision is first and foremost a matter of manhood, including sexuality and fertility. After all it is a form of mutilation, affecting a man's sexual activities.

Other evidence of the habit can be afforded by the mummies. Unfortunately, despite earlier statements, notably by the famous anatomist Sir Grafton Elliot Smith who published the first study on the royal mummies at the beginning of this century, it appears to be extremely difficult in the case of human remains to definitely establish the presence or absence of the foreskin. As Elliot Smith's point of departure was his conviction that "all known adult Ancient Egyptian men were circumcised", he was inclined to find traces where others would be more hesitant.

In the Predynastic and Early Dynastic Periods commoners were probably mostly, if not all, circumcised, as attested by the human remains. Evidence from later – royal – mummies is both scarce and indecisive. Indeed, the physicians who investigated the body of Tutankhamun clearly state: "It was not possible to say whether circumcision had been performed". Elliot Smith came to the conclusion that at least Amenhotep II and probably also Tuthmosis IV had been operated upon. It seemed to him also certain so far as Ramesses IV and V were concerned. However, X-raying in the 1970's proved that king Ahmose certainly, and Amenhotep I probably, did not undergo the surgery. Elliot Smith also remarks on the odd particularity that a royal child of five to six years was possibly (!) circumcised, whereas another young prince of approximately eleven years, and still wearing the side-lock (see p. 33), was certainly not. The latter is according to our expectations, but the former would be extremely confusing. Taken together, and contrary to what one would anticipate, the evidence from the human remains appears to be most ambiguous.

Some two- and three-dimensional representations should also be taken into account. All Old Kingdom statues which are clear in this respect (fig. 37) show distinct signs of circumcision, as do contemporary reliefs of naked workmen, such as fishermen. Archaic depictions, mainly found on ceremonial slate palettes, likewise display circumcised figures. This suggests that in Prehistory the custom was at least widespread, if not universal. It had probably continued to be common during the Old Kingdom. For later times there is hardly any data from sculpture, although naked men are still portrayed, albeit less frequently than previously. Yet, absence of evidence cannot be said to be evidence of absence. Generally there is not a single case in which a boy wearing a side-lock shows the results of the operation. This implies that circumcision of babies, as is practised by the Jews or the Copts within the birth ritual, was unknown in Ancient Egypt.

To summarize, it is evident that in early ages circumcision was possibly general, obligatory for every youth in order to attain social adulthood. That the phallus hieroglyph is depicted as circumcised constitutes an additional indication. In later periods it became voluntary, compulsory only for particular groups such as boys who were to become priests. Perhaps we may extend the group and suggest that it was mandatory for those lads who were expected to become officials, as the Middle Kingdom examples and the Eighteenth Dynasty text concerning Useramun, if correctly interpreted, would indicate. Indeed, most men of whom statues or texts show that they underwent the surgery, such as Ankhmahor, belonged to the upper levels of society. Yet, one or possibly two Pharaohs were not operated upon, although they descended from rulers. The practice thus seems to have devolved into an inaugural rite rather than forming part of a puberty ritual.

What circumcision can be as an element of a full puberty ritual can be seen from its rôle in modern Moslem Egypt. Here then is a brief description of it as it occurred in the Upper Egyptian village of Silwa, located midway between Kom Ombo and Edfu, early in the 1950's.

The ritual begins with a progression through the village by the initiate, together with his comrades, inviting relations, friends and neighbours to attend the ceremony. On the day itself the guests assemble at the boy's house for a meal. The youth sits on the ground, attired in a girl's head cloth around his neck, and the village barber begins to shave his head, continuing according to the value

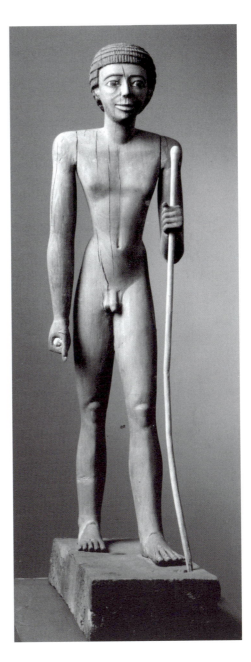

Fig. 37 Wooden statue of Meryrehashtef as a young adult, clearly showing circumcision. From tomb 274 at Sedment, Sixth Dynasty

81

of the money gifts presented to him by the guests. It is conspicuous that during this action the initiate is addressed as 'bridegroom'. Then, before the actual operation, the lad throws off the girl's kerchief, and attires himself in a white robe covered by a green garment, the typical male attire for religious festival occasions. He is encouraged not to cry; otherwise he will be accused of girlishness.

During the days following the surgery the boy receives special food symbolising fertility, such as boiled eggs, dried peas and salted peanuts. At the end of the period, he is taken on a progress along the houses of the community by his peers, all participants bearing palm-tree branches. In front of each house they chant loudly and require a present in the form of food. With this they return to the house of the initiate where his mother prepares from the gifts a meal for them. It is significant that the food is considered to be the contribution of the women of the community.

The ceremony is full of allusions to sexuality and fertility. An interesting detail in this respect is that during the days after the operation the mother takes her son to the Nile and they throw the foreskin, enclosed in a loaf of bread, into the water. However, there is no direct connection with the physical maturity of the initiate, for the boys are only from three to seven years old. Thus the ritual purely performs a social transition from the asexual world of infancy to the male adult society. Henceforth the boy behaves "as a man"; he shall not weep and wail at a burial as the women do, nor shall he show his genitals to anyone except his own mother, whereas before he could walk around naked. But it is not only infancy that he leaves behind; he is also not exclusively part of his parents' household any more. He is now incorporated into the community as a whole. Therefore, it is essential that the entire village takes part in the events.

Evidently, the circumcision itself is no more than one rite within the ritual. It is not even absolutely necessary, for if the foreskin was congenitally contracted or damaged by disease, the ceremony would still be performed, without the operation. Thus it is the social aspect that is the heart of the matter, not the physical side.

It seems not unlikely that a similar custom existed in Ancient Egypt, at least in early times. Unfortunately, our lack of adequate documentation prevents us from recognizing other possible traces of the *rite de passage*. Although circumcision continued to be performed, there is no proof that in later ages a puberty ritual as it exists in our days was celebrated. It should be stressed that this modern ceremony is entirely due to Arabic influences and was not inherited from Pharaonic Egypt.

8 Adolescence and Marriage

Adolescence as a stage of social development and experience seems not to have differed from that of childhood, a situation which still pertains in modern Egypt. During this phase the boys and girls of antiquity gradually accepted responsibility for work, whilst at the same time play elements were progressively eliminated. Whether in this process the puberty ritual constituted a definite turning point is uncertain, the more so since its occurrence is far from certain (see chapter 7).

It has already been noted (see p. 47) that during the Middle Kingdom the age of those engaged in games is not clear any more, whereas in the Old Kingdom the nakedness of boys and girls indicates that they were still children. However, as we acknowledged, the difference may merely be due to the artistic canon. Perhaps the boundaries between children and adolescents were not so sharp. Generally, in so far as they were not part of the training (as for dancers and soldiers), games would have been left to the younger generation, as in our society.

We also demonstrated above (see pp. 42-46) how, from an early age onwards, boys and girls were introduced into their parents' activities, first by rôle play, and later more seriously. Boys receiving a formal education for the scribal profession were an exception, but they gained acquaintance with their craft in the position of apprentices and assistants (see p. 61 ff.).

These circumstances occasioned a somewhat smooth transition, as far as both activities and behaviour were concerned, from the infant into the teenage world. The exact moment at which one became fully adult is difficult to establish. For 'scribes' it was obviously when they were appointed to their first independent office, yet even then Bekenkhons (see p. 61) was still supervised by his father. For peasants and artisans the end of adolescence may have coincided with their marriage and the start of a family. Although, as we shall see, this *rite de passage* was less marked than in modern times, it may have been the greatest change in an individual life.

In how far was heredity decisive for a career? Amenhotep, son of Hapu, probably came from a simple family (see p. 57), whereas Bekenkhons (see p. 61), was the son of the Second Prophet of Amun, the highest but one position in the Theban hierarchy. Two other higher priests, Hapuseneb and Puyemre, who both functioned under Hatshepsut, were of low descent, as was the great man of that time Senenmut, the main power behind the throne. The sons of these men received lower positions in the clergy, particularly within the royal mortuary temples, doubtless due to their fathers' influence.

On the other hand, three viziers from that period, Ahmose, Useramun and Rekhmire, were father, son, and the latter's cousin, almost a dynasty.

Similarly, in the Eighteenth Dynasty we encounter several families of high officials. Sennefer, the mayor of Thebes under Amenhotep II, well-known from his Theban tomb (TT 96) with its impressive grapevine ceiling, was, as will be developed below, the husband of a king's nurse (see p. 121), and, in addition, the brother of a vizier.

Such families can indeed be encountered in every period of Egyptian history, which would seem to contradict the words in the *Instruction of Ani*:

> The head of the Treasury has no son,
> the master of the seal has no heir.
> The scribe is chosen for his hand (i.e. his ability),
> his office has no children.

In accordance with this concept many of the upper classes use their autobiographies to stress their competence, suggesting that their progression up the social ladder was due entirely to themselves. As an instance we can quote a certain Montuhotep, from the early Middle Kingdom, whose stela was discovered by Petrie at Abydos, and is now in Cambridge. He states:

> (I was) one well-disposed and taught by his nature,
> like a child grown up with a father,
> and yet I had become an orphan.
> I acquired cattle, I raised oxen,
> I developed my business in goats,
> I built a house, I dug a pond – the priest Montuhotep.

In other words, he became well-off, despite his humble origins, because of his innate abilities. That he really became an orphan is not certain, for the word can also mean 'simple citizen'. This text dates from shortly after the deepest crisis in Egyptian history, the collapse of the Old Kingdom state, in which many of the social values were lost.

This overthrow of the established order became a theme in the contemporary literature. A famous example is the *Admonitions* (also called *Lamentations*) *of Ipuwer*, which survives on a papyrus now in Leiden. Here we find long sequences of sentences such as:

> The poor of the land have become rich,
> the man of property is (now) a pauper.

Or: The serf becomes an owner of serfs.

Certainly this is the well-attested motif of a world topsy-turvy, which occurs also in Egyptian literature during the succeeding and flowering epoch of the Middle Kingdom. It has not, therefore, to be taken too literally. Yet, it proves that social climbing was envisaged to be possible, and the case of Montuhotep aptly demonstrates this idea.

Apart from birth and talent, there was a third factor that determined the career of a young man, namely, the favour he found in Pharaoh's eyes. For the Egyptians themselves this was the decisive element. In their concepts it was the king himself who appointed the officials, civil as well as clerical and military. Middle Kingdom texts on stelae, for instance, bristle with sentences such as:

> His Majesty put me at his feet in my youth;

> whom the King did know when his nature was still youthful,
>   child of the King by his education;

> whom the King taught to walk.

Such words were not intended to deny that the person involved should credit his later position either to birth or to ability, or to both. It was certainly these which drew Pharaoh's attention to them. But it was the King who ultimately decided whether the young man should attain a high position.

If, in a particular period, the evidence proves that offices became hereditary, it means that Pharaoh's power was substantially diminished. A clear example of this is found on a Second Intermediate Period stela, found in the Temple of Karnak and now in Cairo. It is the copy of a document by which a mayor of el-Kab transferred his office, which had formerly belonged to his father and his uncle, to a relative of high rank in discharge of a substantial debt. Although the various technical details are not all clear, the function was obviously regarded as his private property, and hence inheritable and even saleable.

This is a proof of what happened in times of disorder when the state did not stand firm any more and no Pharaoh held sway. The ultimate reversal can be witnessed during the Amarna Period, when high officials ascribe their career exclusively to the favour of Akhenaten. So May, one of the top administrators, states in his rock-tomb at el-Amarna:

> I will tell you the favours which the Ruler showed me;
> then you will say: 'How great is what He did for this man' ......
> I was an orphan of father and mother,
> it was the Ruler who built me ......

I was without possessions,
He let me acquire personnel ...... etc.

Was May indeed an orphan in his youth? One may doubt it, as in the case of Montuhotep quoted above. The assertion rather belongs to the style of that time. Neither did the theme disappear after the eclipse of this particular Pharaoh.

On a stela, now in Leiden, dating from the early Nineteenth Dynasty, a chief sculptor relates:

I was humble of family, one of small account in his town.
But the Lord of the Two Lands recognized me,
and I was greatly esteemed in his heart ......
He exalted me above the courtiers,
so that I mingled with the great ones in his palace.

The preponderant position of the king diminished once more during the Third Intermediate Period, and with it we find, from the Twentieth Dynasty onwards, an increasing stress on the noble descent of officials and the inheritability of functions. Indeed, power fell mostly into the hands of a small number of families. Herodotus' words: "When a priest dies his son is established in his place" appear to be virtually correct, although Egypt never developed into a full 'caste' society.

In conclusion, it can be stated that the possibility of making a career depended upon three factors: an adolescent's qualities and diligence, his descent and relations, and, above all, upon the favour of Pharaoh. For the mass of the population any advancement in social rank remained impossible; they simply followed their parents in their profession. A distinct condition for attaining high office remained literacy, with the possible exception of one group: active military officers.

The life of common soldiers is described in harsh tones in the *Miscellanies*, but these were exercises for adolescent 'scribes' intended to divert their minds from the temptations of an easy life in the army (see p. 68). Nevertheless, the picture there presented is not necessarily untrue in all details.

I will let you know the condition of the soldier
in all duties he performs.
He is taken to be a soldier as a child of a pole length
(i.e., *circa* 65 centimetres)
being shut up in the barracks,
which are divided among the regiments,
with officers over them.
He is confined and goes not abroad

until he becomes a soldier,
struck down with torments.

Or, in another description:

The man is put to be a soldier,
the adolescent to be a recruit;
the child is brought up (merely) to be taken away
    from his mother's bosom.
When he reaches manhood, his bones are scattered.

Evidently, boys were taken into the army at an early age, perhaps when they were approximately ten years old (less than 1 metre tall). That sometimes happened by force (fig. 38). In a letter in a *Miscellany* we read: "The vizier brought three adolescents, saying: 'Place them as priests in the Temple of Merenptah' (at Memphis). But officials seized the men and took them north, saying: 'They shall be soldiers'". Hence, even young temple servants could be conscripted.

We do not know for how many years they had to serve in the army. The early Middle Kingdom *Instruction for Merikare* even suggests a twenty year stretch:

'Raise your youths', says the king to his son,
'and the Residence will love you.
Increase your subjects with new people.
See, your city is full of new growth.
Twenty years the youths indulge their wishes,
(then) the recruits (?) go forth [to the reserves?];
veterans (?) return to their children'.

Unfortunately, the translation of these sentences is quite uncertain since the text is corrupt. Yet, the figure of twenty years seems to denote the length of time until the return to civilian life. During that period a soldier could marry, as indicated by a *Miscellany* which states:

His wife and children are in their village,
but he (the soldier) is dead, he has not reached it.

Fig. 38 The conscription of recruits for the army. From the Theban tomb of Tjanuny (TT 74), Eighteenth Dynasty

A short term military service for recruits, at the end of adolescence, does not seem to have existed in Ancient Egypt. Soldiering was generally a profession, at least in the New Kingdom.

Some non-commissioned officers, as might be expected, succeeded in reaching subaltern or even higher ranks, and were able to acquire substantial wealth. An example is Ahmose, son of Ebana, who took part in the campaigns against the Hyksos at the very beginning of the Eighteenth Dynasty. In his autobiography, in- scribed on the walls of his rock-tomb at el-Kab, he tells that he was the son of a serviceman, and began his career in a ship's company while still a boy, before he was married. He moved from one vessel to another, and by proving himself a brave warrior he was seven times rewarded, with gold, slaves and fields. Under Tuthmosis I he at last became commander of a naval contingent; not a very high position, but still decisively above the level where he began.

Another successful military man was Amenemhab, by abbreviation called Mahu, the owner of a Theban tomb (TT 85). He followed Tuthmosis III in his Syrian campaigns, captured by his own hand several prisoners, and once saved his master's life on a march near the river Orontes, as he relates in his tomb autobiography:

> The King hunted 120 elephants for their tusks. Then I
> attacked the largest elephant among them, which charged
> against His Majesty, and cut off its hand (trunk), while
> it was alive, before the eyes of His Majesty, while I
> was standing in the water between two rocks.

All this happened when he still held low ranks, but under Amenhotep II he was promoted to 'lieutenant of the army', the highest but one military post, and in this function he commanded the royal bodyguard. That he too acquired wealth is clear from his building of an impressive funerary monument.

These persons are nowhere called 'scribe'. Evidently, non-literates did have the chance to progress, although the possibilities for a distinguished career were certainly better when one started as a military administrator. We have already referred to Amenhotep, son of Hapu, the favourite of Amenhotep III (see p. 57). Another instance is Anhermose, whose advancement we know of from statues and his tomb at el-Mashayikh, in Middle Egypt, not far from Abydos.

Anhermose probably originated from Thebes, as did his two successive wives, since they were "chantresses of Amun, King of the Gods". He lived under Ramesses II and his successor Merenptah, and boasts that as a child he already showed his outstanding qualities. He received a school education, but chose a military profession. Like so many, he started out in a ship's contingent, but also served on land.

As a 'scribe' he moved onto the chariotry, the élite corps. He seems also to have been a good linguist, for he acted as "interpreter of every foreign land". So he must have attracted the attention of the Pharaoh, and at a later stage Merenptah appointed him to the position of High Priest of Onuris, the local god of This, in the region of Abydos.

Certainly, Anhermose was not born into a simple family. His father bears the title of 'scribe of the recruits', that is, administrative officer. That he calls himself 'humble' in his youth is a matter of style, as we have seen above. Yet, his autobiography shows that he was a *homo novus* among the higher clergy. In itself the promotion from officer to priest was not unusual; it was an administrative position, as Anhermose himself stresses, for he declares that he looked after the treasury and the granaries of the temple. For a military man this was certainly a rise in social esteem.

To what extent the accident of birth and to what measure talent contributed to a career as an artist is difficult to assess. Among the necropolis workmen living at Deir el-Medina the position of draughtsman, who was mainly responsible for the decoration of a royal tomb, appears to have become a family post during the Twentieth Dynasty. This is also true for the office of 'scribe (that is, administrator) of the tomb'.

Yet, young craftsmen, although chosen from the sons of the members of the crew, had to be appointed by the vizier, Pharaoh's representative, evidently on the recommendation of the leaders of the workforce. In that respect an ostracon from the site, now in Cairo, is of interest, since it enumerates various objects, mostly pieces of furniture, offered to the scribe and two foremen by a father for "the promotion of his son". Together they constitute a considerable value. In our society such a present would smell of bribery; in Egypt it was perfectly acceptable to offer a *bakshish* in such a situation.

Fig. 39 Painted limestone statue of Ra-maat wearing the gala-kilt with knotted band. From Giza, early Sixth Dynasty

Not for all sons of these workmen, however, was there a possibility of succeeding their fathers. Some became soldiers or peasants, disappearing from the community. Whether this was a sheer lack of luck, or depended upon their abilities, we do not know. That those who stayed were generally better off is clear; the workmen were well paid and less harshly treated than soldiers or agricultural labourers, if the descriptions in the *Miscellanies* are to be believed.

It must have been a culmination point in a boy's life when he entered upon his first appointment, even though it was merely a trainee position. In the Old Kingdom, and once in a Middle Kingdom text, this moment is specifically mentioned. In several autobiographies the words "I knotted the band" occur, always followed by a reference to the reign of the Pharaoh during which the event took place. It is unfortunate that the age of the participant is never indicated.

The expression has been explained as pointing to the so-called 'gala-kilt', the only garment of this period that was worn in conjunction with a linen band. It is shown as a distinctive item of dress, with a pleated wrap-over section normally at the right side, on reliefs and statues of several Old Kingdom officials (fig. 39). Another interpretation is that the term indicates a head-band, which was tied at the ceremony for the first time. Whatever, the phrase is usually followed by the mention of the young man's first office, in one instance by the announcement that he was henceforth educated among the royal children (see p. 59).

Some scholars have taken the phrase "knotting the band" to be an indication of a rite within the puberty ritual, but that seems to be unwarranted. It merely states that the youth attires himself in the ceremonial dress of the civil servants. It is not even clear if it refers to a ceremony, an inauguration ritual, or whether it simply stands as a metaphor for "when I began my career as an official".

From later periods, except for a single Middle Kingdom occurrence of the phrase, nothing is known concerning an inauguration. Hence it is uncertain whether a festival transition was celebrated by which the former schoolboy became an adolescent apprentice.

Probably the start of a married life will have meant a more radical change, since it implied the very end of one's youth. It is therefore even more conspicuous that this passage was not marked by a ritual, i.e. the wedding.

The only indication of such a ceremony occurs in the *Story of Setne* (see p. 2). There it is told how a groom, the son of a general, took his bride, a royal princess, to his house, and according to her narrative "Pharaoh sent me a present of silver and gold, and all Pharaoh's household sent me presents". Then the groom entertains the entire court, after which he goes to bed with his new wife. This at least suggests a wedding as we know it, and as it occurs in modern Moslem Egypt (fig. 40).

However, the story dates from the Graeco-Roman Period. The complete absence of any reference to such a feast in earlier texts or representations seems to indicate that it was rather a late development. There exists no word for 'wedding' in Egyptian, not even in sources such as the love poems where one would expect it to occur. The event is circumscribed as "to establish a household" but that does not imply a ritual. Of the goddess Isis it is once said: "She gives a husband to a widow, a household to a young girl". A married woman is usually called "mistress of the house"; in a few cases "lady of the sitting (i.e. marriage), mistress of the household". Such phrases express the status of 'wife', not the manner in which it came into existence.

91

For the Egyptians marriage was evidently a social fact, not a legal relationship. It was intended for the generation of offspring, and supposed to be based on a mutual sympathy between the partners. In daily life, pressure, or even arrangement, by parents and other relatives may have been decisive. There is no trace of any religious consecration or sanction.

Fig. 40 A bride at her wedding celebrations. From Western Thebes, 1989

Let us look for a moment at the so-called *Marriage Stela* of Ramesses II, the modern name of which suggests that we could find in this text some indication for a wedding. The subject was inscribed on several stelae erected at various sites, for instance in front of the Great Temple at Abu Simbel. It contains a description of how, in Ramesses' thirty-fourth regnal year, the Hittite king, following long negotiations, sent his eldest daughter to Egypt, together with rich presents and numerous attendants as a dowry, in order to marry his fellow ruler. Ramesses rejoiced when he heard about "this marvellous event", and ordered an army and several officials to receive the lady properly. He also prayed to the god Seth to end the current spell of very hot summer weather, to which the deity graciously consented. When the princess arrived, the king was exceedingly happy because she turned out to be beautiful. She received an Egyptian name, and was installed in the Royal Palace. But of a wedding ceremony not a single word is mentioned.

As marriage was neither a legal relationship nor confirmed by a religious sanction, divorce, which was purely a private matter, could hardly have constituted a problem. The ideal state of a loving couple depicted in reliefs and statue groups of every era, the wife putting her arm around her husband's waist or shoulder (see fig. 12) does not agree with the facts as extant records present them to us. Of course, such devoted couples did exist, but divorce was far from rare.

From later periods papyrus documents stipulate the property a woman would receive when this happened, just as deeds were also drawn up in view of an impending marriage. Whether these were drafted at some time before, or even after the commencement of cohabitation is uncertain. Moreover, such documents have not survived from the New Kingdom or earlier. Perhaps oral agreements were then made, and the custom seems to have been that the wife received one-third of the assets acquired during the marriage, whilst she throughout remained the owner of what she had brought in. But even a written record concerning matrimonial property – and that, of course, is not yet a marriage contract – does not seem to have been made. In the case of poorer people it was probably superfluous.

An interesting and unique text in this connection was written on a Deir el-Medina limestone ostracon. In the twenty-third regnal year of Ramesses III, on a particular day, one of the crew called Telmont spoke to the chief workman Khonsu and the scribe Amennakhte, saying: "Let Nekhemmut swear an oath to the Lord that he will not desert my daughter". Then follow the specific words sworn by Nekhemmut: "As Amun lives and the Ruler lives! If I ever will desert in future the daughter of Telmont, I will be liable to a hundred lashes and I will loose all that I have acquired together with her".

We do not know at what stage this oath was sworn, whether before, at, or after the beginning of the marriage. However, it is clear that the stipulations are more stringent than was customary; the young man stands to loose all the common possessions. Perhaps Telmont had good reason not to trust the reliability of his son-in-law. He took the trouble to arrange that the afore-mentioned local authorities and two workmen were present to witness this solemn declaration.

Where the only proof of a marriage was its social recognition, it becomes difficult, if not impossible, to differentiate between couples sharing life and a real matrimonial situation. Yet, in some Egyptian texts a word occurs that is usually translated as 'concubine', suggesting that not every cohabitation situation meant a marriage. In the three cases where we know something about the circumstances, the woman was a second (or later) spouse of the husband, but that does not seem to be indicated by the term.

Other texts distinguish between women who are wives of and those who are 'with' a man. The latter category was common among the lower levels of society during the New Kingdom, and they are the ones who are also called 'concubine'. Some information on this subject can be derived from the legal proceedings of the tomb robberies during the late Twentieth Dynasty. Several women were interrogated, alongside the male accused and witnesses, and their title is sometimes 'concubine', in other cases 'wife'. This may simply be due to the whims of the scribes; it evidently did not make much difference in daily life. Yet, the existence of two terms must refer to some distinction in reality. It cannot be due, as we would expect, to the fact of whether a wedding had been celebrated or not. Therefore, it may have depended upon the stability and duration of the relationship, and consequently, on the measure of its social recognition.

One text from Deir el-Medina sheds light on sexual morals among the necropolis workmen. It is a papyrus record, now in the British Museum, of a large number of charges directed against a chief workman called Paneb (fig. 41). He is accused of having gained his job though bribery, of stealing from the workshop and elsewhere, bullying his subordinates, threatening to kill his former tutor and predecessor, and so on. Even if only a portion of it were true, he was a regular scoundrel. Evidently, he was so, for at a certain moment he was removed from his post.

One of the charges runs: "Paneb slept with Mrs. Tuy, when she was the wife of the workman Kenna; he slept with Mrs. Hunero, when she was with Pendua; he slept with Mrs. Hunero, when she was with Hesysunebef". It was one of his sons who uttered these accusations, and the scribe adds to it that Paneb had also slept with Hunero's daughter, and that his son Opakhte (fig. 41), either the accuser or his brother, had done likewise.

Hardly a very savoury picture of life in the village, even if not all has necessarily to be true! It can be noted that Hunero is said first to have been 'with' Pendua, later 'with' Hesysunebef – only Mrs. Tuy is stated to be a 'wife'. From other sources we know that Hunero and her second 'husband' had children, one of them the daughter mentioned in this text. In later years this relationship floundered: Hesysunebef divorced her, an event recorded on a large limestone ostracon now in the Petrie Museum. Whether the affairs between Paneb and the women were contrary to the will or wishes of the latter is unknown. Anyhow, the term used does not mean 'to rape'.

Fig. 41 Limestone stela of Paneb who (above) adores a coiled serpent, doubtless Mertseger, the goddess of the Theban necropolis; (below) three of his descendants, including (right) his son Opakhte. From Deir el-Medina, Nineteenth Dynasty

It appears that marriages in the workmen's community were not particularly stable. This explains the fluctuations between the terms 'wife' and 'concubine', or 'living with'. The stelae and tomb walls of Deir el-Medina present only the official picture of loving couples and parents (see cover illustrations), the reality may have been different, although we should be careful

95

not to overstress this point. Good marriages did of course occur, as everywhere else in the world, and permanent relationships may have been more frequent than instable ones. The picture conjured up by Paneb's story is exceptional. Reality was somewhere in between this and the rosy image created by the official art.

For our subject, namely the end of adolescence by the foundation of a household, the description of marriage relationships is of importance in so far that the event may be less decisive for the young people's future than it has been in other eras. Perhaps in this respect Pharaonic Egypt most resembles our own days. Nevertheless, marriage, although without being embarked upon through a wedding, certainly meant a fundamental transition in life. Soon the young man would be an expectant father himself, his wife being pregnant, and thus we have revolved full circle to where our study began.

9 The Royal Child

Nothing at all is known about the birth or formative years of royal children, apart from some casual references in narratives and myths. In this respect we have already quoted from the *Tale of the Doomed Prince* (see p. 1) and the myth of the king's divine birth (see p. 1). In how far such literary sources contain elements from real events in the palace is not clear. Neither is the scene from the Royal Tomb at el-Amarna (see p. 4) very illuminating in this respect.

There is an even more intricate problem: who in Egyptian history are undeniably princes and princesses? Those we encounter in the texts are called 'king's son' or 'king's daughter', but these designations have to be taken literally and were, therefore, not hereditary. Grandchildren of rulers, whom we would also term princes and princesses, were generally not so indicated by the Ancient Egyptians.

On the other hand, from the Old Kingdom onwards we find titular 'king's sons' and 'daughters' who are clearly no offspring of the ruler. The origin of this high social rank is easily explained. In the Archaic Period, power was, in principle, entirely concentrated in the hands of the Pharaoh himself. Where he was unable to exercise it, for instance on expeditions to foreign countries, authority was entrusted to his sons since they were closest to his person. Other offspring who did not occupy central positions in the administration were therefore called 'king's son', while those who represented their father bore only their functionary title since that showed sufficiently that they were princes.

Gradually, with the regime's increased exertion of power over the populace, non-royal officials were appointed. At first the 'king's sons' retained some key posts as overseers of the construction projects of the state, the expeditions, and, above all, the government in general, that is, the function of vizier. During the Fourth Dynasty these positions too became progressively occupied by commoners, that of the vizier being the last to succumb to the process. Now it was not self-evident any more that such a high functionary was the king's son, and hence it became the custom, if one was indeed so, to include this information in his titulary. So to be entitled 'king's son' was not an indication any more that one was a prince without employment, but, on the contrary, a top bureaucrat.

However, those administrators who did not belong to the royal family also used princely titles, and when, during the Fifth Dynasty, none of them was of royal birth, all 'king's sons' became titulary princes. For example, Kaemtjenent, a favourite of King Isesi (Fifth Dynasty), who acted as his overseer of building-works and as expedition leader, bore the title of "King's Son and Unique Friend" of the Pharaoh.

A famous illustration of this development, from the Fourth Dynasty, is Hemiunu, a nephew of Pharaoh Khufu. He possessed an impressive mastaba in the cemetery west of the Great Pyramid at Giza, from where derives his fine limestone seated statue, now in Hildesheim, portraying him as a rather corpulent elderly man. Hemiunu was superintendent of works of his uncle, and in this capacity probably co-responsible for the erection of the Great Pyramid. Moreover, he became the monarch's vizier. In these functions he received the honorary title 'king's son', although as a ruler's grandson he had no legal right to the appellation. According to our criteria, he was indeed a prince, but not so far as the Ancient Egyptians were concerned.

The title 'king's son' is therefore to be compared with that of the European 'Prince', which does not only indicate sons of the ruler – and, in modern society, also further descendants – but is also a rank-title of nobility, as in the cases of the Princes of Orange or the Princes of Monaco.

After the Old Kingdom the use of 'king's son' as an honorary title never completely disappeared from Egyptian history, although its frequency varied. In the Eleventh Dynasty, at the beginning of the Middle Kingdom, we hear of no titular princes, nor do actual royal princes seem to have played a public rôle in the state. Likewise, 'king's sons' are seldom encountered during the Twelfth Dynasty, except for those crown-princes who became co-regents of their father, and later on sole Pharaoh.

During the Second Intermediate Period, and continuing into the New Kingdom, some local military commanders, as well as leading members of the clergy in some towns, were titular 'princes'. From the title of one such officer, the 'king's son of Buhen', developed the designation of the Egyptian governor of its African 'colony', the 'king's son of Kush', that is, the Viceroy of Nubia. None of them was ever a real son of the Pharaoh, nor were any of the other military or the religious 'princes'.

The background behind these striking titles is that their holders performed duties directly dependent upon the king. Yet, the same holds true for other top administrators, for instance the vizier, but they are not called any more 'king's son' after the Old Kingdom.

Concerning the real princes of the Middle and New Kingdoms hardly anything has been recorded, except when they themselves became rulers. Only a few others are known to have received governmental positions and by inference political responsibility. It may be, of course, that among those officials who do not mention their father's name a few were actually sons or grandsons of subordinate wives of Pharaoh, but no instance of this possibility seems to have been recorded.

A few king's sons were appointed to the significant post of High Priest of Ptah at Memphis. Among them are: one from the Middle Kingdom, called Amenemhat-ankh, the son of Amenemhat II; one from the Eighteenth Dynasty, namely Dhutimose, probably the eldest son of Amenhotep III; and one from the Nineteenth Dynasty, Khaemwaset (fig. 42), the fourth son of Ramesses II.

Regarding the latter so much evidence has survived that we are able to ascribe to him not only a career, but also, and this is obviously remarkable, a distinct personality. He clearly represented his father in the second capital of the realm, as did his brother Meryatum at Heliopolis, where he functioned as High Priest of Re. Moreover, Khaemwaset, who died in approximately the fifty-fifth regnal year of Ramesses II, seems to have played a leading rôle in the middle period of his father's long reign. Of the many jubilees celebrated by the monarch several were announced by Khaemwaset. He built in and around Memphis, for instance additions to the Ptah Temple and in the Serapeum, where he supervised the burial of more than one Apis bull. Most alluring is his evident sense of history, which entitles him to be called the first Egyptologist. He restored monuments in the Memphite area, such as pyramids from the Old Kingdom, recording his activities in boldly engraved hieroglyphs for posterity. One could almost call him head of a department of historic monuments, as well as director of the country's archaeological service. He searched for tomb inscriptions in order to provide the buildings with 'name plates/museum labels'. Through all these ventures he acquired the fame of a magician, and in later ages he became the hero of the *Story of Setne*. The name Setne is derived from one of Khaemwaset's priestly titles, *setem* or *sem*. Whether he was ever the crown-prince is not quite clear. Anyhow, he predeceased his long-lived parent.

Of the other princes cited above as officials far less is known. From Dhutimose we possess a unique monument, now in Cairo, namely a limestone sarcophagus for a court cat. The inscriptions and representations are fully in the traditional style, as if it had been made for a human being: the 'owner' is depicted as a cat, with a scarf around its neck, seated before an offering table, on which, among other food, is a fat duck. Behind it stands a shabti figure with a cat's head. According to the hieroglyphs the deceased 'lady' was called Tmiao, "The Cat". On the lid of the sarcophagus a text mentions that the receptacle was made by order of the "King's Son and High Priest of Memphis, Dhutimose".

Formerly also the property of the same prince was a whip found among the treasures in Tutankhamun's tomb. Its provenance is not surprising since Dhutimose was an uncle of the boy king.

Of these king's sons, and the few others we ever hear about, all mentions date from the reigns of their fathers. As soon as one of their brothers ascended the throne they drop out of history. In some instances we indeed know that a prince died before his parent: with the high mortality rate a not surprising occurrence. Examples of this are Wadzmose (see fig. 44) and Amenmose, two sons of Tuthmosis I. For the former the father erected a small funerary temple on the Theban West Bank, just south of the spot where the later Pharaoh Ramesses II would build his own mortuary temple, the Ramesseum. The death of both these offspring was the reason why Tuthmosis I was succeeded by the son of a wife of lower rank, the Pharaoh Tuthmosis II.

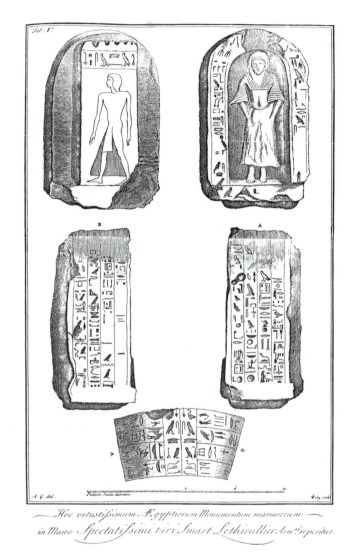

Fig. 42 Figure of Khaemwaset in its naos. Unprovenanced. Now lost, but in the early Eighteenth Century A.D. housed in a private collection in London

Fig. 43 Kenamun's mother nurses Amenhotep II. From the Theban tomb of Kenamun (TT 93), Eighteenth Dynasty

Another prince predeceasing his father was Amenemhat, eldest son and therefore heir apparent of Tuthmosis III. The same is generally believed of the Dhutimose mentioned above, since not he, but his brother Amenhotep IV – who soon began calling himself Akhenaten – succeeded Amenhotep III. Yet, in most instances there is no proof at all for the death of princes. They simply vanish. A large number are only mentioned once, and how many never, we cannot begin to guess. Who, for instance, was the boy whose mummy was discovered in the Valley of Deir el-Medina, or that youth who is supposed to be a son of

Amenhotep II (see p. 33)? What actually happened when one of the brothers seized the crown? That violent struggle sometimes occurred in which several pretenders lost their lives, is more than likely.

Fig. 44 Paheri with his pupil Prince Wadzmose on his lap. From the tomb of Paheri at el-Kab, Eighteenth Dynasty

Generally, the matter of the succession is not at all clear to us. Were only the sons of a particular Great Queen eligible? In the case of the numerous offspring of Ramesses II that indeed seems to be the case, for, although he reigned into his sixty-seventh year and was over ninety when he died, it is far from certain that all twelve eldest sons were deceased when the thirteenth, Merenptah, succeeded. Perhaps the father's decision played a crucial rôle in these matters. Anyhow, when heirs apparent disappear from the records, it is not certain that they necessarily died a natural death, although the sources themselves remain entirely silent on this point.

As regards the 'king's daughters', their position was different from that of their brothers since, with a few notable exceptions, women never held an office. During the Old Kingdom, parallel with 'king's sons', true princesses as well as titular ones are in evidence. The latter are either high ranking ladies-in-waiting, or the wives of top bureaucrats. Whether such women received the title 'king's daughter' in their own right, or on account of the standing of their husbands, is not clear.

In later times, whereas honorary princesses hardly seem to occur, genuine daughters of the monarch feature all the more. With them we encounter two fundamental questions: what rôle did these women play in the inheritance of the throne, and what should be understood by those, in our eyes, incestuous marriages between Pharaohs and their sisters or daughters?

As regards the latter, the only proof for such a relationship is the female epithet "Great Royal Consort". Above we have stressed how difficult it is to define a 'marriage' in daily life in Ancient Egypt, since it was not initiated by a wedding (see pp. 91 ff.). What exactly does it mean if a young royal lady is designated her father's queen? Very probably it only implies that she performed some ceremonies which were specifically reserved for the wife of Pharaoh. Whether a sexual relationship was also involved is highly doubtful, and there exists no proof whatever in an authentic case. The only evidence would be that a child had been the product of such a union, and that seems never to have occurred.

Hence, when one of the Theban *talatat* (that is, small stone blocks from which the temples of Akhenaten were built) shows Nefertiti, offering to the Aten, followed by "the Royal Consort and beloved princess of his [her father's] body Meritaten", we should not conclude that this Pharaoh was married to mother and daughter simultaneously. Moreover, it has been argued that this particular inscription was made when Meritaten was still a toddler, which makes it even less plausible that it refers to a marriage between father and daughter!

Akhenaten's father, Amenhotep III, shows in the later years of his reign a clear preference for his daughter Sitamun, who also bears the title "Great Royal Consort". Probably she represented her mother Teye at certain rituals in which the queen had a ceremonial function. That she also shared her father's bed is not likely, whereas an important rôle of Sitamun reflecting the preference of the old king for her above her brother, with all its political repercussions, would be feasible, albeit not proved.

One detail should be mentioned in this respect. If the function of queen was indeed indispensable in the court ceremonies, one would expect that Queen Hatshepsut also had her "Great Royal Consort", just as female mayors in our days have their mayoress. But such a lady does not occur in the records. How the problems in this matter were solved is a mystery. Hatshepsut's daughter Neferure had indeed a function; not that of 'queen' to her mother, but of the "God's Wife of Amun", one of the most important positions a woman of the royal family could occupy during the New Kingdom.

The second question, what was the rôle of women in the royal family in transmitting the right to the throne, that is: whether the princesses were ritual heiresses – even though the actual power remained in the hands of their sons and husbands – is not so easy to answer. Once more almost all our evidence dates from the New Kingdom. One fact is clear: by far not every king's consort was also a king's daughter; several of the Great Queens were children of commoners.

Yet, marriages between a royal son and his sister did occur, for example, between Ahmose, the first ruler of the Eighteenth Dynasty, and his sister Ahmose-Nofretari. They were both issue of the same couple, whereas in some other instances the royal spouses were half-brother and -sister, as in the case of Tuthmosis II and Hatshepsut. Should such relationships be termed incestuous? The problem is rather complicated. We must at least distinguish between incest, which pertains to sexuality, and exogamy, which relates to conjugal liaisons. Among some peoples where conjugal contacts between particular relatives are strictly prohibited, it may be that sexual relations are even at a premium.

Instead of applying the vague and difficult term 'incest', an attempt should rather be made to understand brother-sister marriages in terms of Egyptian concepts. They have nothing to do with the modern notion of "keeping the blood pure", but such ties are frequent among deities, e.g. the couple Osiris and Isis. Whereas, so far as we know, it did not occur among commoners, at least not officially, a regular marriage between a Pharaoh and his full or half-sister removed him from his subjects and allowed him to approach the divine circle. That may broadly have been the reason for the practice.

During the first years of their life royal children were initially suckled by wet-nurses, and later on looked after by nannies, most of whom were members of the leading families of the realm. Later, during their infancy, they were instructed by male tutors or mentors. Concerning these groups of attendants there is some information from the New Kingdom, particularly, once again, from the Eighteenth Dynasty. Hardly anything has been recorded from earlier ages.

Several ladies who played rôles in the care of royal offspring are mentioned, and even depicted, in the Theban tombs of that period, for they were the wives or mothers of high officials. They are designated "royal nurse" or "chief royal nurse", sometimes elaborated to "chief nurse of the Lord of the Two Lands" or suchlike, with the additional epithet "who suckled the god" (that is, the future king). Evidently, some princes had more than one nurse. In the next chapter we shall see that the husbands and sons of these ladies owed their careers partly to these intimate relationships with the rulers.

In the tomb scenes a royal prince is in some cases portrayed as if he were already king. Of course, these pictures were made subsequently, for it was never quite certain whether a crown-prince would indeed ascend the throne. So, for instance, Amenhotep II is seen in the tomb of Kenamun (TT 93) in full regalia, seated on the lap of Kenamun's mother (fig. 43) – although he apparently was not always the intended heir to the throne. In his right hand he holds, apart from a sceptre, a bundle of strings by which he restrains the bound barbarians placed under his feet. The only indication that the 'king' is in fact an infant is the hand with which the nurse supports his head.

Since the woman is not actually suckling her charge, it is not entirely certain that she was indeed a wet-nurse; she may equally well have been a nanny. That the title 'nurse' in Egyptian is determined by the sign of a female breast is not quite decisive. In another contemporary tomb, that of the military officer Amenemhab, called Mahu (TT 85; see p. 88), his wife Baki is shown clearly breastfeeding a king's son. Most intriguing was the scene in yet another Theban tomb, probably from the time of Tuthmosis IV, which is now lost. According to notes and copies of the wall paintings made in the Nineteenth Century A.D., the wife of the owner was depicted nine times in a row, in each representation sitting on a bed with a child in her arms, some of whom are really being suckled. Probably these babies were members of the royal family.

As stated above (see p. 16), the Egyptian word for 'nurse' is also used, in a masculine form, for male teachers. During the Old and Middle Kingdoms these men were simply styled 'tutor' or 'instructor', and not much is known about them. In his tomb at el-Bersheh a certain Iha states: "I was appointed to the post of instructor of the royal children, for I was a man who knows the ceremonial of the palace, one at the top who dares to approach his Lord". Hence it was Iha's acquaintance with court procedures and his personal relations with the ruler – he was also steward of the royal harem – that gained him his post as tutor. Who the princes were that he educated is uncertain; possibly only sons of a nomarch.

From the Eighteenth Dynasty a number of royal tutors are recorded who occupied prominent positions in the state. So, for instance, Paheri, a mayor of el-Kab and Esna, who acted as teacher of Wadzmose, a son of Tuthmosis I (see p. 99), who is shown wearing a side-lock, sitting on his mentor's lap (fig. 44). According to the inscriptions in his rock-tomb Paheri's father, Itruri, was also tutor of this prince, as well as of his brother Amenmose. From the ruins of Wadzmose's funerary temple (see p. 99) derives a stela of a certain Senimose who also claims to have been the boy's pedagogue. The text of this monument dates from regnal year twenty-one of Tuthmosis III, long after Wadzmose's death. It contains the record, unfortunately damaged, of a legal action concerning Senimose's inheritance, so indeed a matter of many years later. Whether Senimose was still alive at the time is not quite certain; anyhow, for our purpose it is only of significance because it records his title. Wadzmose therefore had three tutors; or even four, since yet another of the instructors of Tuthmosis I's children was the vizier Imhotep, whose mummy and funerary equipment, discovered in the Valley of the Queens (QV 46), are now in Turin. As vizier he may have guided the princes in governmental matters, and it is conceivable that this is expressed by his designation "father-nurse of the royal children", a variant of the simple "nurse of the king's son".

Fig. 45 Black granite statue of Senenmut holding the Princess Neferure. She wears a false beard equating her with the young Theban god Khonsu. From Thebes, Eighteenth Dynasty

The same title is encountered among those of Senenmut, Hatshepsut's favourite and her *éminence grise*, namely 'father-tutor' of her daughter, the

Princess Neferure (fig. 45). He will indeed have originally educated the girl, and later on, after Hatshepsut's accession, may have restricted himself in this respect to lessons in politics, while Senimen, the owner of TT 252 and possibly a relation, succeeded him as teacher. To what extent Senenmut's meteoric rise was due to his office of steward of the princess, whose properties must have been extensive since she was the "God's Wife of Amun" of her time (see p. 103), or to the resulting intimacy with the inner court circle, is difficult to establish. It may equally well have been the other way round, in other words, his appointments being the consequence of the confidence which the Queen placed in him.

Clearly, 'father-nurse' was conceived to be a higher rank than "nurse of the king's son" only. Ahmose-Humay, the father of the Theban mayor Sennefer, was called 'nurse' during his lifetime, but in his tomb (TT 224), posthumously, 'father-nurse'.

Yet a more elevated position was indicated by the title 'god's father', in which 'god' means 'Pharaoh'. Physical fathers of the ruler were so designated, although by no means all, as well as fathers-in-law, albeit only rarely. One of the latter is Yuya, with his wife Thuyu the parents of Teye, Amenhotep III's 'Great Consort', and therefore afforded internment in the Valley of the Kings (KV 46). Their burial was discovered in 1905, with much of its tomb furniture still intact, treasures that now enrich the Cairo Museum.

That 'god's father' became, towards the end of the Eighteenth Dynasty, a priestly title in various temples, for example in that of Amun at Karnak, is of no importance to us here. It is more significant that it was also a title of tutors of crown-princes. From earlier times, namely the Old Kingdom, only one, slightly dubious instance is known. It concerns the famous wise vizier Ptahhotep of the Sixth Dynasty, the author of the outstanding *Instruction of Ptahhotep*. In its introduction, between other titulary, we find "God's Father, God's Beloved, Eldest Son of the King". The latter is, as we have seen (see pp. 97-98), purely honorific, and whether the first epithet indeed means that Ptahhotep was responsible for the education of a later Pharaoh is quite uncertain.

In the New Kingdom 'god's fathers' as tutors of princes were far from rare. Two of them are Heqareshu and his son Heqaerneheh. The first element of their names, *heqa*, that is, 'ruler', suggests that these men were of Nubian descent, although they were of course fully egyptianized. In a Theban tomb (TT 226), which has been ascribed to the father, a unique picture occurs of Heqareshu with four princes – all with side-locks – on his knee (fig. 46). In his son's tomb (TT 64) there is another representation of him, now with Tuthmosis IV in full regalia on his lap, similar to the scene in Kenamun's tomb described above (see

Fig. 46 Heqareshu with four princes on his lap. From Theban tomb 226,
Eighteenth Dynasty

pp. 104-105). In front of him stands the son, Heqaerneheh, the owner of the sepulchre, with one prince before him and six others, now largely destroyed, following him. There has been much discussion as to who these boys actually are, but one thing is plain: Heqareshu bears the titles 'god's father' and "nurse of the king's son" because he had coached the future Tuthmosis IV. The son, however, although tutor of at least three royal infants, and possibly even seven, and himself educated in the palace as proved by his title "child of the *kap*" (see chapter 10), is never called 'god's father'. This is despite the fact that he was close to Amenhotep III, and, particularly, to the Pharaoh's mother, Queen Mutemwia. Perhaps the reason is that when this scene was painted his pupil Amenhotep had not yet become king, even if he indeed was the future King Amenhotep III.

One 'god's father' merits extra attention, namely Ay. Apart from being commander of the chariotry – it is conspicuous that many royal tutors bear such military titles – he was the governor of, first, Akhenaten, and later on, of Tutankhamun. Moreover, he was married to Teye, the wet-nurse of Nefertiti (see p. 16). His relations to the royal family were therefore particularly close. When, after the untimely death of Tutankhamun, no suitable royal heir was available any more, the old Ay ascended the throne. He then incorporated the epithet 'god's father' into his cartouche as part of his private name, probably because this stressed his link to the dynasty and constituted his only legitimation.

A special instructor called "father-tutor of a king's son" was Min, mayor of This and High Priest of Onuris under Tuthmosis III, who built for himself a tomb at Thebes (TT 109). There he is once depicted with a prince on his lap, and on the same wall he is teaching Prince Amenhotep (the later King Amenhotep II) to shoot (fig. 47a). The caption to this painting runs: "Taking delight in the shooting lesson in the courtyard of the Palace of This [by the King's son Amenhotep]"; the last words have been erased, very probably in the Amarna Period. Obviously, a royal palace existed at This where the prince was staying when Min, a trusted servant of Tuthmosis III, who may have been an officer in his youth, coached him in the noble art of archery. A second caption to the same picture states: "He (that is, Min) gives instruction for a lesson in shooting. He says: 'Draw your bow to your ears ....'". The remainder of the text is too mutilated to allow a translation, but the general tenor is clear.

Here we come across an important aspect of the youth of royal princes during the New Kingdom: their sporting activities. Of course, the Pharaoh had always been presented as a warrior and hunter, such scenes implying that he alone was responsible for destroying evil and protecting and restoring order, or Maat. During the New Kingdom, however, these portrayals were augmented by descriptions of the king's prowess as an athlete.

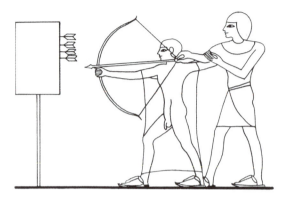

Fig. 47a The sportive king: Min gives an archery lesson to Prince Amenhotep. From the Theban tomb of Min (TT 109), Eighteenth Dynasty

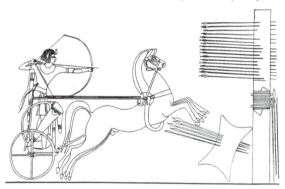

Fig. 47b The sportive king: red granite block showing Amenhotep II shooting at a copper target. From Karnak, Eighteenth Dynasty

The representations and texts showing the ruler's or the crown-prince's physical achievements are not realistic; rather they depict a ritual. Self-evidently, the Pharaoh surpasses everyone; his performances, even when exactly described, have not the purport of records. He does not win a game, since by definition he is invincible. As he is the best hunter or warrior, and by that guarantees the universal order, so his physical exercises are a necessary aspect of kingship.

That many scenes of the monarch shooting at targets from his chariot can hardly be realistic is proved by the fact that he is throughout, in battle, the hunt, and at sport, alone on his vehicle (fig. 47b). Normally two people man the chariot, a charioteer and an archer, and we know that the Pharaohs had their own charioteers. Of course, this would not have precluded them from driving the horses themselves, but to have done so at the same time as shooting at the target would in itself be a remarkable performance. On the other hand, Pharaoh's position forbade the representation of another person with him on the vehicle, his queen excepted. In one scene, on a quiver belonging to King Ay, the draughtsman solved the problem of what to do with the reins by depicting them tied around the sovereign's waist; in most representations this detail is simply left unclear.

In itself the motif of a duel, a contest between two opponents, is not unknown in Egypt, where it is encountered in the Horus and Seth legends. Above we discussed the Middle Kingdom wrestling scenes (see p. 49), and in the contemporary famous *Story of Sinuhe* the narrative occurs of a combat between the hero and a Syrian champion, reminiscent of the biblical account of David and Goliath. But with one exception (see below) a Pharaoh is never shown engaged in such a duel. As a reflection of reality it would make no sense, for the king must always be victorious.

Although the pictures and stories of the ruler's athletic accomplishments are ritualistic, that does not mean that princes were not trained to fit the model. In the New Kingdom at least they were expected to be outstanding warriors, able to shoot and row, to handle horses and a chariot, probably also to swim, which was sometimes necessary during a military campaign. Already from the Middle Kingdom a text, from the tomb of a certain Kheti at Asyut, states: "He (the king) had me instructed in swimming, together with the royal children".

It is particularly of the Pharaoh Amenhotep II that in several texts his physical strength and skill in shooting are related. This occurs so frequently and with so many details that one gains the marked impression that it is more than a mere literary motif. On a stone fragment from the Montu Temple at Medamud, not far from Thebes on the East Bank, near the desert edge, we read that Amenhotep shot an arrow straight through a copper target, so that more than half its shaft stuck out of the back. Then he challenged his officers to emulate him in a competition, which of course none of them could. The text is lacunary and not always clear, the story probably exaggerated and unrealistic, yet it distinctly suggests that this Pharaoh was extremely strong. Moreover, this is the only allusion to a match between the king and his companions.

On another monument Amenhotep's sporting prowess is extensively described. This is the so-called *Sphinx Stela*, one of the most famous inscriptions from the Eighteenth Dynasty. Twice in this laudation it is stated that the Pharaoh had demonstrated his strength while still an adolescent. A translation of the narrative part of the text would seem to be a suitable subject with which to conclude our appraisal of the royal prince. Although, in contrast to the introduction with its formal encomium, the narration itself is not really rhythmic, yet it is written in a genre midway between poetry and prose, sometimes referred to as the "orational style".

> Now his Majesty appeared as king,
> a fine youth who was well-developed,
> having completed eighteen years upon his thighs in strength
> (i.e., without having been ill).
> He was one who knew all the works of Montu (the war god),
> without equal on the battlefield.
> He was one who knew horses,
> one whose like did not exist in this numerous army.
> Not one among them could stretch his bow,
> nor could he be approached in running.

After this general introduction describing the prince, a young man of eighteen years, as already an able-bodied athlete, various of his skills are dealt with, the first of which is rowing.

> Strong of arms, one who did not tire
> when he seized the steering-oar.
> As the stroke for two hundred men,
> he steered at the stern of his falcon-boat.
> One paused after they had covered half a mile
>   (i.e., *circa* 5 kilometres),
> becoming weak, the limbs exhausted, out of breath,
> whereas his Majesty was strong under his oar of
>   twenty cubit in length   (*circa* 10.5 metres).
> He paused and landed his falcon-boat
> only after he had done three miles of rowing
>   (over 30 kilometres)
> without interrupting his stroke.
> Faces were aglow as they saw him do this.

Evidently, the prince was able to handle the large and heavy steering-oar for three miles, whereas the two hundred rowers were exhausted after only half a mile. This is a fair result and looks indeed authentic.

Next comes archery:

> He strung three hundred strong bows,
> comparing the craftsmanship of their makers,
> in order to know the unskilled from the skilled.

These lines are reminiscent of Odysseus' feats on his return to Ithaca!

> He also came to do the following,
> which is brought to your attention.
> Entering his northern garden,
> he found erected for him four targets of Asiatic copper
> of one palm (*circa* 7.5 centimetres) in thickness,
> with twenty cubits (*circa* 10.5 metres) between one post and the next.
> Thereupon his Majesty appeared on a chariot,
> like Montu in his might.
> He seized his bow,
> grabbing four arrows at once.
> He drove on northwards
> shooting at them like Montu in his panoply,
> and his arrows came forth from their back
> as he attacked the next post.

> It was a deed as had never before been done,
> nor heard by report:
> shooting an arrow at a target of copper,
> so that it came forth from it and dropped to the ground –
> except by the king, rich in glory,
> whom Amun had made strong,
> the King of Upper and Lower Egypt Aäkheperure,
> a fighter like Montu.

As here described, it is a dual feat: piercing targets and being able to hit them all while driving his chariot along them. According to some representations, such as the fine granite block found as fill in the Third Pylon at Karnak, and now in the Luxor Museum (fig. 47b), the targets were oxhide-shaped ingots. They are stated to be three quarters of a hand's breadth thick, or, in another text, three palms. This type of ingot is well-known, particularly from the wreck of a ship sunk off the southern coast of Asia Minor, near Cape Gelidonya, and dated to approximately 1200 B.C. Modern experiments have proved that it is hardly possible to pierce such targets: the story, therefore, clearly forms part of the ideology.

The text continues by expounding on the prince's passion for horses, the royal animal of the New Kingdom.

> When he was still a young crown-prince,
> he loved his horses and rejoiced in them.
> He was tenacious in working them,
> learning their nature,

to be skilled in training them,
understanding their temperament.

There follows an exposition as to how his father, Tuthmosis III, learning about his son's devotion to horses, rejoices at it and soliloquizes:

> He will make a Lord of the entire land
> whom no one can attack;
> eager to excel, he rejoices in victory;
> although he is only a charming young man, still without wisdom,
> and not yet ripe for the work of Montu (i.e., military campaigns),
> he ignores already the thirst of the body,
> and loves strength ......

> Then his Majesty said to those who were at his side:
> 'Let him be given the very best horses
> from my Majesty's stable at Memphis, and tell him:
> "Look after them, master them
> trot them, handle them if they resist you'''.

Subsequently, the prince was ordered to take care of the horses of the king's stable. He did as he was told, and:

> Reshep and Astarte (a warlike god and goddess from Asia)
>   rejoiced over him
> as he did all that his heart desired.
> He trained horses that were unequalled,
> which did not drip sweat in the gallop.
> He would yoke them secretly at Memphis
> and stopped at the resting-place of Harmakhis (the Great Sphinx).
> He spent time there, leading them around it,
> and observing the excellence of this resting-place of Khufu
>   and Khafra.

So his trips brought him to the neighbourhood of Giza, where he later on, after succeeding his father – as the narrative states – erected the stela on which this text is inscribed. Indeed the monument was found in the Temple of the Sphinx, now largely destroyed, and there was probably a training course in its vicinity. It leaves us with a vivid picture of the youth who seems to have been the most sporting of all Egyptian princes.

10 The Companions of the Prince

In his *Library of History* the Greek author Diodorus Siculus, of the last century B.C., talks about the companions of an Egyptian prince:

> Now after the birth of Sesoösis (other classical texts refer to him as Sesostris; he is a legendary figure, with some traits derived from Ramesses II), his father did a thing worthy of a great man and a king. Gathering together from all over Egypt the boys who had been born on the same day, and assigning to them nurses and guardians, he prescribed the same training and education for them all, on the theory that those who had been reared in close companionship and had enjoyed the same frank relationship would be most loyal and as fellow-combatants in the wars most brave. He amply provided for their every need and trained youths by unremitting exercises and hardships.

Diodorus then goes on to recount how they began the day by running 180 *stades* (approximately 30 kilometres) and as a result of their training became a most hardened and robust corps of athletes.

Although written much later, this description contains elements from an Eighteenth Dynasty reality. Indeed, some boys, albeit not necessarily born on the same day, were educated with the royal sons, and trained together with them in the arts of war.

Above we have quoted instances of boys educated at court among the princes: Ptahshepses during the Old Kingdom, and some anonymous pals of King Merikare in the First Intermediate Period (see p. 59). From the Middle Kingdom there was Kheti, the later nomarch of Asyut, who was taught to swim with the royal children (see p. 111), as well as Ikhernofret who is recorded as having been raised as a foster child of the king (see p. 61), which probably implies that he grew up among the princes. During the New Kingdom such companions of the King's sons, educated as pages in the palace, were destined to play influential rôles in the government, as will be seen below.

Very probably these young men received a military training, just as the royal princes did, not only in those sports particularly practised by officers, such as archery and chariot driving, but in all kinds of physical exercises. Conspicuous among the military games were wrestling and stick fighting. Actually, the depictions of these activities seem to present "mock battles", ritual rather than real matches. This is confirmed by the locations in which the 'battles' took place: according to tomb scenes in front of a temple, with the best known representation (fig. 48a) indeed occurring in a temple. It is sculpted under the 'Window of Appearance' in the first court of the Great Temple at Medinet Habu.

From this 'window', structurally a wide opening in a wall, the king and his retinue could assist in the events that took place in the courtyard, for instance, the rewarding of valiant warriors and the parade of a victorious army. To the ceremonies there performed belong single-stick fighting contests and wrestling matches, and therefore they are carved in relief under the "royal box". Our illustration (fig. 48a) shows three couples, two wrestling in different stances and one pair single-stick fighting, whilst at the right-hand side the game has ended: the victor raises his arms in triumph, as the disconsolate loser slinks off.

Perhaps the participants in these 'games' were specially trained, not unlike Roman gladiators. In many instances they seem to have been Nubians. The Eighteenth Dynasty tomb of the officer Tjanuni at Thebes (TT 74) depicts a group of such Nubian wrestlers, with the last figure in the row carrying their military standard which shows two contestants grappling with each other. The physique of the soldiers is quite in accordance with the requirements of this sport. That they were also stick fighters is clear from the sticks which they are holding.

The fact that the matches have a ritual character in such representations does not mean that wrestling and stick fighting did not belong to the training programme of army recruits. Moreover, they were practised by boys in the villages, as is still the case in modern Egypt (fig. 48b). The attention displayed in such games by the king and his court at festival occasions, albeit in mock-fightings, stresses the close relationship between rulers and their soldiers during the New Kingdom.

This keen interest of the monarch in the achievement of his troops is also apparent from an inscription dated to the reign of Taharqa, the great Pharaoh of the Twenty-Fifth Dynasty. It occurs on a limestone stela that was discovered in 1977, lying face-down along the desert road west of Dahshur. In this text his Majesty relates how he ordered his army to run daily, evidently as part of its fitness training. There follows a harangue by the king to the soldiers in the usual bombastic style.

After this introduction, however, an obviously realistic description is presented of the work-out on a particular day, the date of which was mentioned at the beginning of the text but is now lost. On this occasion, Taharqa himself came "on a horse", that is, driving his chariot – riding on horseback seldom occurred in Egypt – in order to oversee the physical condition of his men. When they started to run, during the cool hours of the night, he himself raced on foot with them for a stretch. After five hours, at the break of dawn, they reached the Faiyum Oasis, having covered no less than fifty kilometres. The soldiers rested here for two hours, after which they returned to the residence at Memphis. The first arrivals were rewarded with food and drink which they were allowed to partake of in the company of the king's bodyguard, while the officers were presented with valuable objects, for: "his Majesty loved the work of arms that was done for him". Clearly, this particular 'manoeuvre' had been a success.

116

Fig. 48 Wrestling and single-stick fighting: (a) From the First Court of the Medinet Habu Temple, Twentieth Dynasty (b) At Abydos, A.D. 1901

The remark that the sovereign himself joined the runners for some distance seems to be reliable. It shows how he identified himself with the achievements of his army, even taking part in its training. Such a close relationship between the king and his troops, particularly his officers, is found in Egypt from the Eighteenth Dynasty onwards. Above we have mentioned that young men sought a military career since this offered the possibility of catching the Pharaoh's eye during the campaigns (see p. 67). It was especially the companions of the royal prince who could hope for the chance to 'make it'.

117

Another group of royal companions also owed their careers to a personal bond with the ruler. These were the natural children of the ladies who acted as wet-nurses of the king's sons, the foster brothers and -sisters of the princes. Several of them remained in close contact with the sovereign throughout their lives. The bond was conceived to be some sort of physical relationship in which milk took the place of blood. Some of these foster-brothers of the monarch attained leading positions in the state. No wonder then that those men like Kenamun chose to depict in their tombs their mothers suckling the ruler (see fig. 43).

A similar, although less close, affiliation existed between the Pharaoh and the brothers or husbands of their wet-nurses and between sons of a royal tutor ('nurse') and their sovereign. When, as could happen, these youngsters were also educated together with the princes, such ties became all the more close.

During the Eighteenth Dynasty several members of the upper classes boasted that they were "children of the *kap*". The designation already occurs during the Middle Kingdom, with the variant "one sitting (i.e., living) in the room of the *kap*". The word *kap* here indicates a part of the palace, a school or a nursery or suchlike. Children taken into it became some sort of 'pages' in the medieval sense. It was a position which one was as proud of as the pupils of famous public schools in Britain are accustomed to be, and the title "child of the *kap*" was conceived to be one of the most honourable.

Over sixty such boys are known from the Eighteenth Dynasty, after which the title seems to have disappeared. Several of them rose to high office, but certainly not all, for some simply continued in the humble profession of their fathers. Others were foreigners, as, for instance, Heqaerneheh, the son of Tuthmosis IV's tutor Heqareshu (see p. 107-109). Another well-known page was Heqanefer, a local Nubian ruler of Miam (that is, Aniba). He built for himself a tomb in the Egyptian style at Toshka East, south of his city, and he may also be depicted in the Theban tomb of Huy (TT 40), the Viceroy of Nubia under Tutankhamun. Among the African chieftains who bring their tribute to the Pharaoh we see a Heqanefer, the chief of Miam, who flings himself down before his sovereign. However, the common identity of the two is not absolutely certain. As stated above (see p. 107), *heqa* is a frequent element in names of foreigners, and so Heqanefer, 'The Good Ruler", may have been fairly popular in Miam.

The component *heqa* likewise occurs in the second name of a certain Benia, who was also called Paheqamen. He was the owner of a Theban tomb (TT 343), and he too had been a "child of the *kap*". The fact that he was of foreign descent is evident from the non-Egyptian names of both his parents; that he became a fairly well-off civil servant is apparent from his tomb.

Fig. 49 Ramesses III chucks his daughter under her chin. From the Eastern High Gate of the Medinet Habu Temple, Twentieth Dynasty

On account of these and a few other instances it has been suggested that the "children of the *kap*" were, at least in part, those sons of foreign rulers whom the Egyptians transferred to the Nile Valley in order to educate them as loyal servants of Pharaoh. On the death of their fathers they were then installed in their

119

stead. Although this custom doubtless existed, it seems not to be these foreigners who were educated in the "royal nursery". Moreover, most of its pupils were Egyptians, of lower, middle and high rank, and, as we have just mentioned, by far not all later attained high office. Benia, for instance, merely became 'overseer of works', a sort of master builder. Other men who record on their monuments, mostly of a modest nature such as stelae, that they had been in their youth "children of the *kap*", became a draughtsman in the Ptah Temple, a shipbuilder, or even simply a doorkeeper. How highly such persons esteemed their stay at the court's educational establishment is apparent from the frequency with which they record this information. The shipbuilder, Iunena, for instance, does so no less than eleven times in the twelve lines of his stela, now in the British Museum.

Why these humble boys, who remained fairly simple citizens throughout their lives, should have been chosen for the post of 'page' is unknown. Perhaps the reason was that they were born on the same day as the crown-prince. That it was due to their intelligence or to their beauty is unlikely, although their female counterparts who were entitled "Royal Ornament" may indeed have been elected because of their charms.

It has been suggested that girls so designated were inhabitants of the royal harem and thus secondary wives of the king, but that appears not to have been the case with the majority. Indeed, they usually seem to have come from simple families, which make it plausible that they were chosen because of their charms. On the other hand, some of the "Royal Ornaments" were daughters of eminent families, while several married high officials. Evidently, as a group they were ladies-in-waiting rather than royal mistresses.

It may be that these are the girls represented in all their naked beauty on the walls of the rooms high up in the Eastern High Gate at the Medinet Habu Temple (fig. 49). The king is here entertained by them, presenting them with jewellery and playing the *senet* board-game with some; he puts his arm around their shoulder or chucks them under the chin. In the past Egyptologists interpreted these portrayals of intimacy as 'naughty' illustrations of harem life. The illusion is partly destroyed, however, by the discovery that at least some of the beauties were Ramesses III's own daughters, for they are once called "the royal children". Moreover, nudity – even the Pharaoh himself is undressed in these scenes, though wearing a crown – had in Egypt different connotations from those in the Western world (see p. 27 ff.).

Being a son of or married to a "Royal Ornament" was of significance for the promotion of a functionary. For instance, the mother of the vizier Rekhmire was such a lady-in-waiting, as was also the wife of Ramose, the vizier of Amenhotep III. Both viziers are the owners of Theban tombs: TT 100 and 55 (see p. 43) respectively, much visited by the modern tourist. The High Priest of Amun Hapuseneb, under Hatshepsut (see p. 83), was born of such a lady, while the military scribe and later general Tjanuni (TT 74; see p. 116) was married to one. One of the daughters of Menna, a "scribe of the fields" whose tomb (TT 69) is so famous because of its delightful wall paintings (see p. 45), received this rank, as did a daughter of the commander of the marines Nebamun (TT 90), who later in his life was appointed to police captain on the Theban West Bank. It is self-evident that at least some of the royal nurses also became a "Royal Ornament".

The ladies-in-waiting were looked after by the court, certainly until they married. In the tomb of the Theban mayor Sennefer (TT 96) it is stated of one of his daughters, "a Royal Ornament whom he loves, Nefertary", that she was buried by favour of the king with all ceremonies befitting her status. Clearly she died a spinster, perhaps at an early age. Indeed, certain objects found in the Valley of the Queens suggest that some holders of this rank were buried there, amongst the queens and princes. If they were unmarried, the court – that is, officially, the king himself – was responsible for their funeral. In view of the high infant mortality rate this would frequently have been the case, many ladies-in-waiting being still mere children when they died.

In the Egyptian governmental system, in which in theory all power lay in the hands of the Pharaoh, it is not surprising that he surrounded himself with a circle of intimates from his youth. These were men with whom he had grown up, whom he knew and could trust: sons and husbands of his wet-nurse, sons of his tutor, sons of the ladies-in-waiting whom he had met as girls in the rooms and corridors of the palace, and especially the "children of the *kap*" amongst whom he had been educated. And then, too, the soldiers whom he had selected and promoted during the campaigns at the beginning of his reign, or the favourite officers of his father, who had looked after and advised him when he was still a crown-prince.

Such a group, in many instances closely knit, can be found at the head of the state under many Pharaohs. A clear illustration is the ruling set under Amenhotep II, the sportsman whose achievements as a prince were described in the preceding chapter.

Amenhotep succeeded his father, the warrior-king Tuthmosis III, probably after some years of co-regency with him, but still at a relatively early age – he was not the eldest son, for that had been a prince Amenemhat, one of those crown-princes who died before their father (see p. 101). The new Pharaoh inherited the old vizier Rekhmire, who still held office, the third member in succession from one family (see p. 83). After his death Amenhotep did not cleave to this line, but chose one of his personal companions, a certain Amenemope, called Payry ('The Comrade'). He was a son of Ahmose-Humay (see p. 107), a steward of the estate of the 'God's Wife' and husband of a "Royal Ornament". Moreover, Ahmose-Humay, the owner of a Theban tomb (TT 224), had been overseer of the harem, and one of Amenhotep II's tutors. That Amenemope himself also married a lady-in-waiting is according to what one would expect.

His position was further strengthened by the appointment of his brother Sennefer as mayor of Thebes. Theoretically, the vizier ruled the capital, and only in a few instances during the Eighteenth Dynasty did Thebes have its own special mayor. That this post came under the control of Amenemope's sibling shows the concentration of power in the hands of this family, bolstered still further by Sennefer's second marriage to a royal nurse.

Both brothers built impressive tombs at Thebes: Sennefer TT 96 (see p. 84) and Amenemope TT 29. But their preponderant might is most clearly demonstrated by the fact that the latter certainly, and possibly also the former, were accorded the right to be interred in the Valley of the Kings. Amenemope's last resting place was a shaft (KV 48) south of the path leading to the tomb of Amenhotep II, in which fragments of his coffin and clay tablets with his name have been found. Sennefer was perhaps laid to rest in a tomb (KV 42) which had been prepared for Tuthmosis II, who was, however, subsequently buried elsewhere. In this grave some small limestone vases inscribed with the name and titles of Sennefer were found, as well as the canopic jars and a necklace pendant belonging to his wife. Although not decisive evidence, these indications are hard to explain in any other way.

Usually, such figures as a vizier or a Theban mayor remain for us simply names and titles, without any human trait. From the hand of Sennefer there does survive a letter, now in Berlin, addressed to a tenant farmer and, in so far as we can understand it, dealing with the requisition of various materials. It may not be a private matter, however, but one of the affairs of the Amun Temple at Karnak to which Sennefer was attached during the early stages of his career.

More personal, therefore, is a water-colour palette of polished boxwood that belonged to Amenemope, and is now in New York. It has a narrow compartment for paint brushes in the back and on top eight oval cavities for the much used blocks of dry pigments, in various colours. Clearly, it was intended, and actually utilized, for painting. Amenemope appears to have been one of those statesmen and rulers, like Winston Churchill or Queen Wilhelmina, who passed their leisure hours as amateur painters.

A third administrator of King Amenhotep II, besides these two brothers, was the manager of the royal domain Kenamun. He commenced his career as a military officer, accompanying his master on his early campaigns to Syria when Amenhotep was still co-regent. Later on he became the steward of one of the king's most important estates, that in Perunefer, the naval-base and royal residence near Memphis. At the end of his life he became the monarch's financial adviser. On the Theban West Bank he built a fine tomb (TT 93), but he may have possessed a second burial place in the North, a few miles south of Giza, for here many wooden shabti figures of him have been found.

Kenamun was a foster-brother of the king, as the depiction in his tomb of his mother nursing the ruler on her lap proves (see fig. 43). On another wall of his sepulchre some of his relatives are depicted, among whom are Kaemheribsen, who too was the son of a royal nurse, as well as a mayor of This, whose name is lost. The latter is thought by some scholars to be the archer Min who taught Amenhotep to shoot (see p. 109 and figure 47a). Kaemheribsen was the Third Prophet of Amun, hence high in the hierarchy of the Karnak Temple. His ultimate superior was Mery, the High Priest and owner of another Theban tomb (TT 95), who was perhaps a brother of Kaemheribsen and at any rate the son of a royal nurse called Hunay, that is, by inference, a foster-brother of the king. His father had been a High Priest of Min at Coptos, so that he belonged by descent to the clergy.

One more man in a prominent position should be mentioned: the Viceroy of Nubia Usersatet. He too served his royal master as a brave soldier during the military campaigns early in the reign, but he was also a "child of the *kap*" as well as the son of a "Royal Ornament". All this implies that he was close to the king from his youth onwards.

These personal relations are clearly revealed in a private letter which Amenhotep II sent him when he governed Nubia, a message which Usersatet valued so highly that he had it engraved on a sandstone stela erected in the Nubian fortress of Semna. This inscription is now in Boston (fig. 50). At the top the owner is depicted offering to the king who is seated on his throne, his pet lion beside him. The text, consisting of fourteen lines, is dated to Amenhotep's twenty-third regnal year, and stated to be a copy of an order which his Majesty wrote by his own hand "while he was sitting and drinking and making a holiday". Therefore, the tone of the communication is personal and quite informal.

Unfortunately, a large portion of the stela has been broken off and lost, so that the course of the argument is difficult to follow. It seems that the king warns his viceroy against Nubian magicians and denigrates some Asiatics whom they had once defeated as brothers-in-arms. Evidently, the Pharaoh was sitting back and reminiscing of the happy days of his youth. Towards the end he does seem to proffer some direct advice concerning Usersatet's dealings with his Nubian subjects, but this is tied to what seems to be a proverb, the meaning of which escapes us. Anyhow, Usersatet was obviously greatly pleased to receive this token of trust from his royal master.

Fig. 50 White sandstone stela of the Viceroy Usersatet. From the second cataract fortress of Semna, Eighteenth Dynasty

Against this background it is surprising that we know of no Theban tomb for Usersatet. Did he build one elsewhere, perhaps at Aswan near his Nubian domain, where he erected many signs of his activities, or perhaps in the North, near Meidum, where he had once been "Overseer of the House" (of the king), apparently a provincial royal seat? It may be so, but appears less likely since all his important contemporaries had their Theban burial places. Moreover, on some of his monuments his names and representations are erased, which suggests that he fell from favour, either under Amenhotep II or under his son, Tuthmosis IV.

As stated above (see p. 121), Amenhotep inherited some favourite servants of his father. Among them were two prominent military men, Amenemhab called Mahu (see p. 88) and Pekhsukher called Tjenenu. Both were promoted at the end of their careers to "lieutenant of the army" or "of the King"; both possessed finely decorated Theban tombs (Amenemhab TT 85; Pekhsukher TT 88); and both were married to royal nurses. In addition, Amenemhab was a "child of the *kap*"; for Pekhsukher this is unknown. When Amenemhab's wife died, probably at the beginning of Amenhotep's reign, she was, as is stated in his tomb, "buried by the favour of the king. One did for her what is done to a noble one".

124

Alongside these key figures a whole set of minor officials are attested, who were specially bound to the Pharaoh, mostly from his youth on. One of them is the royal butler Maanakhtef, a former "child of the *kap*", later on a court dignitary. There is another butler, Mentiywy, who "followed" Tuthmosis III as a young man and became a good soldier before he officiated in the harem and, later, at court. Perhaps he was a predecessor of Maanakhtef. Another former page is Userhat, who became the "scribe who counts the bread(-rations) in Upper and Lower Egypt", evidently a post in the distribution of food among state officials. He was married to a "Royal Ornament", a rank also granted to one of his daughters.

Among the officers mention can be made of Paser, a troop commander, probably the son of a Nebamun of the same military rank. Educated in the palace as a page, he became chief of the bodyguard of his Majesty "when he was (still) a young prince". Hence he was evidently a member of the inner circle. His Theban tomb (TT 367) was never finished, while his sarcophagus was transported to Sedment in the North and there usurped by a certain Pahemnetjer.

Several more companions of the king from his youth could be cited, for instance Heqaerneheh, the son of Heqareshu, a royal tutor (see pp. 107-109), and himself a mentor of royal princes. But he may have belonged to a later generation.

However, not all mighty officials seem to have been part of this clique. A high personage like Minmose, "director of the great construction projects in the temples of the gods of Upper and Lower Egypt", was probably of low descent and certainly no "child of the *kap*" or the king's foster-brother. Yet he clearly enjoyed a distinguished career. He had accompanied the ruler Tuthmosis III as a military scribe on several campaigns before he became the director of the building activities of the state. The fact that his wife was a lady-in-waiting and his daughter later became a royal nurse, was probably the result of his position, rather than the reason for his success in life. It is characteristic that no Theban tomb is known for him.

Almost all the other companions so far recorded possessed burial places in one particular section of the Theban necropolis, namely the south-west side of the hill called Sheikh Abd el-Qurna. In that area we also find the tomb (TT 97) of another politician who reached the top, without being a member of the select band of the king's companions. This is Amenemhat, a High Priest of Amun, probably the predecessor of the Mery referred to above (see p. 123).

Amenemhat had an unusual career. As the son of a simple artisan connected with the Amun Temple at Karnak, the "chief cobbler Dhutihotep", he became a common priest in the same sanctuary. He long remained inconspicuous, until suddenly, when he was fifty-four years old, he was promoted to the top post in the Theban clergy, probably jumping over the heads of several of his superiors in the process. For what reason he was chosen for the position of High Priest remains a complete mystery; certainly he nowhere refers to any connection with the royal court. His character seems not to have suffered from this unexpected success, as shown by his autobiography which is inscribed on a wall in the inner room of his tomb. It is cast in the form of a wisdom text:

> He says to his children as instruction:
> 'I say now,
> and let you hear what happened to me since the first day,
> since I came forth from between the thighs of my mother.
> I was a priest, and a "staff of old age" with my father,
> while he was living on earth.
> I went in and out at his command;
> I did not transgress what his mouth uttered ......
> I did not neglect the orders which he gave me;
> I did not pierce him with many glances,
> but kept my face down when he spoke to me'.

In short, Amenemhat declares himself to have been an ideal son of his father, and by that he creates the impression that he owed his position neither to his relations nor to the special favour of the ruler, but merely to his own humble righteousness and innate wisdom. Whether this is true we cannot prove, but it is obvious that not all the high and mighty of this reign were former companions and brother-in-arms of the crown-prince, although many indeed were.

11 Society's Perceptions of the Younger Generation

In the preceding chapters we have used various English words for young people. Some of them refer to a specific age, such as baby, toddler, schoolboy, teenager, adolescent; others are vaguer in this respect: kid, lad/lass, youngster, infant, whilst child and boy/girl cover the entire stretch from birth to adulthood

In Egyptian there also exist a large number of designations for the younger generation, even more than in modern English, which is not surprising since the texts span longer than three millennia. Many terms spring up and disappear again during the course of the centuries.

However, with a few exceptions the words do not seem to indicate a particular age. One of them, for instance, is derived from the verb "to wean". One would expect it to describe the period of time between the ages of one or two until five or six years, and indeed that does occur. Yet, the High Priest of Amun Bekenkhons (see p. 61) employed it in one of his inscriptions to denote his entire youth up to adulthood, and in other autobiographies it embraces still later stages of life. Thus it is hardly equivalent with our 'weanling'. Evidently, the label became as vague as our 'lad' or 'kid', not referring any more to a specific age.

Some terms for children seem to imply a social rank. An example is the word used during the Old Kingdom for boys after they had "knotted the band" (see pp. 90-91), that is, for adolescents who already occupied a social position of some importance. Another expression is restricted to young princes. In the *Sphinx Stela* it is used for Prince Amenhotep when he was eighteen years old (see p. 111), but whether it could also pertain to a lower age group is not clear. It has also been suggested that it bears the connotation 'crown-prince'.

Yet another word for a young person is usually taken to mean 'adolescent', but the ages indicated by it vary considerably. Bekenkhons applies it to his youth between ten and twenty years of age; Pharaoh Ramesses II was once called so when he was ten years old; King Taharqa when he was twenty, and the Middle Kingdom official Ikhernofret (see p. 61) when he was as much as twenty-six. Clearly, it does not point to a fixed stage in life.

Even the phrase "my child" can present a problem, as does the English expression. Normally in Egyptian it refers to one's genuine son or daughter, but in a few Middle Kingdom and Second Intermediate Period cases it betokens someone who acts as a son, in supplying funerary offerings for a deceased person, although in reality he is no member of the family but a subordinate or servant in the household.

The vagueness in terminology may correspond with the lack of attention displayed by the Ancient Egyptians for the characteristics of childhood. To them an infant was an incomplete adult, still in a state of imperfection. Yet, the care devoted to the burial of children, even of newborn ones, shows that they were considered to be already personalities. There were also vessels and foodstuffs put in their graves, an indication that they were supposed to live on in the hereafter.

In the later epochs of Egyptian history, infancy was conceived to be a stage of innocence. On stelae from that period erected for those who had died at an early age, the departed states about him- or herself: "I was an innocent child" or "I was young, one who has not yet faults". In a Demotic wisdom text from the First Century A.D., but probably composed in the late Ptolemaic Period, and which survives on a papyrus now in Leiden, we read: "He (i.e. man) spends ten years as a child before he understands death and life. He spends another ten years acquiring the work of instruction by which he will be able to live". That is, only during his adolescence does he reach a level of understanding of life necessary for human existence. This agrees with the words spoken by Tuthmosis III about his son (see p. 114): "He is a charming young man, still without wisdom". And this when Amenhotep was eighteen years old! At that age he was still considered to be "not yet ripe for the work of Montu", i.e. too young for a warrior. Not all societies would agree with this opinion.

We possess at least one text which reveals that the specific nature of a child, as distinct from that of an adult, was not wholly unknown to the Egyptians – although the contents also demonstrate that contemporary society did not want to take it into account. This is the epilogue to the *Instruction of Ani*.

After Ani has uttered all his admonitions to his son Khonsuhotep, the latter replies that he would indeed wish to be as learned as his father. Then he would act as he is taught. Unfortunately, he is not a sage: "Each man is led by his nature". "The son understands little when he recites the words in the books". Certainly, he has learnt them by heart, but that does not yet mean that he is able to observe their lessons. "A boy does not follow the moral instructions, though the writings are on his tongue".

This Ani does not accept. "Rubbish", he says; animals can be trained: "The dog obeys the word and walks behind his master; the monkey carries the stick, though his mother did not carry it; the goose returns from the pond when one comes to shut it in the yard". So why not with the boy? To that Khonsuhotep retorts: You do not really listen to me, father. What you state may be excellent, to do it demands virtue. All that Ani requires, however, is his son's obedience. He does not really want to listen to his arguments, and compares Khonsuhotep with a crooked stick which the carpenter can straighten so that it becomes a useful staff.

Once more the son complains: "Look, you, my father, are wise and strong of hand. The infant in his mother's arms, his wish is for what nurses him". That is, please, father, take my age into account. The last words of Ani, however, continuing the same imagery, run: "When he (the infant) finds his speech, he says: 'Give me bread'".

Such a debate is unique in the pages of Egyptian literature. To our ears it sounds almost modern. The argument of the son is: such an instruction may be ideal but it is too difficult for a boy. In other words: education should make allowances for the age of the pupil. Contrary to these progressive views the father defends the conservative attitude: a boy should obey, if needs be forcibly. In Egyptian society it is the latter standpoint that prevails.

This does not imply that the Egyptians did not care for their children, or did not respect their individual personalities. When we read in the *Admonitions* (*Lamentations*) *of Ipuwer* (see p. 84):

> Look, great and small say: 'I wish I were dead'.
> Little children say: 'He should not have made me live!'
> Look, children of nobles are dashed against walls,
> infants are cast out on high ground,

we have to remember that this is a description of a world topsy-turvy. The passage actually states with force that normally parents looked after their offspring well.

Some were even very proud of them, as is apparent from the text on a granite block-statue of a certain Bekenkhons, a priest of Amun from the Twenty-Second Dynasty – to be distinguished from his namesake, the Nineteenth Dynasty High Priest whose autobiography was discussed earlier (see p. 61). The sculpture was made for him by his son "to keep his name alive"; yet, the texts on it are put into the owner's mouth. Concerning the son he says:

> I already loved him when he was still a small boy;
> I acknowledged him as a proper gentleman.
> As a child I found him already mature.
> His breeding was not in accordance with his (young) age.
> His speech was well-chosen.
> There was nothing uncouth in his words.

To our senses this is an overstatement, slightly embarrassing for a son to hear from his father in public. Yet, it was the son himself who had it incised on the statue. In any case, it does show that children could be highly appreciated.

Three-dimensional expression of the care for a child is found in some other block-statues, mostly dating from the Eighteenth Dynasty. In these an infant is shown sitting between the drawn-up knees of its tutor; only its head emerges above the mantle enveloping his lower limbs. This type of statuary occurs particularly in figures of Senenmut with his pupil the Princess Neferure (see pp. 106-107), although sculptures of him in different attitudes also express a similar emotion (see fig. 45).

Certainly, such representations are not meant to be naturalistic, as the beard of the girl in figure 45 undeniably indicates. They evoke an idea in the form of a 'hieroglyph', and should be compared with the ideogram of the breastfeeding mother used in the designation for 'male tutor' (see p. 16), or that of an infant sitting (as on the lap) with the hand to the mouth, the common hieroglyph for 'child'.

Fig. 51 Grey granite and limestone colossal statue of Ramesses II with the falcon god Hurun. From Tanis, Nineteenth Dynasty

A further step in this direction is the large grey granite and limestone (the face of the bird) group of Ramesses II and the falcon-god Hurun, discovered at Tanis and now in Cairo (fig. 51). In front of the protecting figure of the bird a baby prince is sitting with drawn-up knees and the index finger of the left hand to its mouth, a sun-disk on its head, and a plant in its left hand. Together these elements should be read as: *Ra* (the sun-disk) + *mes* (the child) + *su* (the plant) = *Ramessu* (or, in the Greek form, Ramesses). The representation of the youngster

130

does double service, for it depicts the Pharaoh and, at the same time, stands for the hieroglyph 'child'.

Later on we shall return to the infant in Egyptian art, as one of the means to recognize the concepts concerning childhood. The other avenue of approach is by the way of the texts.

Obviously, children were highly valued and not merely for emotional reasons. Sons in particular were a dire necessity for parents. In the absence of any form of social security, older people, if they were not rich, became dependent upon the younger generation. This is expressed by the designation of a son as "the staff of old age", which we encountered above in the autobiography of the High Priest Amenemhat (see pp. 125-126), but which was common throughout the ages. Moreover, it was the son, especially the eldest one, who was expected to build a tomb, or complete it, for his parents, and to look after their burial – also to pay for all this! In addition, after the ceremony he had regularly to bring offerings to the tomb and to there recite the customary prayers.

An expression which occurs frequently in connection with children is "to cause to live" (or: "to keep alive") the name of the father (see p. 129). It does not mean, as we would expect, to keep the family name alive by producing children and grandchildren, but to perpetuate the memory of the deceased by pronouncing his name when passing his monument! It was a duty for everyone who walked along to do so (see p. 60), but particularly for one's offspring. In fact it was of even more importance than the service to the living father as a "staff of old age".

The social need for a son is convincingly expressed in the text on a pottery ostracon from Deir el-Medina, probably dating from the Nineteenth Dynasty, and which is now in Berlin. It is couched in the form of a polite letter, addressed by the unknown author to a certain Nekhemmut. There were several persons of this name in the workmen's village, and there is no way of knowing which one of them was meant. It is not even certain that a specific person was indeed addressed.

To Nekhemmut.
(May you be) in Life, Prosperity and Health, in the favour of
your august god Amun-Re, King of the Gods, your Lord, every day.
What does it mean that you have got yourself into this miserable position,
in which you are now, not letting anyone's word penetrate into your ears,
in accordance with your haughty character?
You are no man, for you did not make your wife pregnant,
    as your friend did.
And then, you are excessively rich, but you don't give anything to anybody.

131

He who has no children should get for himself some orphan, to bring him
   up. Then he will be the one who pours water upon his hands,
as a genuine eldest son.

Not a particularly 'nice' letter, but clear in its indication of why one needs a son
in life: "To pour water upon one's hands", very probably before the meals; and,
in a wider sense, to serve the father whenever he requires.

   This rendering of service to one's parents is many times mentioned in
autobiographies on the tomb walls. One example belongs to an early Sixth
Dynasty priest in the Temple of the Pyramid of Teti at Saqqara, who was named
Nefersekhemre, in daily speech Sheshi. His mastaba adjoins that of Ankhmahor
(see p. 76), and contains a description of how well the tomb-owner had behaved
on earth. It runs: "I respected my father, I was kind to my mother, I have raised
their children" (that is, his younger brothers and sisters). It does not matter
whether that was true in this specific case; it represents the ideal behaviour of a
son towards his parents, the counterpart of care for one's children.

   In view of the need for offspring it is evident that childlessness was
regarded as a disaster. Particularly for women, but to a lesser extent also for men,
who would have nobody to look after their burial and supply the offerings.
Hence we find the wish for progeny expressed in various ways. One is the text
quoted above (see p. 6), written on the leg of a Middle Kingdom female figure:
"May there be given birth to your daughter Sah". Another manner of uttering the
desire for descendants is the text on the underside of certain scarabs. They are
inscribed with hieroglyphs that have a different meaning from the normal, so-
called cryptograms. The most common sentences run: "Your name may last,
children may be granted to you".

   Yet another proof for the hankering after issue is encountered in a letter
addressed to a dead relative, written on a pot and probably to be dated to the First
Intermediate Period. The container is unprovenanced and is now in Chicago. The
text, in vertical lines according to the custom of that time (see pp. 66-67),
contains a complaint about childlessness. Requests – here: "Cause that there be
born to me a healthy male child" – were frequently addressed to deceased
members of the family, probably shortly after their demise. Written either on
papyrus or on a vessel, they were placed in the tombs. The background is the
world-wide belief that the departed has not yet lost all contact with this earth and
is still able to help or to harm. No wonder then that one turned to them with a
petition for a child!

   Although in general both boys and girls alike were wanted in Egypt (see
p. 20), it is understandable that the author of this Letter to the Dead particularly
begged for a son. The same happened in the text on a stela, now in the British
Museum, which dates from the last century B.C. It narrates the autobiography of
a certain Taimhotep, the wife of a priest of Ptah, and mentions all kinds of exact
dates such as those of her birthday (see p. 14) and of her marriage, when she was

fourteen years old. She bore her husband three daughters, but to the grief of them both no son. Therefore they turned to the deified Imhotep (see p. 57) after whom she had been named, and he indeed harkened to their prayers, revealing to the husband in a dream that he should build for him a chapel. The priest did so, of course, and after some time the ardently desired son was born. Unfortunately, only four years later the mother died at merely thirty years of age.

Let us now turn to child representations in two and three dimensions, of which the reader will find a number described and illustrated in this book. In general, the youngsters are depicted as adults-in-miniature. Their age is indicated by their nudity, in many instances of boys by side-locks, and sometimes by the childish gesture of putting a finger to the mouth. This is to be seen rather as a 'hieroglyph' for child than as a picture of a genuine baby or toddler (see also p. 23).

If portrayed together with its parents or with just one of them, the child's proportions are not realistic, it being frequently too small. In group statues its head reaches to the seat of the adult's chair, or just above it, to his or her knee (see fig. 12), and, in other instances, as far as the shoulder of the main figure. It also happens that all the heads in such a group are at the same level, which suggests an abnormally tall infant. In actual fact the size of the body bears no relation with reality, as compared with that of grown-ups. In reliefs too the youngster could reach to the knee or the thigh of his or her parent (see fig. 18).

If more than one child were depicted, a difference in age between the various siblings is seldom expressed, although the girls are generally more delicately represented than the boys. Rarely does one find traces of the natural plumpness and the proportionally large heads which in reality distinguish the child's body from that of the adult.

This especially holds true for Old Kingdom art, from which numerous portrayals of young people have survived. From the Middle Kingdom three-dimensional figures of children are less frequent. In the Eighteenth Dynasty they again become more numerous, but still show the same general characteristics as in earlier times.

The great break in this respect comes in the Amarna art. Then the artists abandoned the custom of picturing infants in the old symbolic manner by the hieroglyphic ideograph. The Amarna princesses have taken their fingers out of their mouths and behave like real infants by using them instead to point or play. For example, on the altar slab in Berlin (see pp. 25 and 35) the two groups are brought together dramatically by the linking pose of the eldest princess on her mother's knee who looks up at her as she points to the pair on the opposite side (where the middle daughter is also pointing across). The youngest plays with Nefertiti's hair ornament. The princesses are also not all of the same size any more, so that it is possible to recognize their respective ages (fig. 52, and see fig. 13).

A proof of this more realistic interpretation, here to be seen even in the face, is a very small royal head with a uraeus on the brow. Made of siliceous

Fig. 52 Opaque red moulded glass inlay showing two young Amarna princesses. From el-Amarna, Eighteenth Dynasty

sandstone, it is now in Hanover. The scholar who published the piece suggests that it is the remains of a sphinx figure, and because he recognized childish traits he felt inclined to identify it as a representation of Tutankhamun. Similar boyish features are displayed on another statuette of this Pharaoh, in petrified wood, and now in Cairo. Of somewhat riper years is the face emerging from the blue lotus-flower. Sculpted in painted wood this beautiful object was found in the boy king's tomb.

Even if the suggestions that these countenances exhibit childish characteristics are, in each separate case, debatable, taken together they show that the Amarna Period constitutes a new development in the portrayal of infants. This corresponds with a vividness in some contemporaneous Theban tomb scenes, for instance those of Neferhotep (TT 49; see fig. 22). And, although Nineteenth Dynasty art mainly returned to the old principles, the children on our front cover illustration display a greater naturalness than those in Old Kingdom tombs (see, for instance, fig. 18).

Yet, realistic details were never completely absent from Egyptian art. In the Fifth Dynasty mastaba of Nefer and Kahay (see p. 36) there is the scene of a woman sitting at the entrance to a bower and watching dancing girls. Before her stands her little daughter, dressed in a long gown and looking up at her – evidently she was not particularly enthralled by the performance! With her left hand she just touches her mother's hand which rests on the lap: a rare display of tenderness.

Such details are fairly scarce, and far dispersed. Infants are mostly merely pictured as a type, and that a small adult. "The child in Egyptian art" is hardly to be viewed as an interesting subject within the field of art history, and it is not surprising that such a study has never been written.

This agrees with the Egyptians' concepts of childhood in general. Although well aware of the individuality of each youngster, as a stage in life youth was conceived to be "not-yet-adulthood", with full stress on the "not yet". As a necessary transitory stage, without its own value, the aim was simply to prepare the child for the future as quickly as possible, without seeking to promote his or her own innate possibilities. Growing up in Ancient Egypt was thus still far removed from "The Age of the Child".

Nevertheless, offspring were valued, and we can aptly conclude our study with the words of the oft-quoted Ani in his *Instructions*:

> Happy is the man whose people are many;
> He is saluted on account of his progeny.

Amun, give me your heart
Direct towards me your ears
Open your eye
Save me every day
and lengthen for me my lifetime.

A prayer by a certain Penpare, written on the rock near the entrance to the Royal Cache (the so-called Tomb of Inhapi) at Western Thebes.

Part II: Getting old

Acknowledgements

We are most grateful to the many museum curators who have provided us with photographs, in many cases gratis, and permission for their publication. Each institution is fully credited in the List of Illustrations. However, we would especially like to single out Dr. Bettina Schmitz of the Roemer- und Pelizaeus-Museum, Hildesheim, Dr. Stephen Quirke of the British Museum, London, and Mr. Robert Partridge whose help with photographs has been exceptional. Our special thanks must go to Dr. Alain-Pierre Zivie, who most kindly and at great speed sent us two of his superb colour transparencies. One has become our back cover illustration, while the other appears as a black and white figure within the text. Ms Mary Hinkley of the Photography and Illustration Centre, University College London, painstakingly and with good humour, produced our other photographs. Ms Bram Calcoen is to be thanked and congratulated for her skilful line drawings and ever constant attention to detail.

To Anthea Page, Juanita Homan, and Robin Page, Partners of The Rubicon Press, we express our sincere gratitude. Once again, they have given us their habitual encouragement and assistance at every stage of the production.

Finally, we would like to thank all those who expressed an interest in our *Growing up in Ancient Egypt* which encouraged us to write the present volume.

Preface

This second part is the sequel of the first one, and is based on the same principles. As in our treatment of childhood, the present section is also based on many sources, both texts as well as representations. But since it is intended for the general reader, and not for professional Egyptologists, we have refrained from referring to these sources. The bibliography at the end may be of some help, but the reader should bear in mind that it is merely a small selection from the numerous works we have consulted.

As in Part I, our translations are mostly based on those of the admirable volumes by Miriam Lichtheim, *Ancient Egyptian Literature* (Berkeley, 1973-1980); in the last chapter also on her *Ancient Egyptian Autobiographies* (Freiburg/Göttingen, 1988).

Even more than was the case with childhood, old age has been a neglected subject in Egyptology. One reason for that is clear: the Egyptians never stressed that the elderly as such were a source of wisdom, as is the case in other ancient civilizations, such as those of India and China. On the one hand, lack of precursors made our task more difficult; we had ourselves to decide what subjects we wanted to discuss. There are indeed articles dealing with the topics of various chapters – they are quoted in the bibliography – but only a few. That meant, on the other hand, that we felt justified in using the opportunity to investigate all manner of aspects of Egyptian life which are in some way or other connected with old age. The present part is thus to a certain extent an introduction to Egyptology in general. This may be warranted since the elderly were, far more than children, part of the rich panorama of life in those days.

In our choice of illustration we have once again attempted to avoid the obvious, although it was not always easy to evade the well-known pictures. At the very least, all our photographs and line drawings illustrate parts of the text.

February 1996   Rosalind and Jac. Janssen
Revised July 2005

Note to the translations:
Round brackets (   ) indicate: our explanations.
Square brackets [   ] indicate: restorations in the text.

INTRODUCTION
Gerontology

Part II of this book is about getting old. The question immediately arises: who is old? A simple definition is one which we happened to hear on Radio 4's 'Thought for the Day'. "One is old if when bending down to tie up one's shoelaces, one looks around to see what else can be done on the floor before stretching up again". This picture reveals the physical, and also to some extent the psychological aspect of being elderly, as well as being an individual point of view. Of course, there are other, better definitions.

When asked who in our society constitute the old, people are apt to come up with specific ages: for example, those over sixty-five, the moment in life when most of us still hope to retire. Two centuries ago our forebears would have answered very differently, for when old age pensions were first proposed in Britain, by Defoe in the 1690's, and by Dowdeswell in 1772, fifty was the age at which they were to be payable. These are socially constructed boundary lines.

But what is the criterion in societies where people do not know their exact age, as was the case in Ancient Egypt? Then functional definitions are used, based on performance rather than on age. For instance, individuals who cannot any more be fully productive are considered to be old: those not able to execute the full range of tasks appropriate to adults of one's sex and status, and, consequently, have to rely on others for part of their livelihood. The first stage of old age is now sometimes called "young old". The next one, comprising the over 85 age group, is known as "old old", and is often the stage of dependency. Similarly, "the Third Age" has been dubbed "the crown of life", whereas "The Fourth Age", and now even "The Fifth Age", are ones of dependency.

Other indications that one has passed the boundary line are, for instance, for a woman the end of the menopause, and for both men and women the birth of the first grandchild. Further physical indications occur, for example, the appearance of wrinkles and grey hair, or the onset of various ailments, usually in combination with each other. These include arthritis and rheumatism, breathlessness and giddiness, deafness, poor eyesight, forgetfulness, or even senility.

The academic discipline that is devoted to the study of ageing is called Gerontology. It is a relative newcomer to the scholastic fraternity, yet it has already in its short history, produced a wealth of literature. A few of its classic publications are cited in our bibliography.

The enormous growth in gerontology should not surprise us: the rapidly expanding mass of older people in our modern world is one of its most spectacular features. Whereas at the beginning of the Twentieth Century the life expectancy in Britain for men was 44.1 years, and for women 47.8 years, this had risen at the end of the last century to 75.1 and 80.0 years respectively. Britain's ageing population comprises a growing proportion of older people and of very old people, with the 'baby-boomers' set to cause numbers to peak in the 2030's. The problems of global demographic change are presently being highlighted by the world's media and the governments are beginning to address some of the crucial issues.

Getting old exhibits various aspects: biological (what happens to our bodies in the course of our lives, and why); psychological (how do people react to their old age, and how do the circles in which they move react to them); sociological (which social and cultural factors influence the ageing process; what is the place of older people in a particular society). Several key subjects elicit much attention. Firstly, the medical problems, which are the object of a special branch of medicine called geriatrics. Then, for instance, the difficulties connected with retirement, such as a lower income and the loss of regular occupation; or the need for adapted housing, and special homes for those who become totally dependent. Quite a different branch of study is the image of older people in society: formerly preponderantly the aversion against senility and decrepitude, but recently also the attraction of leisure, enjoying a good pension and having the time and resources to travel all over the world. Of particular interest is the foundation of political parties engaged entirely with the interests of the strategic 'grey vote'.

There are three gerontological theories which attempt to explain the ageing experience. Disengagement Theory (1961) states that, as a person ages, a mutual withdrawal takes place between that individual and the society of which s/he is a part. The only possible trace of this attitude in Ancient Egypt is Ineni's withdrawal to a "tent" beside his tomb once in receipt of his old age pension (see pp. 198-199). However, in Ancient India we find the ideal of withdrawal features prominently, although mainly for the élite, and for men. The aged are supposed to retreat to the forest, renouncing all worldly attachments and becoming ascetics who retire into meditation.

Conversely, Activity Theory (1963) claims that in order to achieve "successful ageing" older people need to continue to be active in the same way as they were at mid-life. This theory can perhaps explain the Turin Erotic Papyrus as a picture of successful ageing, rather than its normal interpretation as one of derision (see p. 150).

More recent research focuses on the diversity of the ageing experience. Thus Continuity Theory (1993) argues that a person's previous life course is a clue to understanding their wishes, feelings and activities in later life. So Qenhikhopshef the historian and dreamer becomes the collector of a library in his old age (see p. 268).

A further three theories attempt to explain the attitude to old age in past societies. Prominent Modernization Theory (1972) promoted the myth of a lost "golden age of senescence", a romantic picture based on the notion of a respectful attitude to old age in non-literate societies where older people had a rarity value and were viewed as repositories of vital knowledge. The opposing stance – Revisionism Theory (1997) – envisages an unmitigated progression towards retirement and the modern welfare state. As such the 1990's have almost been viewed by the revisionists as the utopia of a "golden age of senescence".

Over the past decade there has been a new emphasis on the diversity of the ageing experience, based on an older person's health, wealth, and gender. The Diversity School therefore dismisses the notion of a "golden age of senescence" as a myth. When writing the first impression of *Getting old* back in 1996, we unconsciously embraced this model of persistent ambivalence seeing "both attitudes ...... that of respect for elderly men and that of derision for the decaying body" as present in the written documents and in the artistic products (see p. 146).

Some Egyptologists – most notably Professor John Baines – have embraced Modernization Theory in envisaging Ancient Egypt as a gerontocracy where elderly courtiers formed the power behind the throne. However, the pages that follow reveal no trace of this feature which dominates some African societies.

Nor is the wisdom of the elderly stressed, not even in the so-called Wisdom Literature. Being a semi-literate – as opposed to the pre-literate societies of Modernization Theory – the emphasis was placed firmly on the wisdom of the ancestors, particularly the great administrators of olden days.

In the *Instruction for Merikare* (see p. 224), we read:

Copy your fathers, your ancestors,
[for work is carried out through] knowledge.
See, their words endure in books.
Open and read them, copy their knowledge.
He who is taught becomes skilled.

This means that in Ancient Egypt the rôle of the old was decidedly less conspicuous and more ambiguous than in most other great civilizations, such as Imperial China where old age was venerated and afforded a position of power. No doubt this goes a long way to explaining why no books have been devoted to the subject. Nevertheless, it is of fundamental importance to study this aspect of life in Pharaonic society, and the following pages are an attempt to redress the situation.

12 Perceptions of the Older Generation

Some Egyptian texts contain a clear description of what it means to become old. The most famous of them is probably that at the beginning of the *Instruction of Ptahhotep* (see pp. 207 and 216). Ptahhotep, who was a Fifth Dynasty vizier under Pharaoh Isesi, speaks to his sovereign as follows:

> O King, my Lord!
> Old age is here, high age has arrived,
> Feebleness came, weakness grows,
> Childlike one sleeps all day.
> Eyes are dim, ears are deaf,
> Strength is waning, one is weary,
> The mouth, silenced, speaks not,
> The heart, void, recalls not the past,
> The bones ache throughout.
> Good has become evil, all taste is gone,
> What age does to people is bad in every respect.
> The nose, clogged, cannot breathe,
> Painful are standing and sitting.

This is indeed a moving picture of incipient decrepitude! It is even (mis) quoted by Christina Victor in her classic book on modern old age (see bibliography). Yet, it is not unique in the pages of world literature. Ageing is poignantly described in the *Panchatantra*, a famous collection of framing stories, animal fables and rhymed maxims, intended to teach practical politics and worldly wisdom. Created in India in the early centuries A.D., the work is known in several versions and in numerous translations. We quote here from the version of Arthur Ryder:

> Slow, tottering steps the strength exhaust,
>   The eye unsteady blinks,
> From drivelling mouth the teeth are lost,
>   The handsome figure shrinks,
> The limbs are wrinkled; relatives
>   and wife contemptuous pass;
> The son no further honour gives
>   to doddering age. Alas!

Obviously, the impression made by the "old old" is the same in every civilization.

Ptahhotep's lamentation found an echo in the famous *Story of Sinuhe*, the literary autobiography of a fictitious courtier of the time of Amenemhat I and Sesostris I, known from many copies on papyri and ostraca. Its hero, after his flight to Syro-Palestine, dreams about his return:

> Would that my body was young again!
> For old age has come, feebleness has overtaken me.
> My eyes are heavy, my arms weak;
> My legs fail to follow.
> The heart is weary; death is near.

The words seem to be inspired by the example of Ptahhotep. Or should we rather say that the picture of old age was so evident in those days that every author could have found his inspiration in the reality around him?

Yet, this was not the only possible manner in which to portray the aged. There is, for instance, an old magician called Djedi who occurs in the *Tales of Wonder*, featuring in the Papyrus Westcar, a Middle Kingdom collection of stories, now in Berlin (see p. 201). He is greeted by Prince Hardedef with flattering words, such as are eminently suitable for a venerable older person:

> Your condition is like that of one who lives above age –
> for old age is the time of death, enwrapping, and burial –
> one who sleeps till daytime, free of illness,
> without a hacking cough.

Not everyone is therefore seen as a victim of his advanced years, although Djedi was certainly an exception. Was what the Egyptians saw daily around them so frightening that they needed to offset it by such an exaggerated story?

Descending from the lofty realms of poetry to the everyday vernacular, we should now look at the words in the Egyptian language by which the concept "old" was expressed. The most common one is written as *iau*, but, as is habitually the case, its actual pronunciation is quite uncertain. In most texts it is determined by the hieroglyphic sign of an older person – mostly a man, but occasionally a woman – bending over and leaning on a stick. We will discuss it further below (see p. 204 and fig. 80a and c).

A second word, *teni*, seems to carry the same meaning. Linguists, however, teach us that no two words in a language ever express exactly the same nuance. They usually have a different distribution, that is, they are not used in the same type of context. Hence, there will be some distinction between *iau* and *teni*, such as between our "old" and "elderly". But what exactly this could be unfortunately eludes us.

A third word for roughly the same concept, *kèhkèh*, indicates the physical aspect of getting old. Its original meaning may be "hacking cough", reproducing the throaty sound made by old people. As "hacking cough" it appears as the last word of the greeting to Djedi in the Papyrus Westcar, translated above. That it, in a wider sense, points to the bodily state of the elderly can be illustrated by a sentence in a magical papyrus from the New Kingdom, housed in the British Museum. Here the speaker derides his adversary with the words: "Your appearance is that of a monkey after reaching old age" (*kèhkèh*).

Another instance occurs in a literary work from el-Hiba, in Middle Egypt, which is dated to the Twenty-First Dynasty, and now housed in the Pushkin Museum in Moscow (see p. 202). It is a tale concerning the wanderings of an outcast, presented in the form of a letter to a friend of his. In the initial lines the sender, according to the custom, wishes the addressee to reach the 110 years that constituted the ideal age (see p. 202), while "Your body is whole, grown old (*kèhkèh*) with a contended heart, without illness in your frame but continuous gladness and joy in your heart, and without the weakness of old age, you having arrested it". Once again the threat of the deterioration of the body is perceptible behind the words.

It is conspicuous that here both the words for old, namely *iau* and *kèhkèh*, are written with a sign that determines expressions of disease, pain, and such like. Its use, even more than the words themselves, reveal the feelings of the Ancient Egyptians towards old age.

The same sign, perhaps depicting a pustule or a gland, is also used, in combination with the hieroglyph of a man leaning on his stick, in the writing of *iau* in the so-called *Onomasticon of Amenope*. This is a glossary of hundreds of words, arranged in more or less consistent classes, describing all sorts of entities in the world. Several manuscripts of this list have survived, the most complete being known as the Golenisheff Onomasticon. Dating from the very end of the New Kingdom, it is also housed in the Pushkin Museum in Moscow. One of the classes are words for the different stages of the life of human beings. Starting with "man", there follow: "young man", "old man" (*iau*), "woman" and "young woman". The next group comprises various words for children, boys and girls. No special word for "old woman" is listed; one simply used the feminine form of *iau*. The division of life into three stages: young, adult, and old, reminds us of the modern expression "Third Agers" for older people. But for the Egyptians adolescence was a separate stage, distinguished from childhood as well as adulthood.

The deterioration of one's body was feared, as we saw above, but that was no reason to accept the treatment of older persons as inferior beings. In a little known wisdom text we read: "You should not mock an old man or woman when they are decrepit (*kèhkèh*). Beware lest they [take action] against you before you get old". This warning is found on an ostracon now in the Petrie Museum of Egyptian Archaeology at University College London.

"Ostracon" (plural: ostraca) is the Greek word for potsherd. In Egyptology it is used for sherds which are inscribed with a hieratic (cursive form of hieroglyphs) text or a drawing, but also for flakes of limestone bearing a sketch or an inscription in ink. Those that have survived from the Pharaonic Period – and there are several thousands of them – almost all derive from the settlement of the necropolis workmen at Western Thebes. These artisans built and decorated the tombs of the New Kingdom Pharaohs in the Valley of the Kings, as well as the burial places of members of the royal family in the Valley of the Queens. The draughtsmen among them were talented artists, as evidenced by numerous pictorial ostraca (fig. 53). These people lived in a village halfway between those two valleys, which is known by its Arabic name of Deir el-Medina. It is, as will become evident in Part II of this book, our main source of knowledge concerning daily life in Ancient Egypt, and it is the ostraca in particular which provide us with details unknown from elsewhere, for instance about old age.

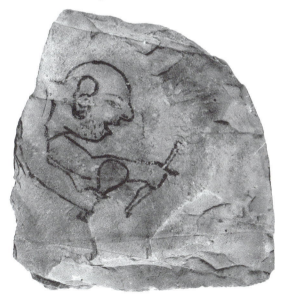

Fig. 53 Limestone ostracon depicting an out of breath elderly workman cutting into the rock. From Deir el-Medina, Ramesside Period

Related to the documents from this village, but yet of a different type, are the so-called Tomb Robbery papyri (see p. 221). One of them, now in the British Museum, relates a story from which it appears that the respect for the old, mentioned in the Petrie ostracon, was by no means a universal practice.

A certain incense-roaster, named Shedsukhons, is interrogated by the vizier. He relates how he was visited by night in his house by some men. They urged him to go with them, and so they went to a tomb, opened it, robbed the gold and silver it contained, and divided the loot among them. Then, not unexpectedly, a quarrel arose concerning the division of the spoils. Shedsukhons' father started meddling in the matter, whereupon one of the thieves retorted: "Oh doddering old man, evil be his old age; if you are killed and thrown into the water, who will look for you?". Not exactly a friendly repartee, but what could the old man expect from such rough scoundrels?

Fig. 54 The elderly Sennefer holding a stick. From the Theban tomb of Sennefer (TT 96), Eighteenth Dynasty

Both attitudes we have observed, that of respect for elderly men and that of derision for the decaying body, are also encountered in the representations. An example of the former is found in the tomb of Sennefer (TT 96), the Theban mayor in the time of Amenhotep II. While in all other wall scenes he appears as a vigorous adult, one portrays him with rolls of fat along his torso (fig. 54). The implication is that he was a venerable elderly man. The opposing facet occurs in the tomb of Paheri, a mayor of el-Kab and Esna under Tuthmosis I. On a wall showing a series of agricultural scenes, we come across a pot-bellied old man with a receding

146

hairline, who is combing flax (fig. 55). Convinced of the value of his performance, he says to a younger colleague who brings a bundle: "If you bring me thousands of bundles, I will still comb them". The other, clearly not impressed, answers: "Hurry up, don't chatter so much, you old baldy yokel".

Fig. 55 An old man combing flax. From the tomb of Paheri at el-Kab, Eighteenth Dynasty

As we stated in the Introduction, wisdom is not particularly stressed as a characteristic of the elderly. Yet, it is not wholly absent from the texts. On a Middle Kingdom stela from Edfu, which bears the autobiography of a priest called Tjeni, we read: "I am a trustworthy man for my brothers and sisters, old of heart, but one who does not know the weakness that belongs to it". That is, Tjeni states that he is wise, but not yet senile.

Such statements are rare. There is, however, one figure who was very probably old and who was believed to possess a deep knowledge of the secrets of life, far above that of most people who are apt to be confused by them. So far as we know, this figure was always a woman. There are not many places where a Wise Woman is mentioned, and those we know of all happen to derive from Deir el-Medina. There she was asked to bring enlightenment into situations in which people felt threatened and uncertain.

By their very nature such matters tend to be mysterious, and the documents which relate them are far from clear. They do not reveal the background of the various incidents and contain allusions which we do not understand. Therefore we can catch no more than glimpses of this particular rôle of older women in society.

147

One ostracon, now in a private collection in France, bears a letter written by a certain Qenkhopshef, one of the necropolis workmen, to a woman called Inerwau, who is otherwise unknown. It runs as follows:

> Why did you not go to the Wise Woman
> on account of the two boys who died in your charge?
> Ask the Wise Woman about the death
> the two boys have incurred.
> 'Was it their fate? Was it their destiny?'
> You shall question (her) for me about them.
> You shall (also) look after the life of mine
> and the life of their mother.
> As regards whatever god of which one will [speak] to you,
> you shall afterwards write me his name.
> [You shall fulfil] the task of one who knows her duty.

Qenkhopshef, evidently the father of the two boys who have died, wonders why Inerwau, perhaps their nurse, did not on her own initiative consult the Wise Woman. He wants to know why they died, and whether his life and that of their mother is now in danger. He especially wishes to hear which deity was responsible for his misfortune, hoping that the Wise Woman can at least give him some assurance in his misery.

Another ostracon, formerly in the collection of the distinguished Egyptologist Sir Alan Gardiner and now in the Ashmolean Museum in Oxford, is more obscure. A woman, whose name is not mentioned, states:

> I went to the Wise Woman,
> and she said to me:
> 'The manifestation of Ptah is with you,
> because of the Light,
> on account of an oath by his wife ......'

In this case the lady who turned to a Wise Woman was visited by what was called "the manifestation of Ptah". What exactly this means we do not know, but such manifestations of deities are also mentioned in other texts. In some instances we gain the impression that they haunted the dreams of those inflicted, but whether that was also the case here remains obscure. Who is meant by "the Light" which seems to be the cause of the lady's distress we likewise do not know. It may be a Pharaoh who is sometimes called so, either the ruling sovereign or the patron of the community, King Amenhotep I, or perhaps the sun-god Re who can also be addressed by this term.

A man seems also to be involved, for we hear of an oath by his wife. Is the lady who wrote the text accused of adultery? One can easily create a whole scenario out of the somewhat scanty evidence, but all we can really understand is that a Wise Woman was consulted in such a situation. She was thought to be able to provide the answers to all kinds of burning questions.

Venerated by some as possessors of esoteric knowledge, or simply considered to be wise, older people were therefore not to be scorned for the deterioration of their bodies. However, as we have seen, they were clearly regarded with disdain by others; despised, or even ridiculed. From Deir el-Medina comes a papyrus, now in Turin, which bears two series of drawings. On the right-hand side are representations of animals in human attitudes, whereas the continuation left bears twelve scenes of an outrageously erotic character. They tell the story of a man, shown with an oversized phallus, visiting a brothel and having intercourse in various positions with a prostitute.

The papyrus as it is now exhibits numerous lacunae, also in the hieratic captions to the scenes, so that the whole is difficult to reconstruct. Fortunately, during the last century, when it was more complete, copies were made and these enable us to recognize what has been drawn. Because of its erotic nature, illustrations of this document have remained taboo, even in the scientific literature, until fairly recently.

There has been much discussion about various aspects of this unique papyrus. It has been suggested that it is mainly satirical, as, for instance, the position of the girl on a chariot would imply, since normally only the king rides alone on such a vehicle. Moreover, it is drawn not by horses but by two naked girls. In another scene the man and the woman are shown in what is known as the Geb-and-Nut position, he lying on the ground, she bowed over him. This could indicate a caricature of a religious representation. However, not all episodes can be explained as being allegorical.

Another question is whether the same man is throughout depicted. The figures show small differences, especially in the shape of the noses, but it is uncertain whether this is intentional. It is usually considered that the man who is here portrayed was past his prime. He is partly bald, with unkempt hair on the back of his head, and he has a stubbly beard. Furthermore, he exhibits clear 'middle-aged spread'. In the first representations he is still vigorous, but later on his energy seems to have gone. He is seen lying under a bed on which the woman, clad merely in a girdle, is stretched out, leaning down to him and trying to seduce him (fig. 56). He appears to be exhausted, as the text, so far as it is legible, confirms. In the next scene the woman, assisted by two girls, carries him away. His phallus, still of enormous dimensions, is now flaccid.

149

Fig. 56 The Satirical-Erotic Papyrus: a girl attempts to seduce an exhausted man lying under her bed. From Deir el-Medina, New Kingdom

It is not absolutely clear whether the bawdy representations deride an older person. An alternative interpretation, put forward by a Gerontologist, is that they denote a picture of "successful ageing" (see p. 140). This would imply that older workmen were considered still perfectly capable of engaging in such types of sexual activity. Whether the story is thought to take place in Deir el-Medina is not certain; more likely the City itself (Thebes, on the east bank) was the location of the brothel. For our purposes it is significant that it is a picture of a man of advanced years. In the next chapter we will encounter more dignified representations of older persons.

13 The Aged in Art

The vast majority of Egyptian representations of men, whether in two or three dimensions, portrays them as healthy, vigorous, and comely; the body is muscular, with wide shoulders and a slender waist. In short, they are seen as ideal human beings. Although minor personal traits can occasionally be recognized, the images are no portraits in our sense of the word.

That is proved by those cases in which we happen to possess two statues of one and the same man. An example is the two wooden statues of the chancellor Nakhti, found in his Middle Kingdom tomb at Asyut. Discovered during the French excavations of 1893, they are now in the Cairo and Louvre Museums. If the inscriptions on their bases did not confirm that they represent the same man, then nobody would have surmised it, for their faces are totally different. That is, although Egyptian art has sometimes been provided with labels such as "realistic", or even "naturalistic", it does not attempt to reproduce reality as a photograph does.

It is against this background that we have to study those statues and reliefs or paintings that have been suggested to depict middle-aged or older men. The age does generally not so much appear from the face, but rather from the build of the figure, which is in some instances that of a corpulent, prosperous looking official. A well-known example is the Fifth Dynasty wooden statue known as the "Sheikh el-Beled" (see p. 204); another is the Fourth Dynasty limestone seated statue of Hemiunu, now in Hildesheim, whose adiposity reflects his successful lifestyle (see fig. 103).

Whether these persons should be called "elderly" is mainly a matter of definition. In view of the low life expectancy in those days (see pp. 167-169), men of over forty, the age at which they reached the pinnacle of their career, were certainly considered to be "young old" (see p. 139), and that is what their statues are intended to show.

In contrast to men, representations of older women are rare. Statues of them are restricted to a few figures of women grinding grain. Generally, it is only from the lower levels of society that women are shown to be old, and they are never depicted as being overweight. The only fat lady in Egyptian art is the famous Ati, the obese wife of the chief of Punt, pictured on the walls of Queen Hatshepsut's mortuary temple at Deir el-Bahri. However, she was a foreigner. The Egyptians clearly considered her figure to be an object of ridicule, as is aptly demonstrated by a lively drawing on a Ramesside ostracon, obviously intended as a caricature.

Male corpulence is not the only sign of advanced age. Others are bending over and leaning on a stick (see Chapter 18), stress on a fat upper torso, even to the extent of what look like pendulous breasts, grey hair, and baldness. The latter characteristic can almost only be seen in representations of workmen, for the upper classes hid it under a wig! If the élite are shown bald, it is not a sign of old age but of belonging to the priesthood. Of course, grey, or even white hair, can only be seen in paintings, which are none too frequent. We will return to this point at the end of the chapter.

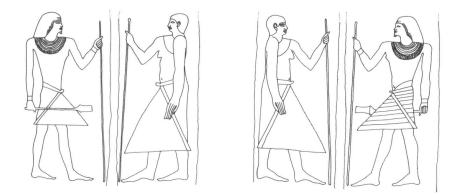

Fig. 57 Two figures of Khentika on both sides of the entrance doorway of his tomb. From the mastaba of Khentika at Saqqara, Sixth Dynasty

In some Old Kingdom mastabas the owner appears on the walls in two different guises: once as a slender, youthful man, and once as an older, corpulent personality. An example can be found in the Saqqara tomb of a certain Khabausokar, called Hethes, which is dated to the Third or early Fourth Dynasty. On both sides of the entrance is a niche where the owner is depicted as a rather obese individual, with a staff in his hand and wearing an elaborate necklace. In a Fifth Dynasty mastaba at Giza, of a certain Rakhaefankh, the owner appears at both sides of the doorway. Left he is represented as an ideal, slender adult, and right as an elderly man with a fat breast and belly. In the Sixth Dynasty tomb of the vizier Khentika, called Ikhekhi, also at Saqqara, so well published by the former Keeper of the Egyptian Department at the British Museum, T.G.H. James, we see the high official in the doorway on both sides depicted twice (fig. 57). He walks into the tomb as a slender adult, whereas on the thickness he walks outwards as a beardless older man, wearing a long kilt and displaying rolls of fat along his body. It has been suggested that the latter picture presents Khentika after his retirement, the other in his prime when he held office.

152

Stout elderly gentlemen also occasionally occur in other Old Kingdom tombs. East of the smaller pyramids that belong to the Great Pyramid of Khufu (Cheops) at Giza, in the so-called East Field, the mastaba of Queen Merysankh III is situated. She was the wife of the Pharaoh Khafra (Chephren) and the daughter of Kawab, Khufu's eldest son. In the offering chamber her father is once depicted, in accordance with his age as a heavily built man.

Another such obese person is represented in the mastaba of Seshemnefer IV, in the Central Field of Giza, South of the causeway of Chephren, reliefs of which are now in Hildesheim. The tomb dates from the late Fifth to early Sixth Dynasty. However, this is a picture of a statue, not of a living person, as appears evident from the accompanying caption. Priests are depicted bringing offerings to it.

Also in Hildesheim there is a wooden seated statue of the Sixth Dynasty, belonging to a certain Hetepi, which came from his tomb in the West Field of Giza. The posture is exceptional: the back slightly bent, the head bowed somewhat forward. Such an attitude occurs with statues of squatting scribes, but that is here not the case. It has been suggested that it is an expression of Hetepi's advanced age. If that is a correct interpretation, it seems to be a unique case.

The final example of a dignitary that we mention from the Old Kingdom occurs in the Sixth Dynasty mastaba of Nefer and his father Kahay, situated at Saqqara, South of the Djoser compound, and nearby the causeway of Unas. On one wall the father is shown as a distinctly corpulent individual, leaning on a stick, whereas on the false door he appears, like Nefer himself everywhere in the tomb, in the traditional slender posture.

In all these cases the persons represented as elderly belong to the élite, whether they are tomb-owners or members of their family. But the walls of the mastabas also bear scenes which show us aged servants. An example is the Sixth Dynasty tomb of Kaemankh, again situated in the West Field of Giza. Two people are depicted preparing bread, one of whom is a naked, bald man with a conspicuously square skull, a short unkempt beard, and a rather fat body. He kneads the batter in a dish for the round loaves his younger workmate, in the register above, is patting into shape.

Two other figures, equally naked and corpulent, with stubble beards, are shown building a papyrus boat in the famous mastaba of Ti at Saqqara, which dates from the Fifth Dynasty. Yet another man occurs on a wall from the tomb of a certain Persen at Saqqara. This relief is now in Berlin. He exhibits a deeply lined face and a rather swollen body, and is busily engaged in carrying a yoke laden with offerings.

Not only men from the lower levels of society show in some cases signs of their advanced years. In the tomb chapel of a Pepinakht, called Heni the Black, at Meir, of the Sixth Dynasty, there is in a corner a depiction of a squatting man. According to the caption, he was inspector of the prophets, treasurer of the god, scribe of the nome, and superintendent of the scribes, and bore the name of Ankhy.

These copious titles imply that he was a middle ranking provincial official. Certainly, the corpulence of Ankhy's body indicates that he was accustomed to lead a quiet, sedentary life!

Proceeding to the Middle Kingdom, another tomb at Meir, namely that of the nomarch (provincial governor) Ukhhotep, son of Senbi, of the Twelfth Dynasty, also contains pictures of some corpulent officials. Two of them are shown standing behind the tomb-owner and his wife, rolls of fat on their bodies indicating that they had attained a comfortable position. A similar figure can be seen standing behind the seated Ukhhotep, while on another wall a stout herald is depicted walking behind two long-horned oxen. A meagre cowherd with spindly legs and a long, round beard conducts the animals to his master. The contrast between the herdsman, shuffling along and supporting his tottering steps on a short, knobbly stick, and the prosperous, well-fed official is striking. Of course, adiposity is in itself no definite proof of advanced age, no more than the meagreness of the cowherd is sufficient to characterize him as elderly. Yet, the contrast is certainly intentional, representing two aspects of old age, one of the poor, the other of those who are well-off.

In the same tomb another elderly man is depicted. Leaning on his stick, he

Fig. 58 A naked pot-bellied old man chats to a shipwright. From the tomb of Ukhhotep (B2) at Meir, Twelfth Dynasty

is standing before a boat on which shipwrights are busy binding bundles of papyrus with ropes (fig. 58). The naked pot-bellied fellow, with a shock of hair over his forehead and a rather long beard, chats away to the workmen, doubtless uttering all kinds of platitudes. This is obviously a caricature of old age, but certainly a fine one.

With the stela of the singer Neferhotep, now in Leiden, we enter quite a different sphere. Actually, there exist two pictures of this musician. The other occurs on a stela of his master, also in Leiden, where he is playing the harp for Iki and his wife. Above the head of the obese, bald Neferhotep a brief song is written. It runs:

Oh Tomb, you have been built for a feast,
you have been founded for goodliness.

This is a typical harper's song of the Middle Kingdom, a composition addressed to the tomb, not to the deceased.

On the other stela the singer also appears as an obese, elderly man. It was devoted to his memory after his death by two friends, a carrier of bricks and a draughtsman who were responsible for its rather mediocre execution. Probably Neferhotep had no relatives, so that his comrades, simple people like himself, performed for him the last rites. His marked adiposity may be due to his sedentary lifestyle. In other instances a corpulent harpist is sometimes depicted as being blind (see fig. 75), which would explain the lack of mobility.

Before turning to the New Kingdom a few words should be said about some statues of Twelfth Dynasty Pharaohs, particularly those of Sesostris III. The heads of these, at least from his later years, have been interpreted as being those of an elderly man, disappointed by life. In their traits, scholars have wanted to see world-weariness, pensive melancholy, and suchlike. This has even been connected with the events of his reign, and thought to be reflected in the literature of that age. Certainly, the artistic style shows profound changes during the reign of this Pharaoh, but whether they reflect his psychological reactions is questionable. It is also not even clear whether these statues represent Sesostris as an elderly man. If so, then it is only his face, for the body also exhibits the traditional slender, youthful figure.

Perhaps the most expressive portrait of a man of advanced years in all Egyptian art is the relief on a limestone block from a tomb, probably at Saqqara, and now in the Brooklyn Museum, New York (fig. 59). On account of its style it can be dated without hesitation to the post-Amarna Period. With his furrowed forehead, the deep line from the nostril to the corner of the mouth, the flabby double chin and the prominent Adam's apple, this unknown personality provides us with a model of the Egyptian view of dignified old age. Note should also be taken of the protruding collar bone, as well as of his skinny wrists and bony fingers. In how far it is a reliable portrait we cannot know, but it is without doubt the most striking expression of the subject of Part II of this book.

Only slightly less powerful is the head of the black granite kneeling statue of Amenhotep, son of Hapu (see pp. 197, 210, and 261), from the time of Amenhotep III. Found at Karnak in 1901, in front of the Seventh Pylon, it exhibits the characteristics of an old man: hollow cheeks, deep grooves from nose to chin, and a meagre neck. That the body clearly expresses old age cannot be said. The inscription, however, tells us that Amenhotep was already eighty years of age. Yet, it has recently been argued that the sculpture was actually usurped from a Twelfth Dynasty statue, with a few minor retouches. On the other hand, a second scholar has rejected this suggestion, considering it to be a genuine Eighteenth Dynasty work of art. This controversy indicates just how difficult it can be to interpret and date Egyptian statuary.

A third piece derives from a house in the North Suburb of el-Amarna, where it was found during the British excavations of 1928-29; it is now in the Cairo Museum. An 18 centimetres high, painted limestone statuette of a man seated on a chair, it is a remarkable example of the art of the period. The toothless mouth, gaunt neck, the grooves from the nostrils downwards, and the prominent collar bones, are

Fig. 59 Painted limestone relief of an anonymous aged official with a close-up of the face. From ?Saqqara, transitional Eighteenth/Nineteenth Dynasty

156

all traits strongly suggestive of an elderly man. Corpulence, on the other hand, is only discretely suggested, as in the statue of Amenhotep, son of Hapu.

Of an earlier date is the picture of the Theban mayor Sennefer (see fig. 54). As we have stated (see p. 146), this is the only depiction in his tomb in which his age is indicated by rolls of fat. In all other instances he is portrayed in the traditional manner as a slender adult. That his advanced age is only delicately suggested, and does not appear in his face, is in accordance with the more restrained style of the Tuthmosid Period.

As for scenes with elderly workmen, we have already mentioned one from the tomb of Paheri at el-Kab (see fig. 55). Such representations are rather frequent in the New Kingdom. We will discuss a few of them.

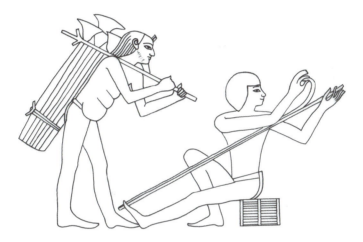

Fig. 60 A naked elderly labourer carrying a bundle of papyrus stems. From the Theban tomb of Puyemre (TT 39), Eighteenth Dynasty

Several persons of advanced age are depicted in the Theban tomb of Puyemre (TT 39), the Second Prophet of Amun in the time of Tuthmosis III. They are herdsmen and artisans, and their age is indicated by a bald forehead, in some cases with a tuft of hair in front, while the remaining locks fall untidily to the nape of the neck. They also have a pointed beard, and exhibit a tendency to flabbiness. An example is a naked labourer carrying a large bundle of papyrus stems on his back, while his younger colleague sits and strips them (fig. 60).

A similar figure is the bent ploughman in the Theban tomb of Nakht (TT 52), of the time of Tuthmosis IV and Amenhotep III. On his thin legs he hobbles

157

behind the team of oxen, trying to steer the plough. In the vintage scene in the same tomb two elderly men are depicted with grey hair and pot-bellies, one picking grapes and the other bending over the overflow from the wine-press.

Not only the élite and the simple workers occasionally show signs of being old. As in the Middle Kingdom, we also come across instances of lower officials. A fine example occurs in the Theban tomb of the Great Herald Antef (TT 155), again dating from the time of Hatshepsut and Tuthmosis III. As part of a series of vineyard scenes we see an overseer sitting on a mat in a pavilion, while a naked girl stands before him, offering him a cup of wine. He is a stout man, with an almost pendulous breast, and is designated as a manager by the staff in his hand. The scene is somewhat damaged, but the essential elements are recognizable. A caption gives the words spoken by the girl: "For your *ka*! Receive the good thing with the *ka* of the Herald Antef!" This rather stilted translator's English is rendered by the publisher of the tomb as: "To your health! Take this and drink to the health of the Herald Antef!'" Whereupon the man, putting the cup to his lips, answers: "How sweet is the wine of the workers. To the *ka* of the Herald Antef as a gift from you, Renenutet."

Higher still on the social ladder brings us to a scene in the Theban tomb of the overseer of the treasury Dhuti (TT 11), which is also of the same period. Before the tomb-owner, who stands adoring Amen-Re, a smaller figure is shown, with rolls of fat on his breast like Sennefer (see fig. 54). This is very probably the father of the deceased. Herewith we are back to our point of departure, namely the top stratum of society. We can now move on to the Late Period.

Perhaps the most famous personality of that epoch is Montuemhat, Fourth Prophet of Amun, Mayor of Thebes, and Governor of Upper Egypt, who flourished at the end of the Twenty-Fifth Dynasty and at the beginning of the next one. Of him a number of statues are known, rendering him in the traditional manner. However, in 1897 a black granite sculpture was found during the excavations of Miss Margaret Benson in the Mut Temple at Karnak, portraying him as an elderly man. Now in Cairo, it is a broken fragment with only the head and shoulders remaining. Hence, one cannot say anything about the body, but the sagging facial muscles certainly suggest advanced age. The work is generally acknowledged as a masterpiece of Egyptian sculpture, although its identity as a representation of Montuemhat has been disputed.

To this statesman has also been ascribed a head, now in the Petrie Museum (fig. 61). Although it also provenances from the Mut Temple at Karnak, the attribution is far less certain. Doubtless it represents an old man with a heavily wrinkled face, but, as recently as 1991, it was suggested that the piece be redated to the Middle Kingdom. Again, this demonstrates the problems posed to us by Egyptian sculpture.

Fig. 61 Black granite head of an elderly man. From the Temple of Mut at Karnak, Twenty-Fifth Dynasty or ?Middle Kingdom

Clearly showing Montuemhat, since it provenances from his Theban tomb (TT 34), is a relief at present in Kansas City. Here he is portrayed offering to Anubis, and he exhibits the features of an ageing man: puffy eyes and sagging cheeks, as well as a bald skull. In almost all other representations from his tomb he displays the idealized traits of a youthful personality. It should be noted, however, that the usual adiposity of elderly men is here not indicated.

In the last centuries B.C. some instances occur of real portraiture, showing individuals as they will have looked in life. Whether that is due to foreign influence, Greek and later Roman, is a matter of discussion. We will here mention only one example. In Baltimore is the head of a statue described as the "Tired Old Man". Its realism is evident. The face displays the resignation, even the disappointment with life that we sometimes encounter in elderly people. Here we are far removed from the reserved manner in which Egyptian art in general exhibits the manifestations of old age.

As mentioned above, one of the means by which advanced age was indicated is greying, or even white hair. The instances are not very numerous because not too many paintings or reliefs have survived. Those we possess all seem to come from the New Kingdom, particularly from the tombs of the necropolis workmen at Deir el-Medina, and these are the ones that we will now cite.

159

Fig. 62 The relatives of the workman Pashedu and his wife. First register: his family; second register: her family; third register: their children. From the Theban tomb of Pashedu (TT 3), Nineteenth Dynasty

A fine example occurs in the tomb of Pashedu (TT 3), from the Nineteenth Dynasty (fig. 62 and back cover illustration). On a short wall beside the entrance to the burial chamber three registers with representations of Pashedu's relatives are to be found. In the top row his father, whose hair is completely white, and his mother, who is grey, are followed by his three brothers who are clearly younger. In the middle row we have first his father-in-law, with pepper-and-salt coloured hair, then his mother-in-law, who is grey. After her comes a lady whose place in the family is not quite clear, and whose black wig exhibits grey ends. The other women in this row, and Pashedu's children in the bottom register, are all too young for grey hair.

In the tomb of the sculptor Ipuy (TT 217), also from the Nineteenth Dynasty and famous for its lively scenes, the deceased is once depicted while libating to the gods. The wall is slightly damaged, but it is clearly visible that Ipuy here has grey hair, whereas elsewhere in the tomb his hair is black.

The tomb of Irinefer (TT 290), another necropolis workman from the Ramesside Period, contains a picture of the deceased and his wife in which both are wearing white wigs. By contrast, on a stela from its chapel, now in Paris, where Irinefer and his wife are shown censing before his parents and brothers, it is his father Siwadjyt, who is white-haired.

There are also a few instances of grey hair from tombs outside of Deir el-Medina. In that of Puyemre cited above, which shows so many balding heads, one man is depicted whose hair at the back of his head is greying. He is busy gutting fish, and has a pointed beard, his forehead being hairless as is usual in this tomb.

Finally, we turn to the Theban tomb of the Viceroy of Kush Amenhotep, called Huy (TT 40), of the time of Tutankhamun (see p. 204). Here a scene occurs in which men and women bring to him the Nubian tribute. One of the men is partly bald, with a ring of hair around the base of his skull, while three of the women are shown with white hair. Below these people, in the middle register, an elderly woman is leaning upon a stick, whose hair is also white (see fig. 81).

The examples we have cited, and which can easily be supplemented, demonstrate that the Egyptians were by no means loath to show old age on their tomb-walls, especially not when persons from the lower strata of society were concerned. This was achieved by the shape of the body or by the colour of the hair. Facial traits indicating that the person represented was old are almost only found in statuary, which by its very nature means: representations of the upper class. The vast majority of two- or three-dimensional figures are shown, however, throughout Egyptian history, as vigorous, slender, youthful persons.

14 Mummies and Medicine

The state of their body is for human beings at its optimum level between the ages of eighteen and thirty. In these years their growth is completed, biologically their organism has stabilized, their skills and reaction times are at their best. After this point, signs of decay begin to appear: reaction time increases, the lens of the eye begins to harden, the efficiency of oxygen transfer in the lungs begins to decline; blood pressure rises since the tissue in the arteries becomes less elastic. Strength and endurance, however, still remain fairly constant into the forties. By the fifth decade of life the signs of old age become more pronounced: blood pressure rises further, tissues becoming even less elastic, strength and endurance decline. In short, old age commences.

Is it possible to trace this development from the study of Egyptian mummies? Did the Egyptians themselves speak about it in their medical papyri? The short answer to these questions is simply: no!

During the last thirty years or so a large number of investigations into human remains, skeletons and mummies, have been published. These have been executed with modern techniques: not only plain radiography, but also particularly computed tomography (CT), as well as DNA analysis and endoscopy. However, the results had been until recently rather disappointing. This is mainly because the scientific methods applied are not yet sufficiently advanced to produce the results which Egyptology requires. An example may serve to indicate what we mean. Investigations of his mummy years ago led to the conclusion that Tutankhamun was at his death between sixteen and twenty-five years old. However, that is precisely what the historical documents long ago suggested. What Egyptologists wanted to know is: what exactly was his age, sixteen or twenty-five years? Recent examination (January 2005) of the mummy with a CT scanner has shown that he was about nineteen years old when he died. The state of the wisdom teeth confirms that. The investigation of the body also showed some fractures, which might suggest a violent death. However, these could as well be the result of the mummification process – or of Carter's handling of the mummy.

The medical papyri, interesting as they are in showing us how advanced Pharaonic civilization was in this respect, do not explicitly deal with the problem of ageing. One of them is the Papyrus Ebers, named after its first modern owner, the German Egyptologist Georg Ebers, who purchased it in Luxor from Edwin Smith and published it in 1875. Ebers was Professor of Egyptology at Leipzig, where the papyrus is now housed in the University Library. He is also known as the author of some historical novels that take place in Ancient Egypt, including the famous *Eine ägyptische Königstochter* (1864), translated into English as *An Egyptian Princess*.

The papyrus named after him is no less than 20 metres long and is therefore one of the longest papyri that we possess. It dates from the early Eighteenth Dynasty and deals with all kinds of medical matters. Actually the text contains a number of monographs and excerpts devoted, among other subjects, to internal diseases and their treatment, to eye and skin disorders, to gynaecological topics, to heart and blood vessels, etc. It also contains a dozen prescriptions for the loss of hair. Since baldness is a common sign of getting old, this is pertinent to our subject. One such prescription advocates the mixing of fat of lion, hippo, crocodile, cat, serpent and ibex. The resultant concoction was then to be anointed to the head to make the hair of a bald person grow.

Another medical text is the Papyrus Edwin Smith, named after the American dealer who acquired it, together with Papyrus Ebers, in 1862. It was presented by his daughter to the New York Historical Society and is now housed in the Academy of Medicine in New York. This surgical treatise is an Eighteenth Dynasty copy of an earlier original, and was published in 1930 by the great American Egyptologist James H. Breasted.

In an appendix, written in a different hand from the rest of the text, we find some prescriptions for ointments said to smooth an old, wrinkled skin when applied to it. They are processed from the legume fenugreek (*Trigonella faenum graecum*), which is washed, dried, cooked and ground. Actually, the paragraphs containing these prescriptions are called "Book for transforming an Old Man into a Youth", but that seems a little overdone. However, maybe the claims are no more outrageous than those associated with modern cosmetic surgery, in particular, some advertisements for a face lift.

All this is interesting, but only marginally connected with the problems of growing old. That life was a precarious matter in those days we have noted in the introduction. A rise in life expectancy during the last century from 44.1 (men) and 47.8 (women) years to 72.4 and 78.1 speaks volumes. What the figures were in the time of the pyramids, or even in that of Ramesses II, we do not know. It was only in the Late Period that the Egyptians in some instances noted the age of death, and that only of some more important persons.

The hardships of those ages are perhaps best illustrated by the report of a mining expedition to the Wadi Hammamat in year 3 of Ramesses IV (*circa* 1150 B.C.). Of the 9268 men, all certainly adults, no less than 900 are reported to have died. And this was a peaceful mission to acquire valuable building stone for Pharaoh's monuments. If this was supposed to be the norm, how large would the chance of reaching old age have been for the mass of the population?

Medical investigations of human remains have certainly taught us something about the health of the people. We know that all kinds of infections were a major cause of disease and mortality, that arteriosclerosis and arthritis made the life of elderly people difficult as in our days; that all manner of diseases, such as

163

bilharzia (schistosomiasis), poliomyelitis, and tuberculosis rendered them victims. However, it is not possible from isolated cases found in some mummies to draw conclusions as to the frequency of these illnesses among the population as a whole.

One point seems to be certain, although it is historical evidence rather than the medical investigations that suggest it: the food situation seems generally to have been satisfactory. Famines did occur, but were not too frequent. The oldest representation we know of occurs along the pyramid causeway of the Pharaoh Unas at South Saqqara and can be dated to the end of the Fifth Dynasty. Here two rows of living skeletons are depicted, men and women and one child. They sit and lie down, exhausted by hunger. In the lower register we see an old bearded man, supported by his wife and son. Altogether this is a moving, realistic picture of what famine meant in those days.

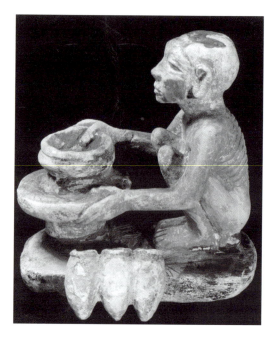

Fig. 63 Limestone statuette of an undernourished potter squatting at his wheel. From the mastaba of Nikauinpu at Giza, Fifth to Sixth Dynasty

Equally realistic, but less poignant, is the statuette of a potter, now in the Oriental Institute at Chicago (fig. 63). It forms part of a group of servant statuettes from the Fifth to Sixth Dynasty mastaba of Nikauinpu at Giza, the exact location of which is at present unknown. The undernourished craftsman, whose meagre back clearly shows his prominent ribs, squats before his wheel, while three of his pots stand ready beside him. Perhaps this piece refers to the same famine as the scene on the Unas causeway.

The worse period for the food supply may have been the First Intermediate Period and the succeeding Middle Kingdom. From that time we have many indications of low Nile inundations and famine. In how far this was really a major problem of those days, or whether it was to a certain extent a literary *cliché* is not certain. Anyhow, medical researches have not yet brought forward evidence that malnutrition was common, although we have to keep in mind that the mummified dead belonged to the upper echelons of society. The depictions of emaciated persons usually show bedouins from the desert. The influence of a lack of food on old age and mortality in Egyptian history is difficult to estimate, however.

At the end of the Twentieth Dynasty many tombs in the Theban necropolis fell victim to robbers. Several papyri (see p. 221) inform us about the investigations and trials of the plunderers. The royal tombs in the Valley of the Kings, however, seem to have escaped this desecration. They were indeed opened and systematically stripped of their contents, but at least partly on the order of the authorities, who used them as treasuries in these economically less prosperous days. The royal mummies were removed from their resting places, unwrapped in order to appropriate their jewellery, then rewrapped, and buried elsewhere. After some moves they ended up in two places, one high up in the cliffs behind Deir el-Bahri (generally known as the tomb of Inhapi), the other in a side-room in the tomb of Amenhotep II in the Valley of the Kings (KV 35).

At the end of the last century these caches were discovered, the tomb of Inhapi in 1871 by the local Abd el-Rasul family, that of Amenhotep II by the French excavator Victor Loret in 1898. The mortal remains of almost all the New Kingdom Pharaohs were brought to Cairo, where they are now on display in the Egyptian Museum. In the following years they were examined by the Australian anatomist Sir Grafton Elliot Smith, and in 1966-73 again, this time by an American team from the University of Michigan using modern methods including radiology.

One would expect that the latter project would have provided us with the answers to several questions, particularly that of the age of death of these rulers, but, unfortunately, that is hardly the case. The subject was studied back in the United States from the X-ray films, but the results are generally far too low. Ramesses II, for example, was stated to have died at fifty to fifty-five years of age, whereas we know that he reigned until his sixty-seventh regnal year. That he would have ascended the throne more than ten years before his birth seems unlikely. Amenhotep III, to quote another example, who celebrated three *sed*-festivals (see Chapter 22), the last in his thirty-eighth regnal year, was calculated to have lived until his thirty-ninth year. Admittedly, the physicians who suggested these ages meant them to be minima, but they are so far out of the known range that they are useless.

There is yet another problem with the royal mummies. Those who re-wrapped them and wrote on the new bandages the names of the Pharaohs seem to have made mistakes. Moreover, when they arrived in Cairo the labelling was not carried out very carefully. Thus, in several cases, there is serious doubt about the real identity.

So it appears evident that the royal mummies, despite the work carried out on them, have not advanced our knowledge concerning the age of death. That some Pharaohs died at an advanced age we know from historical evidence (see Chapter 22), but not from the study of their mortal remains.

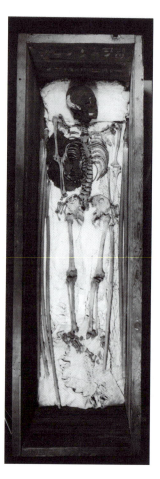

Fig. 64 Skeleton of Idu II lying in his cedar coffin. From the mastaba of Idu II at Giza, Sixth Dynasty

For a better insight into the causes and age of decease we need not so much the study of a single individual, although that will sometimes reveal interesting details, but of large groups, by preference from one period and one site as well as from the same social stratum. For instance, in the museum in Hildesheim is

166

preserved the skeleton of a certain Idu II, a high official of the Sixth Dynasty whose mastaba was found in 1914 in the West Field of Giza. The body was lying in a sumptuous cedar coffin, in which were also some objects including seven walking sticks (see Chapter 18), and two large bundles of "clothing" resting by his feet. All these are housed in the same museum and in 1987 an investigative project took place there. One of us was invited to unwrap the "clothing" and discovered instead twelve linen sheets. At the same time the human remains (fig. 64) were the subject of an extensive palaeopathological study, as a result of which we know that this Idu was a healthy man all his life, although he suffered from chronic inflammation of the middle ear. When he died he was between fifty-five and sixty-five years old. Interesting as all this is, it does not teach us much about old age in Ancient Egypt in general.

For determining the age of death two criteria are used: the pattern of tooth formation, and that of ossification. On account of these three mummies in the Philadelphia University Museum (called PUM II, III, and IV) could be established to have died at 35 to 40 years, at 42 years, and at 8 to 10 years respectively. Again, for our present subject not so very important.

Somewhat more information resulted from an investigation carried out during the 1970's of almost a hundred individuals in various collections in the former Czechoslovakia. Among them were 53 complete human remains, 7 of them 20 to 30 years old, 13 of 30 to 40 years, 6 of 40 to 50 years, 11 of 50 to 60 years, and 8 of even over 60 years. The total is 45, while 8 were classified as juveniles of under 20 years.

This can be compared with the results of a study of the mummies in the British Museum conducted in the 1960's. Of the 35 for which the age could be established, 11 were between 40 and 50 years old, and 9 were even older. While for the Czechoslovakian bodies the average age of the men was 43.7 years, and of the women 41.3, that of the London ones was also between 40 and 45. What is conspicuous is the relatively large group of the over fifties, more than one would expect. However, this is not a random sample taken from the entire population. The percentage of young persons, particularly babies and infants, is far too low. They were usually not buried in the main cemeteries; in some cases they were even laid to rest under the floor of the houses.

Although these particular studies are a good example of what can be done, we have to keep in mind that these mummies provenance from a large number of sites, mostly unknown, and from all periods of Egyptian history. They also tend to belong to the higher classes of society. Poor people were not extensively mummified, that was far too expensive. That among the 45 adults in the Czechoslovakian group no less than 11 came from the workmen's village at Deir el-Medina (see p. 145) is not contradictory to this statement, for these artisans belonged to the best paid people of their time.

Extremely important for our knowledge of the palaeodemography of Egypt was the investigation of approximately 850 individuals from one Predynastic cemetery at Naga ed-Deir. This site, south of Akhmim, was excavated in 1902-03 by the American expedition of George Reisner and Albert Lythgoe, which opened 635 tombs. All contained typical burials of that early period: the bodies, lying on their left side, were in a flexed position. Although the cemetery had already been plundered in Predynastic times, and also disturbed in later ages, the results of this meticulous publication are truly impressive.

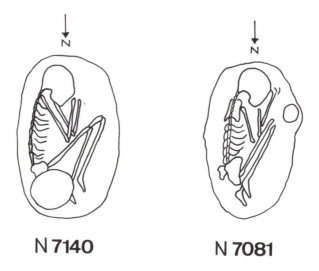

N 7140   N 7081

Fig. 65 Skeletons of elderly women, each accompanied by a pot. From a Predynastic Cemetery at Naga ed-Deir: (a) Tomb N 7140; (b) Tomb N 7081

The excavators were not only able to establish the sex of most of the bodies, but also the age, and incidentally even the cause of death. Examples are Tomb N 7140 (fig. 65a), a woman of between fifty and sixty years old, whose rump was perfectly preserved because it was covered by a large dish, and Tomb N 7081 (fig. 65b), an elderly woman with long, wavy, greying hair, who probably died from chronic constipation.

From a total of 265 persons, comprising 182 sub-adults and 83 adults, the age of 67 individuals could be established as follows: 11 of between 20 and 30 years, 27 of 30 to 40 years, 15 of 40 to 50 years, and 14 of over 50 years, of whom one was even over 60. Clearly, infant and child mortality were high, at 182 out of 265; even more than the figures indicate, because of the habit of burying infants in the houses. The relatively high mortality between 30 and 35 (16 individuals) was of

168

course due to occupational hazards and the risk of childbirth. If one survived this, disease and the factors associated with getting older began to take their toll. Yet, a relatively large proportion of the population (*circa* 10 per cent) appear to have survived into their fifties.

Another investigation, undertaken in the 1970's, was that of the large mummy collection in the Anthropological Institute in Turin, partly from the Predynastic and partly from the Dynastic Period, which derived from excavations conducted at Gebelein and Asyut between 1911 and 1935. The average age of the latter group turned out to be 36 years, while that of the former was only 30 years, so substantially lower than those of the Czechoslovakian and the British Museum investigations. That was caused by a larger proportion of juveniles. The mortality among young adults was very high. At 43 years only a quarter of the Dynastic group was still alive, whereas the Predynastic one had already been reduced to a quarter at 30 years. As is to be expected, the mortality of women up to 30 years was higher than that of men, while later the pattern was reversed. Of the 876 people investigated, 215 had died between the ages of 40 and 60 (24.5 per cent), while only 16 (1.8 per cent) managed to survive beyond 60. On the other hand, 497 (54.5 per cent) had died between 20 and 40 years of age.

One of the most important groups of human remains to have been found in regular excavations derives from the mastabas of the West Field of Giza. One batch of these was discovered by the German excavator Hermann Junker between 1911-13 and consists of 177 skulls, all from the reign of Khufu (*circa* 2620 B.C.) and all belonging to the élite of that time. The collection is now in the Naturhistorisches Museum in Vienna, where it was studied in 1978 by the British dentist Filce Leek. For 50 individuals insufficient data could be collected, while for 27 even the sex remained uncertain. On the other hand, 28 persons were clearly over 40 years at the time of death, representing 17 men and 10 women (1 ambiguous).

Filce Leek also examined a second group of crania from the same cemetery, found by George Reisner in the same period. They had been housed ever since in a storeroom near the Giza Pyramids and were in a bad condition. Of the 62 items, selected at random, only 4 turned out to be over 40 years at death, all these being women. Such numbers are, however, too small to be representative.

The chronologically latest group we will mention derives from 25 tombs, dating from the Seventeenth and Eighteenth Dynasties, excavated in 1934-35 on the Western slope of the Qurnet Murai, East of Deir el-Medina. Some of these tombs contained more than one skeleton. Most of the human remains belonged to girls and young women, but there were also some elderly people. Proper medical research was not carried out on them in those years before the Second World War. Generally, the criterion of the excavator Bernard Bruyère when calling an individual "old" was based on the colour of the hair. One tomb contained a man and a woman, both of whom were grey; two others each housed a "very old man" with white hair. One other "very old man" was bald. It is clear that such statements are not really illustrative for our subject, the normal age of death of the entire population.

That is also not the case with a fairly recent, highly sophisticated investigation. In 1986 the tomb of Maya was (re)discovered by a joint Egypt Exploration Society and Leiden Museum expedition working at South Saqqara. Scattered throughout the rooms and corridors of the lower level, the remains of five individuals were found, evidently those of Maya and his family. Careful reconstruction by an anthropologist has led to the following results. One, fairly robust man, was discovered to have been over fifty years of age; he could be identified as Maya himself, the Treasurer of Tutankhamun. A second man, probably just over forty, will have been Maya's brother, while a sturdy woman of medium height and over fifty years of age was probably his stepmother. Maya's wife Meryt appeared to be a slender lady of between twenty and forty years. The fifth mummy was that of a young teenager, thirteen to fourteen years old.

The investigations here described constitute merely a selection from all the modern researches into the medical aspects of the Ancient Egyptians. It is clear that, until now, the results for our problem, namely causes and age of death, are not overwhelming. A great deal more needs to be done before we reach satisfactory answers to these questions.

15 Households and Inheritance

The position of the aged in a particular society depends to a large extent on their ties with their descendants and relatives, that is, cognates (bilateral kinsmen and kinswomen) as well as affines (relatives by marriage). Hence, much is determined by the kinship structure of the society.

It is common knowledge that many peoples all over the world exhibit strong descent groups, a subject that is widely studied by social anthropologists. The descent may be patrilineal or matrilineal; seldom is it bilineal. Such groups possess all kinds of properties and privileges, and are usually exogamous.

However, strong kinship loyalties run against the demands of a bureaucratic state, and that Ancient Egypt certainly was from the early Old Kingdom onwards. No wonder therefore that we have never found in this civilization any traces of such powerful descent groups. Of course, the Egyptians acknowledged the importance of the family, members of the father's and of the mother's side being principally equal. They also recognized their connections with their affines, as appears clear from the representation of the relatives of a man's wife on stelae and in tombs. In this respect their society was similar to ours. But there were no rights vested in such kinship groups, no more than in our world.

A specific aspect worth mentioning is that, so far as we know, there existed no obligation to marry a particular relative, for instance, a father's or a mother's brother's daughter, as is found in many societies. The choice of a marriage partner seems to have been entirely free. It has been suggested that there was a preference for a paternal cross-cousin, but the proof for this is very weak. Of course, particularly when big financial and political interests were involved, the parents and the wider family pressed the young people to make a particular match. That happens also in our world.

As there were no strong descent groups with their own rights and resources as the basic units of Egyptian society, the main circle in which older people moved would have been their domestic group. In other words, those people who occupy or centre in a common dwelling, sharing many activities such as eating and child rearing, exercising control over family properties, etc. Such a household can be larger than the elementary family of parents and children; it may include unmarried siblings, brothers and sisters, uncles and aunts, as well as the parents or even the grandparents of both spouses, plus other elementary units of the second generation, and eventually servants.

A household ideally passes in the course of the years through a developmental cycle. Beginning with a couple, it grows when children are born. Then these children marry and a third generation enters, unless the custom is, as with us, that newly married people set up their own domestic unit: the so-called neo-local marriage. In this phase the household of the parents gradually decreases, until it ends as it started with just two people. Clearly, this scheme knows numerous variations. For instance, one of the children may at his or her wedding not leave the household but stay as a new elementary unit, forming part of the original domestic group. It may be the eldest son, but it is also sometimes the youngest, and, if there is no son, a daughter with her husband may act as heiress. Every reader can imagine such variations.

Fig. 66 The third entry of the houselist when Snefru was head of the family. From Kahun, Thirteenth Dynasty

Moreover, the lines of division between the aspects of a household are not clear, as we shall see in the following pages. Its members may live under separate roofs, though near enough to each other to form a unit, or under one roof, but eating in each conjugal group. Yet they will generally socialize the children together, and sometimes work together in a common field. The question as to whether these are still domestic groups seems largely a matter of definition.

Turning to the Ancient Egyptian reality, we must state from the outset that of this subject remarkably little is known. It simply did not draw the attention of scholars. What we see resembles so much the world in which we live that it hardly seemed worthy of comment. That may well be a mistake. Admittedly, we possess

172

minimal direct evidence on the domestic group, and it is difficult to establish whether what we have is typical or exceptional. Statistical material, which is so essential for the study of the household, is completely absent. Therefore we can do no better than to present some specific cases.

Among the Middle Kingdom papyri discovered in 1888-89 by Flinders Petrie in the settlement of Kahun in the Faiyum there are parts of a census list. This important document is now in the Petrie Museum and was published by Francis Llewellyn Griffith in 1898. By chance the entries mention one household at successive stages of its developmental cycle, separated from each other by several years.

The earliest entry of the 'household list' records:

> The soldier, Dhuti's son Hori;
> his wife, Satsopdu's daughter Shepset;
> their son Snefru (according to a hieratic sign, a newborn baby).

This is obviously the first stage, a small elementary or nuclear family. The second entry shows significant additions to the household, recording:

> The soldier, Dhuti's son Hori;
> his wife, Satsopdu's daughter Shepset;
> their son Snefru (now designated with the sign for 'child');
> Hori's mother Harekhni;
> her daughters Qatsennut, Mekten, Ese, Rudet, and Satsnefru
> (of whom the last two are also designated as 'child').

Evidently, Hori's mother had come to live in the household, together with her five daughters, the youngest two of whom were still children. Probably this happened after the death of her husband Dhuti. We may also conclude that Hori was her eldest child, for her younger daughters belonged to the same age-group as her grandson Snefru.

A third entry (fig. 66) is said to be a copy of a houselist, dated to year 3 of King Sekhemkare, that is, Amenemhat V, of the early Thirteenth Dynasty. Fundamental changes in the composition of the household have taken place. Its head was now:

> The soldier, Hori's son Snefru.

Probably Hori had died, and Snefru had succeeded him, also as a military man. Yet, he seems still to have been young, no wife of his being mentioned. The household further comprised:

173

His (Snefru's) mother, Satsopdu's daughter Shepset;
his father's mother (Snefru's grandmother) Harekhni;
his father's sisters (Snefru's aunts) Ese and Satsnefru.

The latter was, as we have seen, of approximately the same age as Snefru, although genealogically of an older generation.

A note is appended to the effect that these last three females had entered the household of Snefru's father in a year 2, which can hardly be that of Amenemhat V. For this the changes are too radical. Not only is there the fact that Hori has since disappeared, but it is also clear that three of his sisters have left the domestic unit, probably because they married. Even the last-but-youngest, Rudet, who was in the earlier entry still a child, is not any more there. Only the very youngest and one of her older sisters still belong to the household.

This text presents us with an exceptional insight into an Egyptian household during the Middle Kingdom. Commencing from Hori's nuclear family, it comprised at a certain moment three generations. Perhaps this situation will not have lasted too long, for Harekhni may well have been relatively old according to Egyptian standards. Another change to be expected is the departure of the last two girls by marriage. On the other hand, one might anticipate that Snefru would soon find a wife and start his own nuclear family.

The entries mention only this one son, so that they do not reveal whether sons other than the eldest were accustomed to remain in the household. The daughters clearly married out. However, it is quite uncertain whether this single case can allow us to draw conclusions in general. Regrettably, other census lists are at present still unpublished, some from the New Kingdom workmen's community at Deir el-Medina having also survived.

Hori and his son Snefru were soldiers, hence relatively simple people. More important was Heqanakhte, a well-off landowner at the beginning of the Twelfth Dynasty. Eight of his papers were found by Herbert Winlock in 1921-22 in the passage of the tomb of Meseh, situated at the North side of the bay of Deir el-Bahri. They were lying in the rubble with which the floor had been levelled. How the documents ended up there we will never know, but they were evidently conceived of as being of no value and had therefore been discarded. For us, however, these records constitute an extremely valuable source of information for the period.

Four of the papyri bear letters, the remaining four accounts. For the present subject letter II is the most important. It is addressed by Heqanakhte to his mother and a lady who was perhaps his aunt, and further to his entire household. He speaks, among other matters, about the famine raging in the country, alluding even to cases of cannibalism, although that may well be exaggerated. In this connection

Heqanakhte writes down the quantities of grain that he has allotted to each of the members of his household, and thus we know the composition of this domestic unit.

The household consisted of: Ipi, Heqanakhte's mother, together with her maid; Hetepet, perhaps his aunt, plus her maid; a certain Nakhte, son of Heti, a senior servant and Heqanakhte's agent, together with his family; Merisu, the eldest son, also with his own family; Sihathor, the second son, and Sinebut, the third one, both clearly still unmarried. There were also two younger sons, Anpu and Snefru, probably still teenagers; a woman called Siinut, who may be a daughter; May's daughter Hetepet, whose relation to the others is unknown; and two girls, Nofret and Sitweret, probably also daughters of Heqanakhte. From elsewhere in the correspondence we know that a woman called Iutemhab also lived in the house. She is designated with a word that Egyptologists used to translate as 'concubine'. Perhaps she was Heqanakhte's second wife. In how far her position was legal is a moot point. It should be noted, however, that the mother of Heqanakhte's sons and daughters, his first wife, is nowhere mentioned. She seems to have been deceased. Finally, there was a housemaid called Senen, who in Heqanakhte's eyes had behaved badly to Iutenhab, and whom he orders to be turned out of the house.

All together this is a large domestic group, comprising four generations: a mother and an aunt(?), Heqanakhte himself with a second wife, and several of his sons and daughters, the eldest son with his own family. To this there came some female servants, and the agent with his family as a separate nuclear unit. The entire household will have comprised some twenty or more persons.

But was this really a household? Above we hinted at the difficulties of applying strict criteria. These people may not have eaten together, for they each received their own grain rations. They may even have lived under separate roofs. On the other hand, it is clear from the correspondence and the accounts that they worked on and were responsible for Heqanakhte's estate, his fields and his cattle. In this respect they constituted a unit, in which the two elderly ladies, Ipi and Hetepet, found their place, each with her own maid.

An interesting point is the position of the woman whom we have called Heqanahkte's 'second wife'. He is very anxious that she should be treated well by the family, not only by the servant Senen. Of course, the rôle of a, possibly young, second wife in such a large household is never an easy one. The earlier translation 'concubine' suggests that she was not even regularly married to the head of the family, but that may well be a mistake. One has to keep in mind that, so far as we know and as discussed at length in Part I, there existed in Ancient Egypt no formal sanction on a marriage in the form of a wedding ceremony. All such unions seem to have been 'common law' marriages. In this respect the position of a second wife was no lower than that of a first one. Even so, the opposition of her stepchildren could have made her life very unpleasant.

There is yet a third source for the study of the domestic unit in Egypt. This is of a totally different nature, namely the ground plan of el-Amarna, the city of Akhenaten and Nefertiti. Few settlements in Egypt have been excavated over a larger area, and the best known, namely Kahun from the Middle Kingdom and Deir el-Medina from the New Kingdom, are artificial constructions, created by the contemporary government. Of the main cities it is only el-Amarna of which a considerable portion has been uncovered, sufficient to convey an impression of how its inhabitants lived. There is, moreover, ample reason to believe that life in other New Kingdom cities was not noticeably different.

In 1980 the Swiss architect Herbert Ricke published the results of the excavations at el-Amarna by the German archaeologist Ludwig Borchardt. These had been conducted South of the central temple area in the years just before the outbreak of the First World War. On the splendid plans that accompany this impressive publication we can easily recognize, spread over this entire Southern zone, some large mansions within their compounds. They possess granaries, storerooms, and stables, as well as gardens, in which a chapel for the god Aten had sometimes been erected. In several cases it is possible to distinguish, within its surrounding walls, a second, smaller edifice, which it has been suggested was inhabited by a son and his family. Unfortunately, as the excavations of el-Amarna have produced only a few texts, this hypothesis cannot be proved. The property could as well be that of a steward or agent such as Heqanakhte's assistant Nakhte.

A second type of house, smaller than the main mansions and lacking the extensive outbuildings, but similarly well-constructed and consisting of several rooms, will have been inhabited by what we could term the middle class. These structures are also found in every quarter of the city. A separate upper or middle class district simply did not exist.

Around and between these two types of residences we find wards or clusters of relatively small, cheaply constructed buildings. These display thinner walls and, generally, fewer rooms. Two such simple house groups are here depicted (fig. 67). They are situated West of one of the main thoroughfares, the so-called High Priest Road, named after the mansion of Pawah, a High Priest of Aten, which is situated opposite the block on the East side of the road. Our example comprises two groups, one of four and one of three dwellings, here designated as Group A and Group B. They were not built at one time, but rather after each other in the course of the years, the later edifices filling in the gaps between the earlier ones.

That is clear in Group A. At its South side there is a relatively well-built and roomy property (here indicated as house (c)). It has thick walls, seven rooms, stairs to the roof, and an adjacent garden, probably for vegetables, of which the square plots were still visible during the excavations. This seems to be the earliest structure of the group. Somewhat later house (a) was built, with only five rooms plus the stairs, and the entrance at the narrow alley between the ward and the edifices to the North. Beside the entrance there are two additional rooms, perhaps to be identified as workshops. Between the houses (c) and (a), a small, lengthy dwelling was later inserted (b), with its entrance at its East side, from which the alley could be reached via a court. The fourth and newest house (d), situated beside (b) and its court, is very basic, with five small rooms and thin, rather oblique walls.

The entire group lies adjacent to a wide courtyard in the West, where a

Fig. 67 Two clusters of houses in the Southern zone of el-Amarna.
Nos. N 49.9 and N 50.29

common well was located. This served the inhabitants of several clusters – those further to the West (a sector excavated by the British in 1921-22), as well as our Group B. The latter consists of three, rather poor dwellings. The earliest and best is house (a), which is fairly regularly constructed and has eight rooms. House (b), however, is very small. Between (a) and (b) there was a narrow courtyard, with a stable at its inner end for a donkey, the brickwork trough for which is visible on the plan. The third and latest house (c) has awkward oblique-angled walls. Three of them are solid, but at the North side it shares a thin partition wall with house (b).

What conclusions can we draw from this plan for the relations between the inhabitants of the wards? It is clear that they were closely connected, but that does not mean that they formed a single household. Each family lived under its own roof, and probably ate on its own. Yet, it seems probable that the later arrivals were in some way related to those who built the first houses. The whole situation in these clusters is one which still occurs in Modern Egypt, and many a tourist will have witnessed the picture. One can easily imagine the noise, the smell, and the dirt. The shouting children – whose socialization is more or less a duty of the entire community – and the old men sitting somewhere in the shade (fig. 68). It is in such surroundings that we have to picture the life of older people in Ancient Egypt in so far as they were not rich. That is, the majority of the aged population.

In contrast, tombs and other monuments, such as stelae and statues, show us the ideal life of the upper ten. There too we find the parents depicted as, for instance, in many New Kingdom tombs. Surprisingly, the mothers appear somewhat more frequently than the fathers, particularly when their position promoted the career of their sons. This happened for instance with the nurses of the king. Yet, one would expect to find the father as often, for it was his office that a son habitually inherited. This is not always evident in the accompanying texts, for the father is mostly indicated as *sab*. The word used to be regarded as a designation for a man who lacked any other title and, by consequence, to be indicative of the fact that the son rose to his position on his own merits. Recently, however, it has been suggested that it means something like 'the revered one', expressing the respect of the son for his late father. It is certainly conspicuous that *sab* is never used by a father for his son, nor by a man for himself.

In fact numerous instances are known where sons succeeded their fathers in high offices. A few famous examples may here suffice. The vizier User(amun) (owner of TT 61 and 131) succeeded his father Iahmose (see p. 209), while he in his turn handed over his post to his nephew Rekhmire (TT 100). Hence, three members of one family held this supreme appointment in direct succession. A second example is the overseer of the granary Menkheperresonb (TT 79), who received the position after his father Nakhtmin (TT 87). All these individuals are well-known as the owners of splendid tombs on the Theban West Bank.

Fig. 68 Group of old men sitting in the shade. West Bank of Luxor, 1996

Of course, it was not possible to directly hand over one's office to one's son. For this the consent of Pharaoh, that is, of the government, was needed. Yet, these cases, and there are many more, demonstrate the tendency towards heredity in such appointments. Officially that was not so. In the Eighteenth Dynasty *Instruction of Ani* we read:

> The scribe is chosen for his hand,
> his office has no children.

In reality, however, many high dignitaries succeeded their fathers, or even their grandfathers.

A famous example of the practice of inheriting from one's maternal grandfather occurs in the record for the Khnumhotep family, a line of Twelfth Dynasty nomarchs (provincial governors). Their rock-cut sepulchres at Beni Hasan in Middle Egypt are inscribed with biographies, documenting inheritance of the title over several generations. The tomb of Khnumhotep (II) (No. 3), far the finest at the site, is well-known, particularly on account of a lively scene of brightly clad Semitic bedouin with their donkeys. In 222 short vertical lines the family history is related.

Khnumhotep (I) was appointed by Pharaoh Amenemhat I, hence at the beginning of the dynasty, to rule over Menat-Khufu, a kind of district on the East bank of the Nile opposite the 16th or Oryx nome (province). Menat-Khufu, literally 'wet nurse of Cheops', was originally called Menat-Snefru, a domain already mentioned in the early Fourth Dynasty. It is supposed to be the place where Cheops was born. The Middle Kingdom rulers of the region controlled the Eastern Desert as far as the Red Sea.

Khnumhotep (I) became later on nomarch of the Oryx nome, while his eldest son Nakht succeeded him in Menat-Khufu. Another son, Amenemhat, became under Sesostris I the nomarch of the 16th nome in succession to his father, while a daughter called Beket married a certain Nehri, a high official of the royal residence. It is the son of this couple, named after his maternal grandfather Khnumhotep (II), who succeeded in year 19 of King Amenemhat II his uncle Nakht in Menat-Khufu. He greatly enhanced his power by marrying Kheti, the heiress of the nomarch of the 17th or Jackal nome. So their eldest son, also called Nakht, became the ruler of that province, succeeding his maternal grandfather, while a second son, Khnumhotep (III), ruled in Menat-Khufu.

Although these successions, according to the text, have been confirmed by the king, they seem to have been almost self-evident. For the nomarchs of the Middle Kingdom we can more or less accept this situation, for they were princes rather than officials. In other cases, the automatic succession by a son or a grandson seems to us in general an objectionable practice. But for the *élite* in Ancient Egypt it was the ideal. In the so-called "appeal to the living" texts inscribed on stelae and tomb-walls and addressed to the passer-by, the owner urges the latter to pronounce an offering formula for him, referring to his wish "to hand over your functions to your children". These words are frequently found in Middle and New Kingdom inscriptions, demonstrating that the desire was conceived to be obvious.

In general, children inherited all the possessions of their parents. This applied to daughters as well as to sons, and was one of the main sources of an individual's wealth, the other two being one's own activities and the favour of Pharaoh. That is nicely expressed in the text on a stelephorous statue (holding a stela) now in Cairo. It belongs to a certain Nekhtefmut, a fourth prophet of Amun, who lived during the Twenty-Second Dynasty under Osorkon II. He says:

To me belong the things of my father and my mother,
and of the hard work of my hands.
The rest [comes] from the favour of the kings
whom I served in my time,

there being found no fault of mine.
With them I did what I wanted.

What Nekhtefmut did was to already hand over during his lifetime part of his
properties to his beloved daughter, probably in recognition of the fact that she had
taken care of her parents in their old age. This would explicitly not be deducted from
her share in the inheritance at a later date.

Fig. 69 The lower half of the Second Kamose stela depicting the overseer of the seal Neshi,
the ancestor of Mose. From Karnak, late Seventeenth Dynasty

It was through inheritance that the riches of grandparents and parents were
preserved by their descendants. In particular fields, the major source of wealth in
this agrarian society, could remain in the family for centuries. A striking example is

found in the record of some lawsuits which a certain Mose inscribed on the walls of his tomb chapel at Saqqara in the Nineteenth Dynasty. It is a long and complicated saga that began in the early Eighteenth Dynasty under Pharaoh Ahmose and continued until the reign of Ramesses II.

King Ahmose, the liberator of the country from the Hyksos, conferred upon his faithful servant Neshi as a reward for his services a piece of land, subsequently known as the Hunpet of Neshi. This Neshi is probably the same person as the overseer of the seal depicted at the bottom of the Second Kamose stela, now one of the treasures of the Luxor Museum (fig. 69). It is he who had been responsible for erecting this important monument.

In the reign of Horemhab the estate was owned by six heirs of Neshi, for whom a woman called Wernero acted as a trustee. Her sister Takharu now called upon the lawcourt to divide the lands between the co-heirs, but even after an appeal the decision was that the fields remained undivided. Wernero's son Huy finally received the actual possession of the estate, cultivating the fields year after year.

On his death the property came into the hands of his widow Nubnofret, but her rights were disputed by an administrator called Khay, of whom it is quite unclear whether he belonged to the family. A lawsuit in year 18 of Ramesses II was won by Khay, probably because someone had tampered with the documents. Some time afterwards, our Mose, who was Nubnofret's son, and had now come of age, reclaimed the family property before the lawcourt. Since the papers were forged, he called upon witnesses who were able to prove that he was indeed a descendant of Neshi.

Unfortunately, the end of the text with the pronouncement of the final verdict is lost, but judging by the fact that Mose inscribed the long record on the walls of his tomb we can be certain that he won the lawsuit. The case proves just how strong the force of heredity was in matters of landed property. It also shows how an estate could remain undivided for a very long period.

Such undivided properties are also encountered in one of the most important administrative documents that has come down to us from the New Kingdom. This is the Wilbour Papyrus, now in the Brooklyn Museum, New York. It is a roll over 10 metres long, bearing two texts, both of which concern fields: one of 4,500 lines in over 102 columns on the recto and part of the verso, a second of 732 lines on 25 wide pages on the remainder of the verso. The contents are very complicated, many aspects being as yet not well understood. Text A contains a tax list of numerous fields in Middle Egypt dated to year 4 of Ramesses V; Text B comprises a list of particular types of land in that area.

For our present purpose it is relevant that no less than 131 female names are recorded among the landholders. In a few cases the lady is stated as being dead; sometimes the land is said to be now in the hands of her children. This again serves to prove the continuity of family property over the generations.

Probably, the female owner inherited it from her husband or her father; in the latter case at least three generations would have owned the land. In other instances fields, some also owned by men, are said to be held "together with his/her siblings", which confirms the existence of the undivided landed properties we encountered in the story of Mose.

Such undivided plots are an indication of strong ties between the co-owners. Whether they were tilled by them as a collective we do not know. Nor is it certain that we have here an aspect of the domestic unit discussed above. Even so, it appears that, more frequently than in our society, descendants of one grandfather or great-grandfather, or even a more remote ancestor, constituted a group with a common interest. The rôle of parents and grandparents and their ties with the entire family appears to have been more important in those ancient times than in our more individualistic age. The next chapter will illustrate one special aspect of this social habit.

16 The Ancestors

The Ancient Egyptians held the belief that when a person died s/he did not immediately vacate this world. The deceased was regarded as still being sufficiently near, particularly if he or she had been a forceful personality, to exert an influence on the affairs of the living. Such powerful dead were called *akhu*, and were distinguished from the ordinary dead.

It was a widespread custom to pour water for the deceased at his or her tomb. A Sixth Dynasty inscription from a Saqqara mastaba – it appears on a lintel which is now in the Cairo Museum – testifies to this practice. It is written by the tomb-owner, a certain Nedjemib, who appeals to the living with these words:

> Oh you living on earth, who will pass this tomb,
> libate for me, for I am a master of secrets;
> bring me a funerary offering from your provisions,
> for I am one who loves men.

Moving to the New Kingdom and to the famous *Instruction of Ani*, we read:

> Libate for your father and mother,
> who are resting in the desert valley.
> When the gods witness your action,
> they will say: 'Accepted'.

A similar appeal occurs in a contemporary papyrus containing a copy of the *Calendar of Lucky and Unlucky Days*. For the last day of the fourth month there is noted:

> Make an offering to the *akhu* in your house,
> make an offering to the gods.

The first clause in particular will help us to understand some of the evidence presented in this chapter.

That the instigation to libate for the dead indeed had practical results we know from certain ostraca from Deir el-Medina. In two of them it is related that the vizier came to the Theban necropolis in order to libate for the Kings of Upper and Lower Egypt, clearly the recently deceased rulers. In other texts, listing the days that particular artisans had been absent from their work in the royal tomb, there is noted as a reason for this that they had been libating for their father, or their brother, or their son. We possess no record that they did so for a woman, but that may be pure chance.

Whether this ceremony took place near the tomb or in a house (as the text quoted above stimulates the reader to do) is nowhere recorded. In one case a man even libated on three consecutive days for his father. In another ostracon we read that five men buried a certain Pay, one of whom was his son; three days later three of them, including the son, plus a fourth man, went to libate. Here it is clear that the ceremony took place shortly after death, but that should not necessarily have been so in other instances.

Fig. 70 Limestone akh iqer en Re *stela of Dhutimose. From Deir el-Medina, Twentieth Dynasty*

Recently deceased members of the family were sometimes honoured by having a small stela erected to their memory. About seventy of these stelae, which are usually not more than 25 centimetres in height, are at present known from various sites in Egypt. The vast majority, however, derive from Deir el-Medina (fig. 70). They were set up in houses, invariably in a niche in the walls of the main rooms, but others have been found in the area of the temples and chapels, or even between the tombs.

185

On the stelae we see the dedicatee (seldom two persons) seated, or in a few cases kneeling or standing before a deity. A characteristic is that the venerated dead holds in his clenched fist the stem of a lotus flower, which curves away from his body, the flower looping back towards his nose. In all cases the main figure is designated *akh iqer en Re*, "the able spirit of Re". The word "able" implies that the person (usually a man, but there are instances in which it is a woman) was capable of acting in the Hereafter, being well-equipped with offerings and in possession of the knowledge of the correct spells to facilitate his passage through the Netherworld.

The expression *akh iqer en Re* occurs also on offering tables, on pyramidia, and on some tomb walls (see below), but the stelae are the typical products of the ancestor cult. The representation is indeed so characteristic that the question can be raised as to whether the numerous stelae with such iconographic traits all refer to the ancestor cult, although the crucial words are here absent.

An illustration of this cult is found in a scene in the mid-Nineteenth Dynasty Deir el-Medina tomb of the sculptor Nakhtamun (TT 335). A couple is depicted, seated in a kiosk, with the man holding the characteristic lotus flower. Before him stands the tomb-owner, dressed as a priest, and offering to them. They are designated in the caption as: "The servant of the Place of Truth (i.e., the necropolis workman), the lord of the house" and "His beloved wife, the mistress of the house". The spaces behind the titles, where the names should appear, have frustratingly been left blank. Clearly, however, it is ancestors who are here referred to, even though the words *akh iqer* are absent, and there is no closer indication as to exactly which forebears they are. A more specific instance is another scene in the same tomb, where the "able spirit of Re" Neferhotep receives offerings from Nakhtamun, his wife, and a long row of family members. This Neferhotep was, however, as far as we know, not an ancestor of Nakhtamun, but rather an eminent chief workman of the early Nineteenth Dynasty.

Another aspect of the ancestor cult are the so-called anthropoid busts, also called "ancestor busts" (Petrie's "oracular busts" is a misnomer). These are small human heads, resting on a support. A vague indication of the shoulders is given, but not of the chest or the arms. Their height varies from approximately 1 to 50 centimetres, while the material is mostly stone, although wood, clay, and faience are also attested. Some one hundred and fifty examples are known, about half of which derive from Deir el-Medina. The majority date from the New Kingdom, only a few being earlier or later.

Some heads are bald, or else they show natural hair (fig. 71a). This type is suggested to pertain to Northern Egypt. Others display a tripartite wig (fig. 71b), which is the type of the South. This wig does not imply that a woman is represented for in some cases the skin-colour is the typical dark brown tone of a man. Apart from the hair, the busts wear the broad *wesekh* collar around the support, sometimes with pendant lotus blossoms and buds at the front.

Fig. 71 Wooden anthropoid busts: (a) with short hair. From tomb 136 at Sedment, Eighteenth Dynasty; (b) with tripartite wig. Unprovenanced, New Kingdom

The vast majority of these objects are uninscribed, even when there is sufficient space for an inscription. Only five bear any signs: in two examples the title 'housewife' is followed by a name, and once the titles and name of the goddess Hathor appear. The latter would suggest that a deity is portrayed.

Generally, the heads seem to be of two different sorts. The smaller ones (those under 10 centimetres) are probably merely amulets, whereas the larger examples are actual ancestor busts, being a kind of free-standing determinative of the phrase *akh iqer*.

One ancestor bust is exceptional. Formerly part of the Gallatin private collection, it is now in the Metropolitan Museum of Art, New York, where it is still known as the Gallatin Bust. It is larger than most other examples, being 41.25 centimetres in height. Made of limestone, it is handsomely painted, and although its provenance is unknown, it may very well derive from Thebes or the Theban West Bank. It is such a large head that we are inclined to see it as an actual confirmation of the representation on a stela from Abydos. Here a woman called "the housewife Henut" is standing and libating before a bust placed on a high pedestal. The object in question appears to be life-size.

187

Equally large in proportion to the human figures are two busts carried in a funerary procession, depicted in the Eighteenth Dynasty Theban tomb (TT 78) of the military administrator Haremhab (fig. 72). Although Egyptian art is not bound to natural proportions, the relationship between the busts and their carriers, as well as to that of the mummy-mask that follows them in the cortège, strongly suggests dimensions comparable to those of the Gallatin bust or even larger. However, no such heads of this type are known to us.

Fig. 72 Funerary procession: four men carry a canopic shrine on a sledge (right), two men with anthropoid busts (centre), followed by a man with a mummy mask and a necklace (left). From the Theban tomb of Haremhab (TT 78), Eighteenth Dynasty

If our interpretation of the *akh iqer en Re* stelae and the anthropoid busts is correct, and the fact that so many had been placed in houses makes that highly likely, it means that deceased members of the family were believed to still be part of our world. Like the gods, they too could intercede on behalf of the living, in matters of daily life as well as in the Hereafter. Prayers, and especially gifts of food (funerary offerings), could influence their participation.

That deities were moved by human actions is understandable. A fine example occurs in a letter on an ostracon, sent by a carpenter of Deir el-Medina to his mother. He tells her that he swore an oath to the god to abstain from particular kinds of meat on her behalf. However, he unfortunately broke his vow and is now afraid of the consequences. Other texts confirm that the Egyptians tried to influence the gods by a promise. In the same way they tried to move the spirits of their ancestors, if they felt themselves threatened by a dead person or wronged in this life.

The *akh* one turned to was always a close relation: a parent, child, spouse, or brother, that is, someone who was still remembered, and not an ancestor of long ago. To such a person one would write a letter, either on a bowl that was placed with food in the tomb – so the dead could not miss it – or on an ostracon or a sheet of papyrus.

About a dozen of these so-called Letters to the Dead are known. Usually they are both difficult to read and to understand. This is because some were clearly written under emotional stress leading to many scribal errors. At the same time, their authors were not always highly literate. A particular problem is that the actual subject, known to the deceased, is sometimes only vaguely indicated.

One such letter is written on a bowl, now housed in the Louvre Museum. A mother writes to her son about a person who, when still alive, had threatened to bring a charge against her and her children before the divine lawcourt in the Netherworld. She beseeches her son, who has obviously also died, to denounce the accuser before the court and defend her case. Clearly, the request is preventive. The mother does not state that she has already suffered any evil. In accordance with the situation, it is not surprising that the style of the letter is calm and the hieratic hand rather clear.

Some letters stress that the deceased are dependent upon the living for their sustenance in the Hereafter. This belief is clearly expressed in a series of *Coffin Texts*, those spells written on Middle Kingdom coffins. One of them, CT 38, states: "When I was in the land of the living (says a son to his deceased father), I built your altars, I established your offerings in your funerary domain". That idea we find expressed in another Letter to the Dead, the Hu Bowl (fig. 73).

Found by Petrie's assistant Arthur Mace during the 1898-99 season at the Middle Egyptian site of Hu (Diospolis Parva), this bowl is now in the Petrie Museum. It derives from Tomb Y84, which Mace's notebook reveals to be dated to the First Intermediate Period. Made of red pottery, and some 21 centimetres in diameter, it was broken into five sherds which have now been restored. The letter is addressed to "the sole friend Nefersefki" and can be translated as follows:

The sister says to her brother:
'Full attention! It is profitable to pay attention to the person whom you have favoured (i.e., to me the author of the letter) on account of what is very wrongfully done to my daughter. I did nothing against him (i.e. the deceased person who threatens her). I have not consumed his property. He has not given anything to my daughter. One makes funerary offerings to a spirit (*akh*) in return for interceding on behalf of the survivor. Settle then your account with him who does what is painful to me, for I shall triumph against any dead man or woman who is acting against my daughter'.

189

Fig. 73 Pottery dish inscribed on the interior with a Letter to the Dead. From tomb Y84 at Hu, First Intermediate Period

This is the distressful cry of a mother to her dead brother. She has been threatened by an unnamed person that, after his death, he will bring charges against her daughter. Therefore, she begs the brother for his protection, using the argument that she has looked after him well, providing him with funerary offerings. Now it is his turn to help her.

Far clearer is a long letter, written on a sheet of fine quality papyrus, and now housed in the Leiden Museum. Its provenance is Saqqara, where it was found in the early Nineteenth Century attached to a painted wooden statuette of a woman. Also in Leiden, this, by contrast, is of inferior workmanship (fig. 74).

The Nineteenth Dynasty text is written in a nervous, rapid hand, and bristles with scribal errors, indicating that its author was in a state of high excitement. At the end the text is written in small signs and is greatly compressed as if the author noted his final sentence as an afterthought. It seems that Ankhiry's husband was rather less innocent than he pretends to be! Indeed, the entire letter

*Fig. 74 Painted wooden statuette of Ankhiry against the Letter to the Dead.
From Saqqara, Nineteenth Dynasty*

makes such good reading that it deserves to be quoted extensively:

> To the able spirit (*akh iqer*) Ankhiry.
> 'What evil thing have I done to you, that I should land in the wretched state in which I am? What have I done to you? What you have done is to lay your hands on me, although I have done you no wrong. What have I done to you since I lived with you as your husband, until that day (of your death), that I must hide it? What is there now? What you have attained is that I must bring forward this accusation against you. What have I done to you? I will lodge a complaint against you with the Ennead in the West (the divine lawcourt in the Hereafter), and one shall judge between you and me on account of this letter......
>
> What have I done to you? I made you my wife when I was a young man. I was with you when I held all kinds of offices. I stayed with you, I did not send you away...... "She has always been with me", I thought...... And see, now you do not even comfort me. I will be judged with you, and one shall discern truth from falsehood.
>
> Look, when I was training the officers of the army of Pharaoh and his chariotry, I let them lie on their bellies before you, and they brought all sorts of fine things to put before you. I never hid anything from you in all your life. I never let you suffer, but I always behaved to you as a gentleman. You never found that I was rude to you, as when a peasant enters someone else's house. I never behaved so that a man could rebuke me for anything I did to you......
>
> I am sending this letter to let you know what you are doing. When you began to suffer from the disease you had, I let a head physician come and he treated you and did everything you asked him to do. When I followed Pharaoh, travelling to the south, and this condition came to you (that is, when you died), I spent no less than eight months without eating and drinking as a man should do. And as soon as I reached Memphis, I asked from Pharaoh leave and went to the place where you were, and I cried intensely, together with my people, before the eyes of my entire neighbourhood. I donated fine linen for wrapping you up, I let many clothes be made, and omitted nothing good to be done for you. And see, I passed three years until now living alone, without entering any house, although it is not fair that someone like me should be made to do so. But I did it for you, you who does not discern good from bad. One shall judge between you and me. And then: the sisters in the house (prostitutes), I have not entered in to anyone of them'.

The above chapter has revealed something of the rôle of older people in Egyptian society after their death. Those who were authoritative in life were considered to exert an even more powerful influence from the next world. The beliefs of the Ancient Egyptians meant that the dead were thought to be capable of continuing to intercede, or at the worse to interfere, in the world of the living.

17 The Real and the Ideal Lifetime

In many Egyptian tombs of the New Kingdom a banquet scene is depicted at which a blind harper is represented. The song he sings is inscribed in hieroglyphs on the adjacent wall. These songs were meant to ensure blessedness for the deceased, in the meantime instructing the visitor as to the meaning and value of the mortuary cult.

Fig. 75 Blind harper. From the Theban tomb of Neferhotep (TT 50), late Eighteenth Dynasty

Two such songs are found written before the figure of the harper (fig. 75) on a wall of the late Eighteenth Dynasty Theban tomb (TT 50) of an Amun priest (a god's father; see Chapter 19) called Neferhotep. One of these is rather exceptional. It is a glorification of death and the land of the dead, with hardly any mention of divinities or allusions to celestial topography. The following words are conspicuous:

> As to the time of activities on earth
> this is the occurrence of a dream.
> One says: 'welcome safe and sound',
> to him who reaches the West (i.e. the Netherworld).

This attitude of contempt for life on earth ("a dream") suits the context of mortuary entertainment, but in fact the opposite stance occurs even more frequently. The offering formula, in use from the Fourth Dynasty until the Ptolemaic Period, usually includes the wish for a goodly burial "after one has become very beautifully old". All sorts of additions are found at the end of the sentence, such as "in peace", "on one's seat", etc. A similar desire occurs in the conventional introduction to many a formal New Kingdom letter:

> the gods may give you Life, Prosperity, and Health,
> a long lifetime, and a great and good old age.

A long lifetime! But how old did the Ancient Egyptians actually become? Only a few cases are known. The High Priest of Amun of Karnak under Ramesses II, Bekenkhons (see p. 218) describes his career in detail on one of his statues, now in Munich (fig. 76). From this it is clear that he was active at least until his seventies, and probably until over eighty. In fact, if his actual words are to be trusted, we can calculate a career time-span of eighty-five years from his earliest schooldays, which means that he must have been at least ninety when he died.

Fig. 76 Head of a limestone block statue of the High Priest of Amun Bekenkhons.
From Thebes, Nineteenth Dynasty

195

Fig. 77 Limestone statue of the chamberlain Antef. H. 65 cm. From Abydos, Twelfth Dynasty

A certain Iynofret, the wife of a workman at Deir el-Medina called Sennudjem, mother of ten children, is known from her mummy, now in Cambridge, Mass., to have been over seventy-five years old when she died. Moreover, she was for some time already blind, as she herself relates on a stela which is now in Kingston Lacy (Dorset). She is there represented together with one of her sons, praying to the moon and the sun to be merciful, for they caused her "to see darkness by day", which is said to be due to "the talk of these women" – whatever that may mean.

An Old Kingdom nomarch from the 14th nome in Middle Egypt during the reign of Pepi II was called Pepiankh. He is also referred to as Neferka in his tomb at Meir, where the following words occur:

196

I spent a lifetime until a hundred years
among the living
in possession of my faculties.

Whether this sentence can be accepted at face value, however, is a matter of debate.

The famous Amenhotep, son of Hapu, the favoured courtier of Pharaoh Amenhotep III, states on one of his Cairo statues:

I reached eighty years, great in favour
with the king.

To this he adds:

I will complete 110 years.

This sentiment will be further discussed below.

Finally, there is the evidence from a Demotic Wisdom Text, known as Papyrus Insinger after the Dutch dealer who purchased it in 1895 for the Leiden Museum. The document dates from *circa* 100 A.D., and contains a description of the course of human life:

Man spends ten years as a child before he understands
life and death.
He spends another ten years acquiring the work
of instruction by which he will be able to live.
He spends another ten years gaining and earning
possessions by which to live.
He spends another ten years up to old age
before his heart takes counsel.
There remain sixty years of the whole life
which Thoth has assigned to the man of god.

The ideal lifetime is here a hundred years, but note that at forty man is said to have reached old age!

Many texts refer to a good old age which was really attained, for they are found in tombs and on stelae built or erected by elderly men late in their careers. A few examples may suffice. The famous Ahmose, son of Ebana, was a marine commander who accompanied Pharaoh Ahmose during his liberating campaign to expel the Hyksos from Egyptian territory (see p. 182). In the biography in his tomb at el-Kab he states:

I have grown old,
I have reached old age,
Favoured as before and loved (by my Lord).
I now [rest] in the tomb that I myself made.

Fig. 78 Wooden cubit-rod of Amenemope. From Saqqara, late Eighteenth Dynasty

Some years later, under Tuthmosis III, we have the case of Ineni, who held the post of Overseer of the Granary. He was the builder of the tomb of Tuthmosis I and of a pylon and two obelisks at Karnak. In his own Theban tomb (TT 81) he relates:

I reached the old age of an honoured man,
while I was daily in the favour of His Majesty.
I was fed from the table of the king
with bread from the royal repast
and beer likewise,
and fat meat, various vegetables and fruits,
honey, cakes, wine and oil.

198

Obviously, Ineni as a favoured servant of the king received these commodities as a sort of state pension (see Chapter 21).

These last two men and many other dignitaries relate how happy their old age was because of the favour of Pharaoh. A different boon is mentioned by the chamberlain Antef, who is known from a statue in the British Museum (fig. 77). The son of Sobkunu and Seneb, he served under Sesostris I. On one of the stelae from his offering chapel at Abydos, also in the British Museum, he says:

> I was granted to reach old age,
> with all my children holding office in the palace.

A long life was considered to be the gift of the gods. A certain Amenemope of the late Eighteenth Dynasty wrote on his cubit-rod, found at Saqqara and now in Turin (fig. 78):

> May they (the gods) give me a beautiful
> lifetime upon earth
> in the favour of the Lords Gods
> and a passing of old age without sorrows.

Even more explicit is a New Kingdom hymn to Amun, written on a papyrus housed in the Leiden Museum:

> (Amun,) who lengthens the lifetime and shortens it.
> He gives more above what is destined to him
> whom he loves.

Some Egyptians expressed a wish to pass their days in old age near the god in his temple, (probably dozing in the sun, or in the shadow of a wall, but not inside the sanctuary itself, for that was out of bounds to the laity). An example is Amenysonb from the time of Pharaoh Khendjer of the Thirteenth Dynasty. He erected a chapel at Abydos, two of the stelae of which are now in Paris and one in Liverpool. On one of the Louvre stelae (fig. 79), he says:

> The works you have done (namely, cleansing the
> Osiris temple) have now been viewed.
> As the sovereign favours you, as his *ka* favours you,
> spend your old age well in the house of your god.

Fig. 79 Limestone stela of Amenysonb. From Abydos, Thirteenth Dynasty

A similar sentiment is expressed centuries later on the stelephorous statue belonging to Nekhtefmut (see p. 180) of the Twenty-Second Dynasty. He states:

> You (Amun) have received me in my old age
> as an elderly man in your august house.

and:

> You will reward me in a beautiful high age,
> while I daily see Amun as I want.

Above we saw that in the late Papyrus Insinger the ideal lifetime seems to be a hundred years. In the Pharaonic Period it is frequently stated to be 110 years. Examples range from the Old Kingdom until the Late Period, but most date from the Nineteenth and Twentieth Dynasties. They occur on stelae, on statues, and on tomb walls, but also in literary texts. A variety of examples can be quoted.

In Papyrus Westcar (see p. 143) Prince Hardedef tells his father, King Snefru, about the magician Djedi:

> He is a man of 110 years,
> who eats 500 loaves of bread
> half an ox for meat,
> and drinks 100 jugs of beer, to this very day.

We have already seen that Amenhotep, son of Hapu wished in his eighties to attain 110 years. A century later, Bekenkhons, whom we calculated may have lived into his nineties, states on his Munich statue:

> May (the god) give me a beautiful lifetime
> after 110 years.

This is evidently spoken by Bekenkhons as the statue wishing to endure after death. Whatever, the sentence shows that 110 years was a standard expression.

In a New Kingdom schoolbook (see p. 232), there is a poem in which the pupil addresses wishes to his master in the form of a studied sequence of sentences. Obviously these were considered to be high art:

> May you multiply happy years,
> your months in prosperity,
> your days in life and well-being,
> your hours in health,
> your gods pleased with you;
> they being content with your utterances,
> and a goodly West having been sent forth to you.
> You are not yet old, you are not ill.
> May you complete 110 years upon earth,
> your limbs being vigorous,
> as happens to one who is praised like you
> when his god favours him.

Similar sentiments occur in the introduction to the *Tale of Woe*, the literary composition of Papyrus Pushkin 127 mentioned above (see p. 144):

> May he (the solar god Atum) cause you to reach
> 110 years upon earth,
> your body whole, growing old with a contented heart,
> without illness in your limbs,
> but with continuous gladness and joy in your heart,
> and without the weakness of old age,
> you having indeed arrested it.

What a beautiful wish this is!

In year 50 of Ramesses II, a scribe named Ptahemwia, travelling with his father, visited the Fifth Dynasty pyramids of Abusir. They also entered the beautiful mastaba of Ptahshepses at the site, excavated in the 1960's and 1970's by a Czech expedition. On one of its walls Ptahemwia, clearly an ancient vandal, recorded their visit, including the words:

> That we may reach 110 years, we pray you
> (the goddess).

However, the wish to live 110 years does not relate to a king. This is evident from the Great Papyrus Harris, now in the British Museum (see p. 234). It is a list of what Ramesses III had donated to the temples, drawn up by his son and successor:

> You (Amun) allotted to me a kingship of 200 years.
> Establish them also for my son who is (still) on earth.
> Make his lifetime longer than that of any other king
> in exchange for the benefactions I have made
> for your *ka*.

The ideal of 110 years also found its way into the Old Testament. In Genesis 50, verse 22, we read of Joseph:

> So Joseph dwelt in Egypt he and his father's house;
> and Joseph lived a hundred and ten years.

This is stated again in verse 26. For Joseph that is understandable as he lived in Egypt, but it is also twice stated of the successor of Moses, namely Joshua. In Joshua 24, verse 29, and Judges 2, verse 8, we read:

> And Joshua the son of Nun, the servant
> of the Lord, died,
> being a hundred and ten years old.

It will be obvious from this chapter that, as in all societies, the actuality in terms of age attainment fell somewhat short of the desire. The real and the ideal lifetime were indeed completely different matters in Ancient Egypt.

Sticks and staves were of great significance to the Egyptians. "There was scarcely any object in the life of Ancient Egypt that was so commonly in use, that was used in so many different ways, and that took so great a variety of forms". So wrote Henry Fischer, then Research Curator at the Egyptian Department in the Metropolitan Museum of Art, New York, in a 1978 review article.

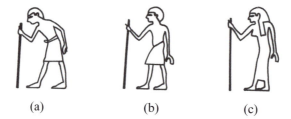

(a)   (b)   (c)

Fig. 80 Hieroglyphic signs: (a) for elderly and old age, clearly distinguished from (b) that for an upright dignitary; (c) picture of an old woman once used in writing the feminine word for old age. From the mastaba of Ti at Saqqara, Fifth Dynasty

    Staves were a symbol of dignity for men in power. An example is that held by the Fifth Dynasty priest Ka-aper in his famous wooden statue in Cairo, commonly referred to as the Sheikh el-Beled (see p. 151), the name given to it by the Arab workmen at the time of its discovery. Women did not usually carry staves; instead they are sometimes depicted holding a stick in the shape of a long-stemmed lotus, such as that of Queen Ioh in the Wadi Shatt er-Rigal relief (see fig. 85).

    Staves were also a support for the elderly, both men and women. A comparison can be drawn between the hieroglyphic sign showing a bent man leaning on a stick, which is well-distinguished from that of an upright dignitary with a stick (fig. 80a and b). In a few cases the sign portrays an old woman (fig. 80c). There are also depictions of real elderly women leaning on sticks, such as that of an old crone with dishevelled white hair who appears as one of a group of tribute bearers in the Theban tomb of Huy (TT 40), the Viceroy of Nubia in the reign of Tutankhamun (fig. 81).

    In accordance with the many tangible forms, there are also numerous words for sticks and staves. A study, published in 1976 by the Egyptian scholar Ali Hassan, lists seventy-four different names. However, it must be acknowledged that some are merely variants; others are very rare, perhaps mentioned only once, while yet more denote what <u>we</u> would call 'sceptres'. By comparison, modern Egyptian Arabic knows sixteen words for a staff or stick.

Some types are typical for a certain period. In the Old Kingdom the officials carry a long, slightly tapering staff, called a *medu* (fig. 82). By contrast, in the New Kingdom many of these artefacts have a curved projection at the top, either the natural fork of a branch, or else an imitation. Certain servants carry specific staffs. Shepherds, for example, are portrayed with a crooked or a curved staff. It is also particularly in the New Kingdom that staffs are inscribed and covered with copper and gilded tips at each end.

Fig. 81 Women bringing the revenue of Nubia to the Viceroy Huy. One of them, with white hair, is leaning on a stick. From the Theban tomb of Huy (TT 40), Eighteenth Dynasty

All sorts and types were placed in tombs, some being real objects used in life, whilst others are merely dummies made specifically for the burial equipment. Three pertinent examples of burials containing sticks and staves can be cited. The first are those found in the burial of a woman called Senebtisi. Her tomb at el-Lisht, situated close to the pyramid of Amenemhat I, was excavated in 1906-7 by the Metropolitan Museum of Art Expedition. A simple shaft-and-chamber tomb, it was nevertheless exceptional because of its rich contents which were practically undamaged. Despite its situation, the objects and in particular the coffins prove that Senebtisi was buried during the Thirteenth Dynasty rather than the early Twelfth. Two sets of staves were discovered, one in a box which had suffered badly from exposure, and the other <u>in</u> the coffin with the body which were, by contrast, well-preserved. The latter consisted of six staves of various types, now in the Metropolitan Museum of Art (fig. 83). In itself it is surprising to find staves in a female burial, because most of them she could not have used in life. Perhaps the underlying reason was that every dead person was believed to become a (male) Osiris.

Fig. 82 Wooden figure of a standing man holding a medu-*staff. From Saqqara, Sixth Dynasty*

Fig. 83 Wooden staves of Senebtisi. From the tomb of Senebtisi at el-Lisht, Thirteenth Dynasty

Our second instance is the intact tomb of Kha, the architect of Amenhotep III, discovered at Deir el-Medina in 1906 by the Italian archaeologist Ernesto Schiaparelli. Kha possessed ten sticks and staves of varying diameters, four being very thin and the remainder solid. Two of the latter are decorated with bronze inlays and incised with the name and title of their owner. In addition to *medu*-staves, there are six forked examples; in three cases the protruding element had been artificially fixed, whilst in the others it was natural. Two of Kha's walking sticks had been broken and repaired in antiquity by winding papyrus bark around the breakage. Obviously they were both precious and well-used!

Thirdly, we have the burial of Tutankhamun with its amazing total of 130 sticks and staves, seventy of these being of the *medu*-type. A large bundle of them was found, leaning against the wall, between the first and second catafalques. Some were ornamented with bark, while others were gilded or even embellished with gold. Special attention should be paid to four ceremonial staves which are real works of art, their lower ends being decorated with beautifully carved figures of Nubians, and, in one case, a Nubian and a Syrian back to back. In stuccoed, gilded, and painted wood, the face and arms of the Nubians are made of ebony, those of the bearded Syrian of ivory. Sadly, all Tutankhamun's sticks and staves still await definitive publication.

Their fundamental rôle in daily life led to a particular metaphoric use of the staff, especially of the *medu*. On a Fifth Dynasty stela in Cairo, the owner, a certain Hemmin, calls himself a "pillar of old age". A similar expression occurs on the Twelfth Dynasty stela of Nesmontu, now in Paris. In his laudatory autobiography the owner states of himself:

> I was a support of the aged,
> a nurse of the little ones.

Yet another phrase, encountered in the Old Kingdom, is "staff of old people". This concept developed into a fixed expression: "staff of old age", in which "staff" is written with the word for *medu*. As we shall see, the idiom carried a specific meaning.

The oldest known instance of its use is found in the *Instruction of Ptahhotep*. As stated above (see p. 142), Ptahhotep was a Fifth Dynasty vizier, but the earliest text of his *Instruction*, which is now in the Bibliothèque Nationale in Paris, dates in fact from the Middle Kingdom (see p. 216). It is in this text that the phrase "staff of old age" occurs. Therefore, it has been suggested that this is a later addition. After setting forth the evils of old age (see p. 142), Ptahhotep asks the king:

> May this servant be ordered to make
> a 'staff of old age',
> and let his son step in his place,
> so as to tell him the words of those who heard,
> the ways of the ancestors
> who have listened to the gods.

A second instance from the Middle Kingdom occurs in the tomb of the nomarch Dhutihotep II at el-Bersheh, who was a contemporary of Sesostris II and III. Dhutihotep's father Kay is portrayed standing face to face with him and stating, according to the text above the figures, that 'my lord' and my god' (i.e., the king):

> made my son to be chief of his city
> and overlord of the Hare (the 15th) nome
> in the place of him who created me.

In other words, Dhutihotep must have directly succeeded Nehri, Kay's father and his grandfather. Could this perhaps have been because Kay was too old to shoulder the duties of a nomarch? The son then says of his father:

> He made me to be chief of his city
> and overlord of the Hare nome
> in the place of him who begot him.
> He (Kay) was the 'staff of old age'
> of his father (Nehri),
> he made me to be chief of his city.

Fig. 84 Representation of Hetepherakhet on the right side of the entrance to his mastaba-chapel. His eldest son, pictured as a boy, is clinging to his staff. From Saqqara, Fifth Dynasty

The figures of father and son both hold *medu*-staffs in their hands. This face-to-face depiction is the antithesis of the usual Old Kingdom scene where the tomb-owner, either sitting or standing, is portrayed with a diminutive figure of a son clinging to his father's staff (fig. 84). Such a gesture of dependence is here transposed into one of equality.

The phrase "staff of old age" also occurs in administrative texts. In a Kahun papyrus (see p. 173), a father, an overseer of priests, certifies that he hands over his office to his son:

> to be a 'staff of old age', for I am old.
> Let Pharaoh appoint him immediately.

There are also three instances of the phrase known from the New Kingdom. One features in a narrative concerning the installation of the vizier User(amun) as the successor of his father Iahmose (see p. 178). It is written on a wall in one of the son's Theban tombs (TT 131).

It relates how, during a throne-session King Tuthmosis II makes an allusion to the age of his vizier. The courtiers, standing around the throne, answer him:

> You have perceived, O Sovereign, our lord,
> that the vizier has reached old age.
> Some bowing down came to his back ......
> It may be useful to your two lands
> to look out for a 'staff of old age'.

Then Pharaoh orders the search for a suitable candidate, and the courtiers, after having considered several possibilities, suggest the vizier's son User(amun), for:

> Intelligent and of good character,
> he is suitable for a 'staff of old age'.

The king agrees with them and confirms:

> I have recognized your (Iahmose's) son User(amun)
> as efficacious and persevering and righteous
> [through] your instruction ......
> May his virtues serve you,
> so that he be to you a 'staff of old age'.

This is a composition of the 'Königsnovelle' type, the name given by Egyptologists to a particular literary genre in which an important historical decision by the Pharaoh is related. This could be, for instance, the building of a temple, the dispatching of an expedition, or the commencement of a war. The usual setting is a session of the king's council, either political or military, during which the king makes a speech. His advisors reply with cautious considerations or objections, and then the king takes a bold decision – which of course turns out to be the right one.

The second New Kingdom example of the idiom occurs in the autobiography of the High Priest of Amun Amenemhat, from the reign of Amenhotep II. Cast in the form of a wisdom text, it is inscribed on a wall in the inner room of his Theban tomb (TT 97). He tells his children:

> I was a priest, and a 'staff of old age' with my father
> while he was living on earth.

This father, called Dhutihotep, was a simple lay priest, overseer of sandal makers in the Temple of Karnak. So it appears that even humble temple servants had a 'staff of old age'.

That not only high officials received such a helpmate, is also clear from our third instance, a sentence in the autobiography of Amenhotep, son of Hapu (see p. 197), written on his limestone block statue in Cairo. Describing his early career as a military administrator, he states:

> I recruited the young men of my lord,
> my reed pen counted their numbers by millions.
> I made them into companies
> in the place of the members of their families
> a 'staff of old age' as his beloved son.

In conclusion it can be stated that "staff of old age" is a figurative expression to describe a son who was appointed, by the Pharaoh or by a bureaucrat, to act as the deputy and future successor of his father, while the latter still officially retained his authority. It seems to have been a special administrative title and as such is attested only from the Middle Kingdom and the Eighteenth Dynasty. The phrase itself reflects the prominent rôle of staves in the life of Ancient Egypt.

19 The 'God's Father'

One of the most curious titles from Ancient Egypt is that of the 'god's father'. An exact rendition of the Egyptian phrase *it-netjer* is 'father of the god'. Earlier Egyptologists habitually translated the expression as 'divine father', but that is not correct. Regrettably, this error is sometimes still perpetuated today. The god here is actually the king, although, as we shall see, it is very seldom the preceding Pharaoh who is so designated.

The origin of the epithet is unknown: perhaps it started out as a court title, later, by the time of the Old Kingdom, becoming an honorary one. Indeed, a peculiar characteristic is that although the term remained in vogue throughout Egyptian history, it changed its meaning several times. The connecting element was that it designated a high rank thus defining the relationship of the bearer with the king. That may be a family tie, or also the ideal fathership as the tutor of the future Pharaoh, but should not necessarily be so. A chronological survey citing specific instances will serve to illustrate this point.

The Sixth Dynasty Pharaoh Pepi I married the two daughters of a local ruler at Abydos named Khuy. At the same point their brother Djau became the vizier. The girls both received the new name of Ankhes-en-Meryre (literally "She-lives-for-Meryre", Meryre being the *prenomen* of Pepi I). They subsequently became the mothers of the successive Pharaohs Merenre and Pepi II, the latter of whom is credited with a ninety year reign (see p. 246). On account of his strong ties to the monarch, Khuy was called "god's father, god's beloved". Here in fact the title can simply be interpreted as father-in-law of the king.

Several other persons from the late Old Kingdom and the succeeding periods are called "god's father", but for what reason we do not know. That they were all related to the Pharaoh is unlikely. That is only the case with some of them. During the First Intermediate Period the Vizier Shemay erected a series of stelae in the Temple of Min at Coptos, all of which are inscribed with royal decrees. From these it appears that Shemay was married to a royal princess called Nebet, and perhaps for that reason he bore the title "god's father, god's beloved". The same designation is also given to the son of Shemay and Nebet. But in this case they were not fathers-in-law, but rather a son-in-law and grandson of the reigning king!

Later in the First Intermediate Period and during the early Eleventh Dynasty the title underwent a distinct change in meaning. In the temple of the deified Heqaib (the surname of an Old Kingdom governor and caravan leader Pepinakht) on the island of Elephantine at Aswan, three fragmentary quartzite statues were found during the excavations of the great Egyptian archaeologist Labib Habachi. One is totally uninscribed, another bears the name of Wahankh Antef, an early ruler of the Eleventh Dynasty, while the third carries the inscription "gods' father (note the plural here) Montuhotep-aa", the name being in a cartouche. All three statues are clearly in the same style and were probably made by the same sculptor. Although Montuhotep-aa was certainly not a Pharaoh, this statue portrays him as a man dressed as a king in the royal kilt and seated upon a throne. The explanation seems to be that he was the father of two rulers, namely Sehertawy Antef (I) and Wahankh Antef (II). Therefore *it-netjer* here indeed designates the (non-royal) father of a king.

Fig. 85 Rock relief of Montuhotep II and his mother Ioh faced by the "god's father" King Antef and the chancellor Khety. From Wadi Shatt er-Rigal, Eleventh Dynasty

The same meaning is encountered in an Eighteenth Dynasty inscription on a block from a building of Amenhotep I at Karnak. This lists the names of earlier Pharaohs, still revered in later ages. Those of the Eleventh Dynasty rulers Nebhepetre (Montuhotep II) and Seankhkare (Montuhotep III) are followed by that of "the god's father Sesostris". He can be identified as the non-royal father of Amenemhat I, the founder of the Twelfth Dynasty.

Montuhotep II is also depicted on a spectacular rock relief in the Wadi Shatt er-Rigal, situated some four kilometres north of Gebel Silsileh on the west bank of the Nile (fig. 85). It was here that the sandstone was quarried for the king's innovative mortuary temple at Deir el-Bahri. The large incised relief, which measures some 2 metres high by 2.15 metres wide, portrays a practically life-sized King Nebhepetre Montuhotep, followed by his mother Ioh, with before him "the god's father, god's beloved, the son of Re Antef". The name is written in a cartouche, and the figure is clearly dressed as a king with the royal kilt and bull's tail, the *nemes* headdress, and the royal uraeus on his brow. The chancellor Khety follows directly behind him, his right hand upon his breast in a respectful position of salute. Who this Antef was is not clear, but it is conceivable that we can identify him as Montuhotep's bodily father. This Antef had indeed been kinglet at Thebes, but he was never King of Upper and Lower Egypt. Therefore he was theoretically not the predecessor (= the "father") of Montuhotep. What is announced in this scene is probably the divine marriage of Ioh that led to the birth of a new (the Eleventh) Dynasty.

The early Thirteenth Dynasty, which is now called the late Middle Kingdom, has as its two most prominent rulers the brothers Khasekhemre Neferhotep (I) and Khaneferre Sebekhotep (IV). They were the sons of a commoner named Haankhef. The father is designated on their monuments and scarabs as *it-netjer*. Here again the title seems to point to the (non-royal) father of the ruling Pharaoh, but as far as we know this is the last instance in Egyptian history.

The Eighteenth Dynasty witnesses a fundamental change in the meaning of the title, many important persons now being called *it-netjer*, with the implication of advisor of the sovereign or elder statesman. Some examples are: various High Priests of Amun, such as Amenemhat (see p. 210), who enjoyed an unusual late career under Amenhotep II; viziers, such as Rekhmire under Tuthmosis III; and Viceroys of Nubia, such as Usersatet, a childhood companion of Amenhotep II.

A suggestion has been made that the designation now means tutor of the crown-prince (or princess). A fine example would be that of Senenmut, the favourite and *éminence grise* of Queen Hatshepsut, who lists among his many titles that of "steward of the estate of Princess Neferure", the young daughter of the monarch. On earlier statues he calls himself "father and (male) nurse" of the princess; on one of them the text reads:

> I brought up the eldest daughter of the King,
> the god's wife Neferure, may she live,
> and I was given to her as 'father of the goddess',
> because I was so useful to the King.

It should be noted that Hatshepsut is here referred to by the masculine designation "King", whereas Neferure bears the feminine epithet "goddess".

Probably the statue on which these words were inscribed dates from a later stage in Senenmut's career, when his pupil needed not so much a "nurse" as a mentor. The statue in question is now in the Chicago Field Museum of Natural History (fig. 86). Made of diorite and some 53 centimetres high, the standing

Senenmut here carries the princess on his arms. Although numerous of his statues show him with badly damaged features, this is one of the five known examples to have survived entirely intact.

Fig. 86 Diorite statue of Senenmut carrying the Princess Neferure. From Karnak, Eighteenth Dynasty

The dignitary Heqareshu, who lived slightly later in the Eighteenth Dynasty, is depicted in the Theban tomb ascribed to him (TT 226) in a unique wall-painting with four princes – all with sidelocks – on his knee. In his son's tomb (TT 64) there is another representation of him with Tuthmosis IV in full regalia, on his lap (fig. 87). His titles above include those of "(male) nurse of the king's eldest son Tuthmosis (IV)" and "god's father". In front of him stands his son Heqaerneheh, the owner of the vault, with one prince before him and six others, now largely destroyed,

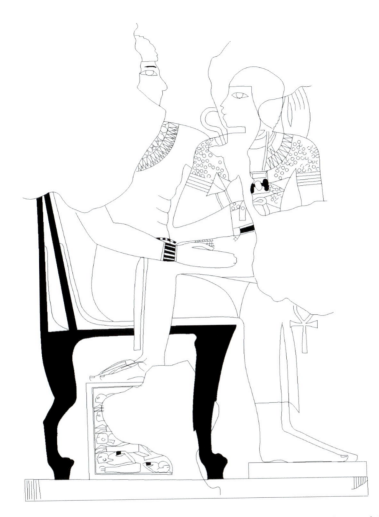

Fig. 87 Heqareshu with Tuthmosis IV in full regalia on his lap. From Theban tomb 226, Eighteenth Dynasty

following him. Father and son were doubtless the tutors of young royals – the father of the future Tuthmosis IV and the son of at least three, and possibly even seven, royal princes. However, it is not certain whether it was indeed the educational aspect that was here expressed by the term "god's father". The son never bears the title which could perhaps be explained by the fact that when this scene was painted Heqaerneheh's pupil Amenhotep, if he indeed was the future Pharaoh Amenhotep III, had not yet become king. However, in general doubts can be raised whether *it-netjer* ever means more than spiritual 'father' of the sovereign, that is, elder statesman.

From earlier times there is only one, highly dubious, instance of *it-netjer* as a title of a tutor of a crown-prince. The epithet is borne by the Fifth Dynasty vizier Ptahhotep (see pp. 142 and 207), at least in the manuscript of his famous *Instruction* known as Papyrus Prisse, which is now in the Bibliothèque Nationale in Paris. This version is the most complete, differing considerably from the other three known copies. The designation occurs in the introduction to the actual maxims where, between other titulary, Ptahhotep calls himself

> god's father, god's beloved, eldest son of the king,
> of his body, governor of the city and vizier.

The combination of "father" of Pharaoh as well as "eldest son" seems very strange until we remember that the latter is purely honorific. Whether the first epithet indeed means that he was responsible for the education of a later Pharaoh is quite uncertain, especially as it is equally unsure whether Ptahhotep himself was really so called. At least we know of no relationship of this vizier to a crown-prince. Could it already in this case be an honorary title equivalent to elder statesman such as it was later to become?

Confirmation of such an honorary title is found in Genesis 45, verse 8 where Joseph says of himself that God made him to be "a father of Pharaoh". This would seem to be a correct translation of *it-netjer*, as it clearly has the meaning here of advisor or elder statesman.

It may be that the many high dignitaries occasionally called 'god's father' played a (minor) rôle in the education of princes. An example is Aper-el, the "forgotten vizier" of Amenhotep III, whose tomb was rediscovered in 1976 by a French expedition working at Saqqara. He was certainly not the king's father-in-law, but seems to have been a tutor of his son Amenhotep (the future Akhenaten). At least he is once called in his tomb "nurse of the royal children".

There is a possibility that some high priests initiated their royal pupils into the secrets of temple ritual, and likewise that high officials may have imparted the code of politics. A modern example of the latter practice is that of the *Raadpensionaris* (Grand Pensionary, that is Secretary of State) of Holland Jan de Witt, who acted as one of the tutors of the Prince of Orange. The young man in question was later to become *Stadhouder* in the Netherlands and King William III of England.

Fig. 88 Ay shows off his new red gloves, a reward from Akhenaten and Nefertiti. From the tomb of Ay at el-Amarna, Eighteenth Dynasty

The most famous 'god's father' is Ay, the high official who eventually became Pharaoh at the end of the Eighteenth Dynasty. Before him the title was borne by Yuya, the father of Queen Teye, the "Great Consort" of Amenhotep III, and the mother of Akhenaten. Hence Yuya was really the father-in-law of the reigning Pharaoh. Whether this was the reason for his title, or whether it was granted to him because he was a special advisor of the monarch remains uncertain. Anyhow, he and his wife Thuyu were even afforded a burial in the Valley of the Kings (KV 46).

Ay was married to another Teye, the wet-nurse of Nefertiti. That he was also the tutor of Akhenaten and later of Tutankhamun is not quite certain. But his relations to the royal family were particularly close. Again, we are uncertain whether he owed the title 'god's father' to a post as tutor of two kings, or to his prominent position at the court of el-Amarna.

The famous recompense scene in Ay's private tomb, situated to the east of the city, depicts his official investiture by Akhenaten and Nefertiti. In one particular vignette we see him, weighed down by gold collars, proudly showing off his brand new red leather gloves (fig. 88). Gloves were extremely rare imports in Ancient Egypt: they are seldom depicted on New Kingdom reliefs, another instance being those worn by the military general Horemhab in his Saqqara tomb, and are known only from tangible linen examples found in Tutankhamun's burial. Their presentation to Ay is therefore a clear indication of the high esteem in which this bureaucrat was held. Indeed, it is even possible that we can identify Ay as the spiritual father of the whole Amarna movement.

When he became Pharaoh after the untimely death of Tutankhamun, the by now elder statesman took the epithet *it-netjer* into his cartouche as part of his private name (*nomen*). Probably he felt that this stressed his link to the dynasty and constituted his only legitimation. However, Ay's emphasis on the title may very well equally be what brought it into discredit for statesmen, for in this position it now disappeared.

However, one notable use of *it-netjer* does occur in the Nineteenth Dynasty when Ramesses II calls his father Seti I his "god's father, god's beloved". Here, exceptionally, the title is used for a royal father!

This apart, it had from the Middle Kingdom onwards a totally different meaning: indicating a lower priestly rank. Henceforth, it remained the only use of the title. Its relative status clearly emerges in the famous Late Twentieth Dynasty *Onomasticon of Amenope* (see p. 144) in the section listing all categories of priests and temple employees, starting with the highest grades and descending to menial occupations such as butchers and milkmen. The series begins with prophets (literally "god's servants"), the highest ranking priests, followed by *it-netjer* and then *wab* (literally "pures"), the ordinary priests. From this it appears evident that 'god's father' occupied a transitional position in the hierarchy.

An apt illustration is found in the long career of Bekhenkhons (see fig. 76 and pp. 195 and 201), the High Priest of Amun at Karnak under Ramesses II. After a primary school education and a training job he passed four years as a *wab* priest. Perhaps this was simply a part-time post during his training as an administrator.

Then he started to climb the hierarchical ladder as an *it-netjer*, at which level he stayed for twelve years. Afterwards he became successively Third Prophet of Amun, Second Prophet, and finally High Priest. It is clear that 'god's father' marks the transition to the higher echelons of the priesthood.

One of Bekhenkhons' successors was a man called Rome-Roy, who was active under Merneptah and his descendants. He describes his career on one of his statues now in Cairo. As a *wab* priest he was chosen, he states, because of his eminent qualities to be introduced to the function of *it-netjer* in order to serve the *ka* of the god.

This is an indication of what we now have to understand by the title. At a certain moment in their life, some of the *wab* priests were inducted as *it-netjer* to serve the cult images of the deity, hidden away in the innermost sanctuaries, where ordinary priests were not allowed to enter. These *wab* priests could indeed serve the processional statues, but remained excluded from real responsibilities and, unlike the *it-netjer*, were not initiated into the secrets of the cult.

It will be evident that 'god's father' could refer to several quite different positions and functions during the long period of Egyptian history. Yet, the word 'father' retained throughout the notion of veneration, whether it referred to a real father (-in-law) of the reigning king, to a wise advisor of the sovereign, or merely to a priest who was initiated into the secrets of the god.

In Chapter 4 we argued that the position of the elderly in a particular society depends to a large extent on their ties with their descendants. Older people without offspring are therefore rather helpless. They are forced to rely on the care and assistance of neighbours and distant relatives, generally less reliable than one's own children. Hence, if one wishes to avoid the situation that one will eventually be alone, it is necessary to generate offspring. Children are the insurance against the deprivations of old age. But what if one is not lucky in this matter? There are in general three possible strategies for the childless: adoption, divorce and remarriage, and polygamy.

Adoption certainly occurred in Ancient Egypt, but we have no idea how frequently. This is not helped by the fact that it is sometimes difficult to distinguish true adoption from the practice of taking a foster-child. In this connection a letter on a Deir el-Medina ostracon is of relevance. Dating to the Ramesside Period, it is now in Berlin. The unnamed sender states:

> He who has no children should get for himself
> some orphan to bring him up. Then he will be
> the person who pours water upon his hands,
> as a genuine eldest son.

Whether this refers to a formal legal adoption is very much an open question. But it certainly reveals a means of acquiring essential care in old age.

In general not much is known about adoption. A special case was that of the Divine Adoratrices, particularly during the Third Intermediate Period. These women were envisaged as being the consorts of the god Amun; they were therefore nominally, perhaps in many cases also actually, head of the Karnak Temple with its extensive properties and large personnel. Since they had to be virgins, they adopted their successors, who were the sisters or daughters of the rulers. This proves that formal adoption was not unknown.

One papyrus, dating from the late New Kingdom, provides us with information concerning the legal formalities. Originally in the possession of Sir Alan Gardiner, he donated it in 1945 to the Ashmolean Museum, Oxford. The text, deriving from Middle Egypt, is known as "The Adoption Papyrus" and consists of two parts.

The first lines relate how in year 1 of Ramesses XI, on the exact day of his accession, a certain Nebnofre adopted his wife as his own daughter. The reason was that their marriage had remained childless. In this way Nebnofre could leave all his properties to his wife after his death, and claims of his siblings would be invalid. The adoption took place before witnesses, while the sister of Nebnofre was also present.

Seventeen years later the present document was drawn up by the wife. She relates in the introduction what we have summarized above. She continues by telling that Nebnofre, together with her, had purchased a female slave, who had subsequently given birth to two girls and a boy. Doubtless, Nebnofre was their father. The wife took care of the children, probably because Nebnofre had by then died, and they in turn behaved well towards her. She had then married the eldest girl to her younger brother Padiu, at the same time emancipating her. Now she adopts her brother, emancipates the other two slave-children and adopts them too, declaring that all four should inherit equally from her, while Padiu will act as the trustee. He has, in exchange, to look after her in her situation as an elderly widow.

There has been much discussion concerning the correct interpretation of this text, for the scribe was incredibly incompetent. Gardiner called the language "barbarous" and the composition of the document "execrable". Although in most of the text the words are those of the woman, he almost always uses the masculine pronoun, so that it has been suggested that it was Nebnofre who adopted the children. We believe, however, following Gardiner, that the above is a correct reconstruction of the events. Evidently, adoption was a means to provide for a childless woman after she became a widow.

Another method to try and acquire offspring in old age would be to divorce a childless wife and to marry another woman. Divorce in itself was easy. Since there seems to have been no ceremonial wedding, it was possible to dissolve the tie with hardly any formality. In the Leiden Letter to the Dead quoted above (see pp. 190-192), the husband stresses that he did not send away his wife whom he had married as a youth. That was clearly not self-evident. Note that, so far as we know, the marriage had remained childless. At least, no offspring are mentioned.

Divorce seems to have been particularly common among the mass of the population during the Ramesside Period. This is revealed by the Tomb Robbery Papyri, an archive from the later reigns of the Twentieth Dynasty dealing with the investigations and trials of the people who had plundered several private and some royal tombs. Among the culprits were many labourers and lower grade priests, but also a few more influential persons. We find some indications of what may be divorce in these papyri. Once a woman even testifies before the Court:

> I am one of four wives (of a goldsmith Ramose),
> two being dead and another still alive.

It is of course not certain whether Ramose had divorced the latter, and whether such separations without a formal wedding could be called 'divorce' is a matter of terminology. Moreover, it is nowhere stated that such 'divorces' took place because of the woman's inability to bear children. Yet, that certainly seems a possibility.

None the less, 'divorces' for such a reason were clearly not the general practice. From Deir el-Medina, the Village which has yielded so much relevant information on real life, we know of at least two important men who never had their own offspring. One is the scribe (administrator) Ramose, from the reign of Ramesses II. He was obviously a notable and a rich man, for he built no less than three tombs for himself and erected many stelae and statues. Although he could easily have afforded a second wife, he adopted a young scribe called Qenhikhopshef, who acted as his son and successor.

Another example is the chief workman Neferhotep, whose marriage with Ubekht also remained sterile. The couple first adopted a certain Paneb, the son of one of the workmen, but he grew up to be a particularly nasty intriguer and bully. Later on they chose as *protégé* a slave-boy called Hesysunebef ("His lord may praise him") (fig. 89). That proved much more successful. This man remained loyal to his former master and mistress, and when he was later set free and married he called his son after the former and his daughter after the latter. What is relevant here is that the marriage of these two seems to have remained stable despite their childlessness.

Fig. 89 Relief of Hesysunebef with a pet monkey, on the side of a fragmentary seated statue of Neferhotep and his wife Ubekht. From the Theban tomb of Neferhotep (TT 216), Nineteenth Dynasty

It is mostly difficult to ascertain whether in a particular case we have to do with divorce when a tomb-owner appears to have had more than one wife. For instance, in the Nineteenth Dynasty tomb of the High Priest of Onuris Anhermose (see fig. 94) at el-Mashayikh (situated not far from Abydos, near the modern town of Girga, in Middle Egypt), two successive wives are recorded. One of them is called on a statue: "his former wife". Does that mean that he had divorced her, or did she die before he remarried? Perhaps the latter, for we would not expect her to appear on the tomb walls if the marriage had broken down.

Somewhat clearer is the situation alluded to in an ostracon from Deir el-Medina. There a man lists the objects which remained in his house: "after he left Wabe, his first wife". He seems to have moved into a new partnership, while being unable to take with him his valuables, for the list enumerates a fair number of bronze objects, mainly vessels but also a razor, and their total worth is not insignificant. It is, however, by far not certain that the man had left his wife because she remained childless.

Fig. 90 Mery-aa and his wives: (above) Mery-aa himself with his ?first wife Isi; (below) his five other wives. From the tomb of Mery-aa at el-Hagarseh, Ninth Dynasty

Generally, the Egyptians were monogamous, only the king being accustomed to have a plurality of wives. On the other hand, there is no indication that polygamy was forbidden. Certainly not by law, but it seems not to have been frowned upon. Nowhere in the wisdom texts do the authors utter objections,

223

although they stress the value of marrying. There exist a few indications that among the upper classes polygamy did occur, and it may well be that the wish for male offspring was behind this practice.

The strongest argument for the occurrence of polygamy is the depiction in a tomb of two wives, as in the case of Anhermose, although, as we have seen, that in itself is no proof. Perhaps more convincing is the case of Mery-aa from el-Hagarseh (near Sohag) in whose Ninth Dynasty tomb no less than six women are portrayed, all called "his wife" (fig. 90). Five of them appear to have had children. That he divorced all five is highly unlikely; he certainly would not then have had them depicted in his tomb. The childless wife Isi seems to be the most important, featuring on several walls. Was she perhaps the first, and did she remain barren?

In this case a multiple marriage seems certain. In all others it is no more than a possibility. Whatever, it was certainly rare, but its public acknowledgement in a tomb like this suggests that it was socially acceptable. Another example may be that of Khnumhotep II, the son of Nehri (see pp. 179-180). In his tomb at Beni Hasan two wives are mentioned, but, as with Anhermose, it may be that the first had died before he married the heiress of the 17th nome.

Once again, it is one of the Tomb Robbery Papyri that provides us with a rather clear instance. In a list of women involved in the affair, one of them, who is named Herer, is said to be the wife of a guard of Pharaoh's Treasury. The next one, in the following line, is called "his other wife, which makes two". This strongly suggests that the guard was living with both women at the same time.

It is time to return to our main subject, namely, the care of the elderly. It was particularly the position of single women that caused difficulties. Therefore, the wisdom texts devote some attention to widows. So, for example, the *Instruction* addressed to King Merikare, which dates from the First Intermediate Period. There the author says to his son, the future Pharaoh:

> Do justice, then you endure on earth;
> Calm the weeper, don't oppress the widow,
> Don't expel a man from his father's property.

Then there are the words of the New Kingdom *Instruction of Amenemope*:

> Do not encroach on the boundaries of a widow,

and elsewhere:

> Do not pounce on a widow when you find her
> in the fields.

That means, when she is gleaning on your land. This situation reminds us of the famous Old Testament picture of Ruth and Boaz.

In all these cases it is not stated that the widow is old. Even young widows without the protection of a husband were considered to be vulnerable, but that held especially true for those who were elderly.

The famous Vizier Rekhmire (see p. 178) states in his autobiography in his Theban tomb (TT 100) among a catalogue of his good deeds:

> I have protected the widow who had no husband.

Further on, he says:

> I provided for the old one while I gave [him my staff],
> causing the old women to say: 'That is good'.

One of the most stringent duties of every high official towards the aged was to bury the dead. To declare that this had been carried out belongs to the traditional subjects of a Middle Kingdom autobiography. For example, the priest Wepwawet-aa, from the time of Sesostris I and Amenemhat II, writes on his stela, erected at Abydos and now in Leiden:

> I buried the old ones in my town.

In many instances this common sentence in the 'moral profile' is followed by its counterpart:

> I brought up the children.

Care for both vulnerable categories, the older and the younger generation, is thus juxtaposed.

Another aspect of the relationship between the generations is found on the Twelfth Dynasty stela of the police officer Beb, also in Leiden. He says:

> I handed over my office to my son
> while I was still alive.
> I made for him a testament
> in excess of what my father had made [for me],
> my house being established on its foundation,
> my fields being in their place.

That this was appreciated by the son appears evident from the following line:

> It is my son who made my name live upon this stela.

Note that the stela was erected by the son, despite the words; he thus demonstrates that he has fulfilled his filial duties.

In one case such behaviour even extended to the preceding generation. On a statue from the Late Period, now in Rome, which belongs to a certain Hor-Re and was erected by his grandson Teos, the grandfather speaks:

> He (the grandson) erected the statue beside Hathor,
> the Mistress (that is, in her temple),
> after he had interred me in a beautiful burial.
> He renewed the burial, with ointment and linen
> from the temple, after thirty-three years.

Evidently, long after his death the young man still showed his care for and devotion to his grandfather.

A unique illustration of the love of a son for his father is found in the tomb of Djau at Deir el-Gebrawi, from the time of Pepi II. Djau was a nomarch of the 12th Upper Egyptian nome and the successor of his father, who was also called Djau with the "beautiful name" Shemay. On the walls of his tomb father and son are once depicted of equal height and standing face to face, the father with a *medu*-staff in his hand (fig. 91). In a text elsewhere in the tomb the son says:

> I made that I was buried in one tomb
> with this Djau (the father),
> in order to be with him in one place,
> not because I did not have
> the means to make two tombs.
> I did it in order to see this Djau daily,
> in order to be with him in one place.

All the preceding, and even this last instance, remain on a high, rather idealized level. But what about the everyday reality? Unfortunately, the evidence is not abundant. One example is a stela found in the temple of Amen-Re at Amara-West, which is some distance South of the Second Cataract, deep into Nubia. Dating from the late Ramesside Period, a second prophet of that temple called Hori, who erected the stela, relates two different dispositions. Firstly, he declares that all the properties of his father, consisting of fields, meadows, slaves, etc., will go to his sister Irytekh. Secondly, the mother of Hori states about all the goods left to her by her husband (Hori's father) that:

they may be given to my daughter, for she has
acted for me when I was old.

Did, perhaps, Hori not want to care for his ageing mother, and had he for
this reason promised his properties to his sister Irytekh, who had looked after the old
lady and, therefore, inherited from her?

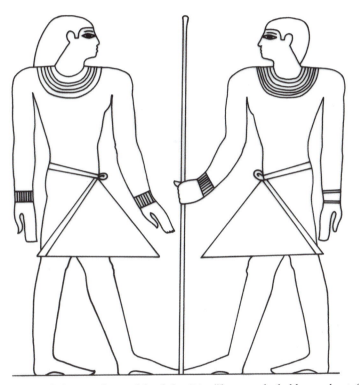

Fig. 91 Djau stands face- to- face with his father Djau/Shemay, who holds a medu-*staff. From
the tomb of Djau at Deir el-Gebrawi, Sixth Dynasty*

As always, the ostraca from Deir el-Medina present a picture of the reality.
In one of them, now in Glasgow, and probably dating from the reign of Ramesses
IV, the necropolis workman Usekhnemte ("Wide of Strides") declares that he has
given all kinds of goods to his father. Some of them were luxuries: cakes, meat, fat
and honey, to which he added clothes; others were basic food, bread and beer. In

particular he gave him 2½ sacks of emmer-wheat monthly, over a ten month period. As is so many times the case, the figures are somewhat mysterious, for Usekhnemte says that the total amounted to 27½ sacks. That is either eleven times 2½, or ten times 2¾ sacks!

The editor of the text suggests that the son here serves as the 'staff of old age' of his father. Whether he would ever have called it so is doubtful, but clearly he was not mean. His own monthly ration consisted of 4 sacks of emmer (*circa* 300 litres), of which more than half was handed over to his father. This would have been more than sufficient for the old man's personal needs, leaving even room for some dependant or servant.

Fig. 92 Limestone ostracon relating the charity shown by a man to a divorced woman. From Deir el-Medina, Twentieth Dynasty

Another case is mentioned in an ostracon now in the Petrie Museum (fig. 92). It is dated to the second year of Sethnakht, the first ruler of the Twentieth Dynasty. In the first lines we are told that, when Hesysunebef (see p. 222) divorced his wife, the author, whose name nowhere occurs, gave her every single month over a three year period 1 *oipe* (*circa* 20 litres) of emmer-wheat, in total 9 sacks. He also records that he paid her for a shawl which was so worn out that it was refused on the market. Why this was written down, even to the extent of recording the names of some people who handed over his grain to the woman, that is, who were witnesses to his charity, we do not know. Had the woman perhaps died, and did the author of the ostracon claim the inheritance?

Not all children were generous towards the older generation. In a famous papyrus, now in Oxford, a lady called Naunakhte formulated her last will. Before a large section of members of the community, she declares that she has brought up her nine children and given them all that was appropriate for those in their station. Now, however, that she has grown old, not all of them have looked after her. Therefore, she disinherits one son and three daughters. Of one daughter who will still inherit she specifies:

> She shall have her share in the division of all my property, except for the *oipe* of emmer-wheat, which my three male children and one daughter have given to me, and except for my one *hin* (*circa* ½ litre) of fat which they have given me in the same manner.

This reveals that four of the children provided their mother, very probably on a monthly basis, with a minimum quantity of bread-grain and some fat. Certainly, it is less than Usekhnemte gave his father over a ten month period, but on the other hand it may have been adequate for an elderly lady. Moreover, it was not all Naunakhte received, for further on she records the landed property she had inherited from her first husband, a storeroom from her father, and the *oipe* of emmer which she collected together with her second husband. There is no doubt that she was not dependent upon the help of her children, but that was not a reason to forgive those who neglected their filial duties.

The Greek historian Herodotus describes in his *Histories* of *circa* 450 B.C., the various ways in which the Egyptians differed from other peoples. One of these is:

> It is not obligatory for the sons to feed their parents if they do not want to do so, but for daughters it is a strict obligation, even if they do not want it.

The 'father of history' is here not clear. As stated above, looking after and caring for one's parents is a moral duty, not enforceable in law. That the obligation was more stringent for girls than for boys is not confirmed by our source material.

In the late Papyrus Insinger (see p. 197), in a rather obscure passage, it seems to be stated that the obligation ceases if the parents behave like fools; then one is allowed to abandon them. Was that what Herodotus had in mind when he spoke about the sons? Or did he misunderstand his Egyptian informant, as was so many times the case?

That some children neglected their elderly parents we have seen. We could know that beforehand; it is only human. How many times it happened remains, of course, hidden. Actual life is hard to pinpoint. All we encounter are numerous examples of sons who want to be seen in their stereotyped inscriptions as virtuously caring for their ageing fathers and mothers.

21 Old Age Pensions

In the preceding chapter we discussed the care of the elderly by their immediate family, especially the children. The question now arises as to whether the state looked after its servants in any particular fashion when they became too old to work. Of course, the state did not maintain <u>every</u> old person; such an old age pension is even in our society a recent development. But are there traces of a pension for those who were directly in the service of the state? Two possible groups emerge: the necropolis workmen at Thebes; and the soldiers and their commanding officers.

Dealing firstly with the former category, evidence occurs on a limestone ostracon now in Turin, dated to a particular month of year 7 of Ramesses II. The quantities of grain are recorded – both barley and emmer-wheat – which in that month were issued to the workmen and their chiefs. This grain constituted the basic wages. Among those who received it four women are mentioned. Perhaps they were simply the female slaves of the community who occur in many similar lists, but there they are always called "slaves". Alternatively, could the women here be the widows of deceased workmen?

This is not too bizarre a suggestion. In other such grain-distribution lists there occasionally occurs a person called a "widow". The incidences are unfortunately rare and not quite unambiguous. Yet, it seems possible that the authorities, who were responsible for the entire upkeep of these very special workers, also gave some food to their widows. Of course, we have no means of telling whether these ladies were elderly.

That older men among the builders of the Royal Tomb received a monthly grain-ration – lower than that of the ordinary workmen, but certainly still adequate – is proved by several of the grain-accounts. These men are explicitly called "old". Whether they still produced some work we do not know, but the payment seems to have been some sort of old age pension.

Of course, these people, the widows and the "old" men, were still partly dependent upon their family. The grain they received was merely a basic support, providing bread and beer.

That the state was responsible for the support of its soldiers is self-evident. In a world without money that had to be done by providing them with all they needed. An easier method was to allot to them pieces of land, together with cultivators. That system was widely followed, for instance, in Ptolemaic Egypt, but it was also customary in Pharaonic times. Soldiers were settled on the fields the government provided, while they could be called up for active service at every moment.

This is a payment, not a pension. If, however, the fields remained in the actual possession of the soldiers when they became too old to fight, then it almost became a pension. However, as we saw above (see p. 210), in some cases the obligations fell to the son, who acted as "staff of old age" for his father.

In the so-called *Miscellanies*, anthologies composed by teachers and used as schoolbooks during the New Kingdom, the desirable position of a scribe (that is, of an official) is contrasted with that of all other occupations.

One of the chapters describes the course of life of a common Egyptian:

Man comes forth from the womb of his mother,
and he runs to his master;
the child is in the service of a soldier,
the young man is a fighter,
the old man is made to be a cultivator,
the adult man to be a soldier.

"Old man" means here "veteran", as is explicitly the case in other similar texts. From the viewpoint of a scribe his fate is deplorable, but the reality behind it is that the veteran receives a field on the yield of which he stays alive, although he has to toil hard to do so.

Another *Miscellany* talks about various persons whom, says the author, one should not ridicule. One of them is a certain Amenwashu:

Have you not heard the name of Amenwahsu, a veteran of the Treasury?
He passed his life as a controller in the workshop beside the armoury.

It is not clear whether this passage refers to a former soldier or to a low level civil servant, who obtained a place in a workshop in order to keep himself alive. One can feel how the scribe looked down upon such a position. Yet, the old man Amenwahsu was not left to depend on the benevolence of his friends and family.

Above (see p. 198) we have quoted the Eighteenth Dynasty high official Ineni. He receives daily, he tells us on the wall of his Theban tomb, all kinds of food from the king's table. This also constitutes some form of old age pension.

Another way of providing for elderly servants was that Pharaoh appointed them to priestly offices. These positions may, in some cases, have been no more than prebends, although some others seem to have carried real duties.

As an example we can cite the soldier Maya, who served under Tuthmosis III. He was buried in the 10th Upper Egyptian nome (later called Antaiopolites), and it will be from there that the fine limestone seated statue provenances, which is now in Berlin (fig. 93). Maya is here depicted wearing a heavy double choker of gold ring beads, and four armlets on both his wrists and upper arms. Those on his wrists are of a special type. All this jewellery constitutes the 'gold of honour' with which kings of that period were accustomed to reward their gallant soldiers.

In what rank Maya served his sovereign he does not state. Apart from referring to the award he mentions on the seat of his statue only his later titles: "governor and chief of the prophets". It has been suggested that these are merely honorary designations, attached to sinecures, which were granted to him as an old age pension.

There are more examples of elderly soldiers who received such offices in the temples. A certain Amenemone, for instance, who lived at the very end of the Eighteenth Dynasty and was buried somewhere at Saqqara – the exact location has

Fig. 93 Limestone statue of Maya wearing the 'gold of honour'. From ?Akhmim, Eighteenth Dynasty

233

recently been rediscovered, and many elements from the tomb are now housed in museums all over the world – was first an army general. Later he was appointed steward of a funerary temple of Tuthmosis III, probably situated in Memphis. Whether this was a sinecure is not clear, however.

This is, by contrast, rather certain in the case of two former generals from the reign of Ramesses III. They are mentioned in the Great Harris Papyrus, the longest papyrus roll that has survived, being over 40 metres in length (see p. 202). Housed in the British Museum, it records the gifts donated by the king to various temples. In the last section, devoted to small temples, we come across a certain Inushefnu, "who had been a general" and was now in charge of a chapel of Rameses III in the temple of Min at Akhmim. Similarly, we read about a man named Dhutemhab, also a former general, who was in charge of a chapel in the temple of Wepwawet at Asyut. Little doubt exists that these two positions were prebends.

Less clear is the matter of a certain Amenhotep who was High Priest of Onuris, the local god of This, during the reign of Tuthmosis IV. On his stela, now also in the British Museum, he relates that he had been accustomed to accompany the ruler on his campaigns to Syro-Palestine and to Nubia. Probably this was in his capacity as stablemaster, that is, he was responsible for the horses of the chariotry. Hence, he was an army officer. When later appointed High Priest, he was in charge of the management and the finances of the temple, a position for which his work as chief of the royal stables may have prepared him. In how far his function was real or merely a sinecure is hard to establish, but it was certainly granted to him as a sort of pension. It should be noted that two of his sons, who are also represented on the stela, themselves became charioteers; evidently in the wake of their father's early employment.

Another High Priest of Onuris who enjoyed a similar career under the following dynasty is Anhermose (see p. 223), who lived under Ramesses II and his successor Merneptah. His rock tomb at el-Mashayikh, the cemetery of ancient This, contains important wall reliefs (fig. 94).

According to his autobiographical inscriptions there, Anhermose started his career, after a very successful school education, as a military administrator in the chariotry corps. Later on he acted as "interpreter of every foreign land" for the king, and it was in this capacity that he attracted Pharaoh's attention. So he was introduced into the leading circles of the realm. This led, later in his life, to an appointment as High Priest of Onuris, although he was probably a Theban by birth. It may be that he even adapted his name to his new position, for Anhermose means "child of Onuris".

As regards his appointment, he relates how he was chosen by the god, which means singled out by an oracle from among a group of suitable persons put forward by the king. It was an administrative post, as we saw above; Anhermose himself assures us that he was not a ritual leader of the temple cult, but rather looked after the treasury and granaries of the temple.

234

Evidently, the function was bestowed on him as a reward for his loyal and efficient service to Pharaoh. In how far we should call it a pension office is not clear; but Anhermose also received a prebend of the same type as that of the two generals discussed above for he was steward of a chapel of Merenptah in the temple of Onuris.

Fig. 94 Anhermose dressed as High Priest. From the tomb of Anhermose at el-Mashayikh, Nineteenth Dynasty

That the transition from the army to the priesthood was not considered to be uncommon, even not to positions in the daily cult of the gods, is evident from the Coronation Decree of Horemhab. This text is written on the back of the diorite statue of Horemhab and his wife Mutnedjemet, now in Turin. The Pharaoh relates how he had set the land in order following the turmoil of the Amarna Period, rebuilding the temples that had fallen into disrepair, providing them with statues of the gods and regular offerings, endowing them with fields and herds, and equipping them with priests "from the pick of the army". Evidently, becoming a priest after serving as a soldier was not so exceptional as we would think.

Finally, mention can be made of the career of a certain Nebamun, known from the tomb he built in the Theban necropolis (TT 90). Originally he was standard bearer of the ship called Meryamun ("Beloved of Amun"), which constituted a middle-rank military post. In his sixth regnal year Pharaoh Tuthmosis IV issued a palace decree, a copy of which is inscribed on one of the walls of the tomb. It was addressed to the commander of the fleet, a position not unlike that of the First Lord of the Admiralty, and it runs:

My Majesty has ordered the receiving of a goodly old age, in the favour of the king, while care is taken of the standard-bearer Nebamun of the royal vessel Meryamun. He has reached old age while following Pharaoh in steadfastness, and being better today than yesterday, in performing what was put in his charge, without being reproached.

I have not found any fault in him, although he was accused as an offender. Now my Majesty has ordered to appoint him to be police chief on the West of the City (of Thebes), in the places Tembu and Obau, until he will reach the blessed state (of the dead).

Fig. 95 Nebamun (left) receives his appointment to police chief from the royal scribe Iuny. From the Theban tomb of Nebamun (TT 90), Eighteenth Dynasty

This decree, together with the standard symbolizing the police force of Western Thebes, was handed over by a royal scribe called Iuny (fig. 95). Evidently, Nebamun received a pension position, although it may not have been a sinecure. It should be noted that his brother was also a chief of police on the Theban West Bank. Clearly the king wished, now that Nebamun had been cleared from the accusations brought against him, that he should enjoy a quiet and well-provided for old age.

Thus it appears evident that the government and Pharaoh himself looked after the elderly, especially former military men. How widespread this concern was we have no means of telling. Certainly, however, it did not extend to every older person in Ancient Egypt. The concept of an old age pension for every citizen was still millennia away.

22 Long-lived Kings

The age at which the Pharaohs died is generally unknown. All we can recognize is the number of years they ruled, or, rather, the highest year-date of these monarchs – which is not necessarily their last year. How old they were when they ascended the throne we can at best only estimate.

There are indications that the Egyptians believed that a king, when he became older, lost some of his magical potency, and that it was necessary to renew his forces. Such a renewal was the *sed*-festival (Egyptian: *Heb-sed*).

What the Egyptian word *sed* meant is unknown. In the Graeco-Roman Period the festival is called, as well in Demotic as in Greek, the "feast of thirty regnal years". The common rendering "jubilee" is not quite correct. Indeed, in most instances the ceremony took place in the thirtieth regnal year of a Pharaoh, after which it was regularly repeated every third year. At that moment most rulers will have been about fifty years old. Of Tuthmosis III we think that he was 46 years, of Amenhotep III that he was 47 years, while Ramesses II is considered to have been 55 years. This gives us an indication of the age at which, according to the Egyptians, a man became old. However, some rulers may have celebrated the festival at a far earlier moment in their life.

To establish which Pharaohs actually organized a *sed*-feast is far from easy. There are two reasons for this. Firstly, there are numerous mentions of what we might call "fictitious" celebrations: wishes to reach the date, which are so worded as to make it seem that it was already so far, or promises by the gods that it will be attained. Such expressions of wishes and promises created to the Egyptian mind the notion that it was already a reality. But this is not so according to our concepts.

Then, secondly, many texts and representations of the *sed*-festival actually refer to a celebration in the hereafter in which the ruler participated after his death. A clear example is the replica in stone of the temporary buildings erected for the feast, which are included in the complex of the Djoser-pyramid at Saqqara. To our mind these buildings, or scenes of the festival, which were particularly common during the Old Kingdom, constitute no proof that the pertinent king really celebrated the *Heb-sed*.

Our knowledge concerning the events of the festival is rather limited. There are no descriptions of the ceremonies, and only a few more extensive representations have survived. The earliest of these is found in the Fifth Dynasty Sun-Temple of King Neuserre at Abu Ghurab, North of Abusir. Originally two series of scenes existed, but of one of them sufficient has been preserved to venture a reconstruction (fig. 96). It should be noted that it is highly unlikely that Neuserre really celebrated his *Heb-sed*.

Some additional information has reached us from the reign of Amenhotep III, particularly from his temple at Soleb in Nubia (*circa* 200 kilometres South of Wadi Halfa). Unfortunately, however, its remains have not yet been adequately published. In the tombs of the high officials of this reign at Western Thebes, some scenes from the festival are also depicted, mainly those in which these persons themselves played a prominent rôle.

Fig. 96 King Neuserre carried in the Upper Egyptian palanquin. From the Sun-Temple of Neuserre at Abu Ghurab, Fifth Dynasty

The third series dates from the early years of Amenhotep IV (the later Akhenaten). He built East of the Karnak Temple, outside the present enclosure wall, a structure which was specially devoted to his *Heb-sed*. After his reign the building was dismantled, and the blocks of the walls used to fill up the interior of some pylons in the Amun Temple. From here they have been recovered as a result of modern

239

reconstruction work. These are the so-called *talatat*, perhaps named because their length is three times (three = Arabic: *talata*) that of a human hand.

The temple, called Gempaaten (literally "The Sun-disk is found") began to be excavated in the late 1970's by a Canadian expedition. At the same time as its scanty remains were being exposed, an attempt was made to reconstruct the scenes on the *talatat*. From what we know at present of this building we can derive some information concerning the festival. Once again, it is dubious whether this Pharaoh indeed ever celebrated such a feast.

The last and perhaps most complete representation is found at Bubastis, in the Delta. In the temple there, Osorkon II, the most prominent ruler of the Twenty-Second Dynasty, erected a gateway decorated with scenes of the *Heb-sed*. Although more of these have survived than in the earlier cases, they too present only a partial picture of the events.

Fig. 97 Limestone lintel depicting the Sed Festival of Sesostris III. From the Temple of Montu at Medamud, Twelfth Dynasty

These four series of representations are vastly different. That is due, apart from their incomplete state of preservation, to the evolution of the *Heb-sed* over the centuries. The distance in time between Neuserre and the Amenhoteps is *circa* a thousand years, and that between the latter and Osorkon is again *circa* five hundred.

240

No-one can expect the ceremony to have remained unchanged over such a stretch of time.

A few elements appear to have been characteristic for the festival. They occur also separately and outside the four series. But what is not depicted is the very beginning of the feast, namely, its announcement throughout the country sometime before. During the following months the divine statues of the temples were assembled and transported to the capital. This event is depicted in the tomb of a priest at el-Kab where a boat under sail is seen towing the sacred barge of Nekhbet, the goddess of this city, with the image of a deity in a shrine. The accompanying text tells us that in year 29 of Ramesses III the vizier was ordered to bring the goddess to the North. On the arrival in Ramsestown, in the Eastern Delta, the king himself came to take the front-hawser of the barque, a detail we know of only from this caption but which certainly conforms to reality.

For several days during the festival the ruler was seated on a throne in a pavilion, a scene which is depicted numerous times (fig. 97). He is shown once wearing the red crown of Lower Egypt and once with the white crown of Upper Egypt. In the representations these two are combined, the king being pictured twice, back-to-back. Generally, the actual ceremonies seem to have taken place twice, once for each part of the country.

During the rites the Pharaoh was clad in a special, enveloping cloak, which was conspicuously short, reaching to above the knees. The starched garment, which stood away from the neck, was decorated with coloured squares, and worn over a sort of feathered undergarment. In his hands he holds a staff and a whip. This attire is so characteristic that we can recognize statues in which the king is so represented (see fig. 99) as referring to his festival, either a real or a "fictitious" one. In later times, from Amenhotep III onwards, a longer, likewise all enveloping cloak replaces the earlier short version.

During the *Heb-sed* several processions took place, in which the Pharaoh was carried around in a palanquin. According to the scenes from both Abu Ghurab and the Gempaaten, the litter of the sovereign of Upper Egypt was basket-shaped (see fig. 96), while that for Lower Egypt was square. The latter looks not unlike the famous carrying chair of Queen Hetepheres, the mother of Cheops, which is now in Cairo. The processions in which the king went around brought him to the temporary chapels in which the gods of all Egypt rested during those days, and where he brought his prayers and offerings.

A conspicuous rite, also many times depicted, is the so-called ceremonial course of the king, by which he asserted his dominance over the entire country. He is clearly running, probably between or around half-round constructions which are sometimes shown in the representations (fig. 98), and of which three-dimensional replicas can be seen in the Djoser complex. On this occasion, the king is not shown in the *Heb-sed* costume, but mostly in his habitual kilt. However, the course seems also to have been an element of ceremonies other than this festival.

241

Fig. 98 Limestone block depicting Amenhotep III running the ceremonial course before Amun-Re. From the Open Air Museum at Karnak, Eighteenth Dynasty

Finally, the ceremonies contain allusions to a secret rite symbolizing the king's death and resurrection. In it a bed with lion's feet played a rôle, but exactly what is uncertain. Since the rite was obviously secret we possess no more than allusions as to what actually happened.

In the past Egyptologists believed that the *Heb-sed* was a sort of civilized survival of a ritual that was supposed to have been common throughout Black Africa, during which a ruler, as soon as he displayed signs of becoming old and weak, was killed. However, no trace of this practice has ever been discovered in Egypt. Moreover, recent research has demonstrated that elsewhere in Africa such a ritual murder hardly occurred. Usually, it was executed in theory only, or a boy acted as substitute for the ruler. On the other hand, since it was believed that his magical potency, so necessary for the prosperity of his land and people, diminished, opponents of the government would use the opportunity to attempt to murder the king. That may also have happened in Egypt, as we shall see below.

In the shadow of this great state ceremony simple daily life went on. That is aptly demonstrated by a text on a stela in the British Museum of a certain Nebipusenwosret, who played a rôle during the *sed*-festival of Amenemhat III in the Twelfth Dynasty. In the middle section, at the end of some biographical notes, we read that he made use of the opportunity presented by the presence of the priests of Osiris in the capital at the *Heb-sed* to send this stela with one of them back to Abydos, certainly in order to have it erected there.

How many Pharaohs really celebrated one or more *sed*-festivals we do not know; this is not a wonder in view of the complications mentioned above. A few doubtful instances may suffice to illustrate the problems.

That Amenhotep IV celebrated the feast in Thebes before his move to his new capital el-Amarna, which would mean, about his third regnal year, is doubtful despite the building of Gempaaten. It would have been excessively early in his reign. On the other hand, the features of the king and the queen in the representations on the *talatat* were not exaggerated as they subsequently became in later years, which proves that the scenes indeed date from early in his reign. It has been suggested that he celebrated the feast together with his father, whose third *sed*-festival in his regnal year 37 is certain. But for this hypothesis there exists no positive proof at all.

A much discussed problem is that of Hatshepsut's festival. Her own reign was certainly not long enough for her to have celebrated a thirty-year festival, but it has been suggested that she counted, not from her own accession, but from that of her father Tuthmosis I. There are indeed vague indications of a *Heb-sed* in her regnal year 16, but definitive proof is as yet lacking.

We can only be certain that the festival took place if, for instance, dated records of its proclamation have been preserved, or dated dockets on jars in which the food for the feast was sent to the capital; or also when we possess mentions of the date of a second or third celebration. Without such evidence the actuality of the event remains doubtful.

At present only a dozen instances are fairly or quite certain. That means that for several kings, of whom we know for certain that their reign lasted for more than thirty years, no proof of a *Heb-sed* is available. An example of these is Amenemhat II, whose rule lasted at least thirty-five years. This silence may mean that, for whatever reason, no *sed*-feast was held; it may equally well be due to a lacuna in our documentation. This is less strange than it might seem to be. Of the so well-known Pharaoh Amenhotep III, for instance, we possess not a single text dated between his regnal years 11 and 30, and hardly any private documents from this period.

One point is clear: the *sed*-festival sheds light on the Egyptian conceptions of what was needed by an ageing Pharaoh. By the extensive ceremonies his power over the country and its inhabitants was renewed.

Let us now discuss some of the kings of whom we know, from their *Heb-sed* or other evidence, that they enjoyed a long-lasting reign. The earliest king of whom it is rather certain that he celebrated *sed*-festivals, and who may therefore have enjoyed a long reign, was Qa'a, the last ruler of the First Dynasty. This is almost all, however, that we know of him. He seems to have reigned only sixteen years, which rather contradicts the suggestion of a long reign. If this is correct, it may be that a *sed*-festival in those early days was not yet celebrated in the thirtieth regnal year.

That Qa'a indeed reached his *Heb-sed*, and even his second, appears evident from the inscription on a sherd from a schist bowl found in Djoser's Step Pyramid. The words: "second time of *Heb-sed*" are clear; admittedly, the name of the Pharaoh has almost totally broken off, but the slight traces fit this name among those of the early Pharaohs.

Qa'a was buried in Umm el-Qa'ab, the cemetery of the early kings on the hills above Abydos. There his tomb, from which no clearly dated material is known, was surrounded by the subsidiary graves of his retainers. One of the mastabas excavated by Walter Bryan Emery at Saqqara in 1953, which has been ascribed to Qa'a, was probably simply the burial place of one of his officials. More we cannot tell about him; the first long-lived king remains a shadowy figure to us.

The next ruler, for which our evidence decisively suggests that he reigned into old age, is Pepi I, from the Sixth Dynasty. He certainly celebrated a *sed*-festival, as is proved not only by a statue in ceremonial dress now in Brooklyn (fig. 99), on the base of which the words "first time of the *Heb-sed*" are incised, but also by some rock inscriptions in the Wadi Hammamat. Three of them also mention the "first time" of the *sed*-festival, but the fourth explicitly states: "Year of the 18th occasion, third month of the third season, day 27: first time of the *Heb-sed*".

The date requires an explanation. In the Old Kingdom the years were not yet reckoned after the regnal years of the king, as in later times, but after a two-yearly census of oxen and small cattle. Hence they were called: "Year of the x-th occasion" (of the counting), or "Year after the x-th occasion". This would mean that the "Year of the 18th occasion" of Pepi I was his regnal year 36. However, it is not certain that the census always took place every second year. Actually, we know that this was not the case; it could happen in two (or more?) successive years. So we cannot be sure about the date of this *Heb-sed*. It may be that it was celebrated earlier, perhaps in Pepi's thirtieth year.

In the Wadi Magharah, in the Sinai, a tablet has been found dated to the "Year after the 18th occasion". The text lists the names of the expedition leaders of that year. At the top are two scenes: one shows the king smiting his enemies, the other depicts the ceremonial course. The latter suggests that a *sed*-festival really took place around this time.

Regnal year 36 or 37, if that was indeed meant, is not the highest date we know of for Pepi I. An inscription in the travertine ('Egyptian alabaster') quarries of Hatnub, near el-Amarna, makes mention of "King Meryre" (the *prenomen* of Pepi) and of "the 25th occasion". That could mean that he reigned for at least fifty years. Even if he came to the throne at an early age, he was evidently a long-lived Pharaoh.

Fig. 99 Travertine ('Egyptian alabaster') statuette of Pepy I. From Saqqara, Sixth Dynasty

Pepi I's reign is considered to be the culmination point of the Old Kingdom. Evidence of his building activities have been found throughout the country. The name of his pyramid at Saqqara, *Mn-nfr-Ppi* ("The Beauty of Pepi endures"), was later used to indicate the nearby capital in the form Memphis. For all his deeds, including expeditions into the desert, he had clearly sufficient time in his long reign, even if it lasted somewhat less than half a century.

Pepi's son Merenre reigned only a few years, and was succeeded, after his untimely death, by his half-brother Pepi II, the son of Pepi I's second wife (see p. 211). First his mother acted as regent, together with her brother Djau, for Pepi was still a child. The famous and exquisite statue of travertine ('Egyptian alabaster') in the Brooklyn Museum, showing him, with full regalia, sitting on the lap of his mother, reflects this situation.

The later tradition attests that Pepi came to the throne in his sixth year, and that he reigned till he was a hundred years old. This seems hardly likely; it sounds too much like the ideal lifetime (see Chapter 17). Yet, he was certainly one of the longest reigning Pharaohs.

A graffito in his pyramid temple at Saqqara South is dated to "the 31st occasion". It records a ritually correct burial. Whether it refers to the entombment of the king is not clear. If it was that, then he would have reigned over sixty years, but this has to remain hypothetical.

Of course, Pepi II celebrated *sed*-festivals. A rock inscription at Elephantine mentions the second, but without a date. Also, some names of officials are composed with the words *Heb-sed*, such as that of the Vizier Ni-heb-sed-Neferkare (Neferkare: Pepi's *prenomen*). Yet, all this is less than one would expect from such a long reign. There is no inscription of the monarch from his later years. In that period the dissolution of the state began, which would soon afterwards lead to the collapse of the Old Kingdom. In how far the advanced age of Pepi II was a factor in this process we have no means of telling.

From the Middle Kingdom the evidence concerning long-lived kings is more extensive. It begins with the Eleventh Dynasty ruler Montuhotep II Nebhepetre, who reunited Egypt after the First Intermediate Period. He reigned at least forty-six years, and certainly celebrated a *Heb-sed*, but in what regnal year is uncertain. Perhaps it was in his year 39. In the Wadi Shatt er-Rigal, near the relief mentioned above (see p. 212 and fig. 85), there is another representation of the monarch, this time in the garment of the *sed*-festival. Beside it there is written: "39th regnal year", but it is not quite certain that this refers to the feast. Several statues have been found in the ceremonial garb, some of which were erected along the causeway to his mortuary temple at Deir el-Bahri (fig. 100). Unfortunately, none of them bears a dated inscription.

It is uncertain in which year Montuhotep defeated the Herakleopolitans and reunified Egypt. Some scholars would like to see a connection between these events and the change of the king's Horus name, first from Seankhtawi to Netjerhedjet, and later to Sematawi ("He who Unites the Two Lands"). The last name would have been used from the moment that unity was restored, perhaps from year 30 onwards, while the first change is connected with the defeat of the Tenth Dynasty, after regnal year 14. That is, however, rather speculative. On the other hand, it is certain that Montuhotep Nebhepetre belongs to the long-lived Pharaohs.

The first sovereign of the Twelfth Dynasty was Amenemhat I. It has been suggested that he was previously the Vizier under Montuhotep IV, the last Pharaoh of the Eleventh Dynasty, but that is no more than a possibility. The name was a common one in the Theban area. We possess no information on how he gained power.

Amenemhat reigned until his twenty-ninth year. From the famous *Story of Sinuhe* we know that on a day in year 30 he was murdered, probably during the preparations for his first *sed*-festival. Whether his opponents objected to the rise of the new dynasty is uncertain, but if that was the case they were unsuccessful. The crown-prince Sesostris, who was on an expedition to the Western desert – conceivably in order to collect cattle for the feast – rushed back to the capital and seized power. That the moment for the attack on the king had to do with his supposed weakness before his potency was renewed by the ritual is well possible.

Fig. 100 Limestone statue of Montuhotep II Nebhetepre in his Heb-sed garb. From the causeway of the Montuhotep Temple at Deir el-Bahri, Eleventh Dynasty

247

A famous literary composition from these days is the so-called *Instruction of Amenemhat for his Son*. It was written by a royal scribe in the early years of Sesostris I, but it well expresses the disappointment of the father in his friends:

Do not trust a brother, know no friend,
make no intimates, it is worthless.
When you lie down, guard your heart (that is, your life) yourself,
for no man has adherents on the day of woe.

Sesostris I reigned for forty-five years, but only one *sed*-festival of his is known. Its date, year 31 (without a month or day) occurs in a graffito at Hatnub, belonging to a certain nomarch called Amenemhat, son of Nehri. He relates how he came to the quarry in order to fetch stone for the monarch. There are also undated references to a first *Heb-sed*, for instance on the beautiful White Chapel of the king at Karnak, now rebuilt in the Open Air Museum there. However, such casual mentions are in themselves no proof that the feast actually took place. Of later celebrations we do not hear anything, although the reign certainly lasted long enough for them to have taken place.

The time of Sesostris I seems to have been far from peaceful. His foreign policy was mainly directed to the conquest of Nubia and the defence against the Kingdom of Kerma, South of the third cataract. All this does not give the impression that he particularly needed to renew his forces in his later years, even though he must have become old in Egyptian eyes. Anyhow, we merely hear about a *Heb-sed* in his year 31. Why not in year 30 is a mystery.

As already stated above (see p. 243), we know of no *sed*-festival under Amenemhat II, despite a reign of thirty-five years. Generally, there is not much information on this period. Yet, one of the titles of the nomarch Khnumhotep II, found in his tomb at Beni Hasan (see p. 179) and which relates to his appointment as governor over a sub-nome in regnal year 17, may perhaps point to the feast. It contains an unknown word, written three times with a half-round sign that resembles the object between which the king was running during the ceremonial course (see p. 241 and fig. 98). That is all the indication we have for a possible *Heb-sed*.

The next two Pharaohs, Sesostris II and III, reigned for too short a time to have celebrated the festival, namely twelve and *circa* twenty years respectively. Nevertheless, the latter is depicted in his ceremonial dress sitting in the pavilion, once with the red and once with the white crown. The scene occurs on a lintel from the Temple of Medamud (fig. 97), which is now in the Cairo Museum. The gods of the two halves of the country, Horus and Seth, hand over to him the symbol of the festival. This is one of the numerous "fictitious" representations.

Finally, the last great Pharaoh of the Twelfth Dynasty, Amenemhat III, reigned for over forty-five years. The documentation on his *Heb-sed* – only one is attested – is scanty. In the round top of a stela belonging to a certain Seniankh, which was found at Naga ed-Deir, the date is given as "Year 30 under the Majesty of Nimaatre" (the *prenomen* of Amenemhat III). In a different hand there was later added, in small signs and lightly incised: "*Heb-sed*". And on a stela now in the British Museum a certain Nebipusenwosret relates that he took part in the celebration of a *sed*-festival, but without mention of a date. That is all, apart from some representations and aspirations; there is no royal inscription recording the feast.

The reign of Amenemhat was peaceful. It was characterized by a large number of expeditions, to the Sinai and other places in the Eastern desert, but not by many military actions. Why this Pharaoh celebrated no more *sed*-festivals is a riddle. Did he think that his health was so good that he did not need to renew his magical potency? Or is this yet another example of our lacunary documentation? At present no satisfactory answer is forthcoming.

Four kings of the New Kingdom reigned sufficiently long to reach the time for a *Heb-sed*. The first one of these is Tuthmosis III. He succeeded his father when he was still a young child, while his aunt Hatshepsut, the widow of Tuthmosis II and daughter of Tuthmosis I, acted as regent. Some years later she herself ascended the throne, without ever deposing her nephew, who also became her son-in-law. During his youth it was Hatshepsut who held sway, although formally they reigned together. Whether she actually celebrated a *sed*-festival is not clear (see p. 243).

In Tuthmosis' regnal year 22 she disappears; how, and why at that particular point, we do not know. Immediately, the king started on the first of his many military campaigns into Syro-Palestine, which led to the famous Battle of Megiddo. In total he would lead his victorious army sixteen times into the field, the last in his year 42. On account of these exploits he is sometimes referred to as "the Napoleon of Antiquity".

In between his various expeditions Tuthmosis found the time to celebrate at least three *sed*-festivals. The third one is mentioned on one of the faces of the erroneously named Cleopatra's needle, the obelisk in London on the Embankment. Originally, it was erected at Heliopolis, together with its companion which now stands behind the Metropolitan Museum of Art, in Central Park in New York. They were placed before the Temple of Re on the occasion of the monarch's third *Heb-sed*. Under the Emperor Augustus they were transported to Alexandria, from where one came to London in 1878, the other to New York in 1881.

There is little evidence for Tuthmosis' *sed*-festivals. A stela at el-Bersheh, from year 33, mentions "the beginning of millions of very many *Heb-seds*", which is usually connected with the second occasion. No date is known for the third, and later ones, if they ever took place, have left us without any documentation. Yet, Tuthmosis reigned for fifty-four years, long enough to have celebrated more of these feasts. At his death he will have been nearing his sixty-fifth year, so he was according to Egyptian concepts certainly long-lived.

The second Eighteenth Dynasty Pharaoh we will discuss is Amenhotep III, "the Dazzling Sun-Disk". He came to the throne as a child of eight or ten years. Therefore, during his first regnal years the country was governed by his mother

Mutemwia, a minor wife of his father Tuthmosis IV, who was ruling with the help of others. Among these may have been the commander of the chariotry Yuya (see p. 217), whose daughter Teye would eventually become Amenhotep's wife.

For the king's three *sed*-festivals fairly extensive documentation exists, particularly in the Soleb Temple, at Karnak (see fig. 98), and in the Theban monuments of some of his high officials. For instance, Amenhotep, son of Hapu, a military officer, mentions in his funerary temple that he was appointed, at the end of the first *Heb-sed* in year 30, to a honorary office, indicated by an archaic title which may literally mean "canal-digger". Nefersekheru, the steward of the royal palace at Malkata, in Western Thebes (in the vicinity of Medinet Habu), where all three festivals were celebrated, depicted in his tomb (TT 107) some of the scenes in which he played a rôle. So too did the steward of the queen, Kheruef (TT 192). All this would not yet be a decisive proof for the feasts having taken place, but from the many hundreds of jar-dockets found littering the site at Malkata they become a certainty. These are the dated inscriptions on the vessels in which the provisions for the banquets held during the feasts were sent to the palace.

When the king died, shortly after his third festival, he was not yet fifty years of age; to our concepts not yet an old man. Even so, he is depicted in his later years as elderly (fig. 101), which may have been due to a fatal disease. He was succeeded by his son Amenhotep IV, who soon took the name Akhenaten and launched a violent and systematic attack on the traditional divinities of Egypt. Although, as related above, he built a temple for his *sed*-feast at Karnak, it is doubtful whether he actually celebrated it (see p. 240).

The longest-living Pharaoh of the entire history of Ancient Egypt was Ramesses II. His lengthy reign as well as his achievements made a lasting impression on his successors. On a stela from his year 4 at Abydos, which is dedicated to Osiris, Ramesses IV declares: "You (the god) shall double for me the long lifespan and lengthy kingship of King Usimare-Stepenre (that is, Ramesses II), the Great God. Indeed, more numerous are the deeds and benefactions which I have done for your temple in order to supply your sacred offerings ...... in these four years than what King Usimare-Stepenre, the Great God, did for you in his sixty-seven years". These words clearly demonstrate the awe and wonder in which the later Pharaohs looked back to their great predecessor.

In accordance with his long reign Ramesses II celebrated more *sed*-festivals than any other king, namely fourteen; although the last one was perhaps only announced and never actually took place. They started in his regnal year 30, and were then regularly repeated every three or four years. Curiously enough, we have no representations of any of these feasts, nor statues of the king in festive attire, although Ramesses II has generally left us with numerous attestations of his many years. All we know about these occasions is that they were announced; the first five by his son Khaemwaset (see fig. 106) and a vizier, the remainder by a vizier alone. The inscriptions recording the announcements have survived at several sites in Upper Egypt, but for some unknown reason not in Lower Egypt.

250

Fig. 101 Limestone unfinished triad identified in the 1990's as Amenhotep III, Teye, and Beketaten. From el-Amarna, Eighteenth Dynasty

Since Ramesses was not anymore a child when he ascended the throne – he will have been at least twenty-five years old – he must have lived until he was over ninety. He is famous (or perhaps rather infamous) for the number of children he fathered: fifty-two sons and forty daughters, produced, not surprisingly with various wives. The most important of these was Nefertari, the first consort, to whom the smaller temple at Abu Simbel was dedicated, and then Isinofre, the mother of Ramesses' beloved daughter Bentanat and the princes Ramesses, Khaemwaset, and Merneptah. It was the latter, son number thirteen, who would eventually succeed his father. Some of the sons, for instance Khaemwaset, had already acted for some years as regents, for it appears that the king, when he became old, was not any more capable of ruling himself.

Ramesses will not have been the only Pharaoh to have had such an extensive family, yet none of the others lays such a stress on his offspring. In this respect, as in many others, he was evidently an unusual monarch, whose era saw the last flowering of Egyptian history.

Fig. 102 Ramesses III: (a) face of granite standard-bearing statue. From the Karnak cachette, Twentieth Dynasty; (b) head of his mummy. From the Deir el-Bahri cache, Twentieth Dynasty

The final Pharaoh of the New Kingdom to have occupied the throne for a considerable length of time was Ramesses III. Although he too ascended when he was not any more so young, perhaps in his early thirties (fig. 102a), he reigned for just over thirty-two years. His first *Heb-sed* was celebrated, as we would expect, in his regnal year 30. There is not much documentation to support this fact, but in an administrative papyrus in Turin we come across the remark that in year 29 the Vizier passed Thebes to the North in order to bring the gods of Upper Egypt to the feast.

In his year 32 Ramesses will have started the preparations for his second *Heb-sed*. At that time, a conspiracy centred in the Royal Harim took place. In this a minor queen and her son, together with several court officials and high dignitaries, devised a plot to murder the Pharaoh while he visited Thebes to take part in a religious festival. Whether the attack met with complete success is not clear, but soon afterwards, Ramesses "flew up to heaven", perhaps as a result of the attempt, although his famous mummy shows no trace of any wound (fig. 102b). Probably, the conspirators hoped to make use of the king's loss of magical powers during the month before the renewal of the *sed*-ceremonies, as was the case with Amenemhat I. They too met with no success, for once again it was the crown-prince, this time

Ramesses IV, who seized control.

It is conspicuous that, according to the papyri recording the conviction of the culprits, they had tried to use magic. This confirms the suggestion that they considered the ruler to be weak and vulnerable. Whether there was a political motif we have no means of knowing; certainly, no text makes any mention of it. That rivalry in the harim played a vital part is no more than a plausible hypothesis.

One of the most extensive sources for the events during a *sed*-festival are the representations on a gateway in the temple of the cat goddess Bastet at Bubastis (see p. 240). This structure was erected by King Osorkon II in his regnal year 22, and the text in which this is stated appears to be an exact replica of that of Amenhotep III on his festival monument at Soleb. That in itself is sufficient reason to doubt whether the feast ever occurred at this date. Other evidence that could prove the reality is absent.

So our series must end as it began with Qaʻa (and Neuserre), namely, with a query-mark. Did this *Heb-sed* ever really take place? What could have been the clearest proof of a long reign for Osorkon II is actually not clear at all. As we have seen, to distinguish between fact and fiction is not always so easy.

23 Aged Administrators

In this chapter our aim is to present to the reader some elderly officials at various levels of Egyptian society. Of course, the number of aged statesmen and executives from whom we could choose is boundless. Actually, almost everyone who became powerful enough to leave monuments, whether stelae, statues, or tombs, will have been older, although we seldom know exactly how old.

A Pepiankh-the-Middle, a nomarch and priest of Hathor from Meir, who flourished in the time of Pepi II, wrote in his autobiography on the wall of his tomb: "I spent the time till a hundred years among the honoured living ones in possession of my *ka* (i.e. well provided for). I spent a great part of this time as chief priest of Hathor ...... to see her and to perform her ceremonial with my hands". In giving us a figure Pepiankh is an exception, but that these "hundred years" refer to reality is more than doubtful (see Chapter 17).

From all the numerous possible aged administrators we have chosen a few concerning whom something more can be said than that they simply became old and attained a high position. Each of them represents a particular facet of Ancient Egyptian civilization, so that this last chapter also offers the reader a range of views on life in those times. Our elderly subjects will be discussed in chronological order.

Our first choice is Hemiunu, Vizier and Overseer of all Works of the Pharaoh Khufu. This means that he was responsible for the construction of the Great Pyramid, the largest of all pyramids on the Giza plateau. He was the son of Nefermaat, who was also his predecessor as vizier, a royal prince whose impressive mastaba was situated near the pyramid of Meidum. Since this was the burial place of Huni, the last ruler of the Third Dynasty, it may be that Nefermaat was his son. Anyhow, Hemiunu certainly belonged to the royal family without actually being the son of a Pharaoh. When he is called "son of the king of his body", this is purely an honorific title.

In the early Old Kingdom the viziers were taken from the sons of Pharaoh. Only his own children possessed sufficient magical powers to represent their father. In the Fourth Dynasty the circle from which they were recruited was enlarged, but still restricted to blood relations of the king. That may be the reason why the famous Imhotep, the builder of the Step Pyramid at Saqqara, never became a vizier: he was merely a commoner.

The power concentrated in the hands of these early viziers such as Hemiunu (see p. 151) was considerable. He was head of the entire administration of the state; responsible for the building works on temples and the royal funerary complex, for which he had the authority to call up *corvée* workers throughout the country. He was director of the state finances; organizer of expeditions into the deserts and to foreign countries; in fact, only the supervision over the temples and over military affairs remained exclusively in the hands of Pharaoh himself.

Fig. 103 Limestone statue of the elderly Vizier Hemiunu. From the mastaba of Hemiunu at Giza, Fourth Dynasty

That he was such a heavy-weight in the state is reflected by Hemiunu's lifesize seated statue which was found in his tomb in the Western Field of Giza, and is now in Hildesheim (fig. 103). The tomb itself is one of the largest in this area (*circa* 53 by 27 metres), which is in accordance with Hemiunu's position. The limestone statue was discovered by Junker in 1912 in a small, closed room, a so-called *serdab* (Arabic for "cellar"), behind one of the false doors. Tomb robbers had entered it in antiquity and broken off the head, which was found almost intact at its feet; only a small fragment was lost and had to be restored. The eyes, however, made of crystal and affixed with gold, had been wantonly smashed from their settings.

When found the statue still presented traces of its original colouring: black hair and a red-brown body. It shows an aristocratic type of man, in what was then a novel attitude: both hands on the legs, in contrast to the preceding style in which the subject held one hand before his breast. The corpulent body, indubitably a realistic trait, denoted the elderly administrator. In its monumental pose it can certainly claim to be one of the masterpieces of Old Kingdom art. Standing before it in the Pelizaeus Museum, one can easily conjure up the power and authority of this aged statesman.

What we know about our second subject, Uni, is of a totally different nature. Certainly, he too became an elder statesman, for he served under three Sixth Dynasty Pharaohs: Teti, Pepi I, and Merenre. That means that he must have lived for over sixty years at the most conservative estimate. His fame in Egyptology he acquired by his autobiography, inscribed on the wall of his tomb-chapel at Abydos (now in the Cairo Museum), where it was discovered by Auguste Mariette, then Director of Egyptian Monuments, in 1860. The text is of a highly literary character, with rhythmic and poetic features, and contains reminiscences of the famous Pyramid Texts. Sentences of it were copied in a composition on a statue from the Twenty-Sixth Dynasty, demonstrating that the Egyptians themselves recognized its literary calibre. Yet, it certainly relates real history.

Uni, who is actually called in several texts Uni-the-Elder, probably because he had a son of the same name, enjoyed an exceptional career. He started in the palace administration, where he quickly gained the confidence of the king. He requested and acquired permission to bring from the Tura quarries, some kilometres South of Cairo, a white limestone sarcophagus and a false-door with its lintel, two door-jambs, and a libation-table, to be placed in his mastaba. The sarcophagus is now lost, but the false-door was found in the tomb and is also now in the Cairo Museum.

A decisive moment in Uni's career came when a plot was discovered in the harim in which the Royal Consort was involved. It was Uni who, on order of the Pharaoh, alone acted as judge, without any colleague, even the vizier, although it was with a high juridical executive that the official report was drawn up. That Uni was allowed to hear the secrets of the harim was a clear proof of trust and appreciation on the part of the king.

Then, he was placed at the head of a large army, assembled from all over Egypt, and which included Nubian mercenaries. At that time Egypt did not possess a standing army nor a professional officer corps; local administrators (the nomarchs) commanded the contingents of their districts, while Uni, although certainly no military man, devised the plans and supervised the organization.

The action culminated in the defeat of the "Sand-dwellers", as the inhabitants of Syro-Palestine are here called. Although it literally indicates Bedouin, it is used in this text in a wider sense. A hymn in the autobiography describes the victorious return of the troops:

> This army returned in peace,
>> after having razed the land of the Sand-dwellers.
> This army returned in peace,
>> after having ravaged the land of the Sand-dwellers.
> This army returned in peace,
>> after having attacked its strongholds.
> This army returned in peace,
>> after having cut down its figs and vines. ......

Notwithstanding the triumph, Uni had to be sent five times, since the unruly Sand-dwellers revolted time and time again. Once he employed a conspicuous ruse. He transported half his troops by ship along the Mediterranean coast, landing them behind the enemy lines, while the remainder of the army proceeded over the road. So encircling his opponents, he crushed them and killed them all.

Rising yet higher in the administration, Uni was appointed to the position of governor of all Upper Egypt, from somewhat South of Memphis to the border at Elephantine. He was sent to Nubia to fetch a sarcophagus for Pharaoh Merenre and a pyramidion for his pyramid. The sarcophagus, a grey diorite monolith, has indeed been found in the tomb of this king at Saqqara South. On another occasion Uni journeyed to Elephantine for a granite false-door, a libation-stone, lintels, and other elements of Merenre's pyramid. Yet another expedition went to Hatnub, to fetch a great altar of travertine ('Egyptian alabaster'). For its transport, he had built a barge of acacia wood, and he succeeded in delivering the altar in a record seventeen days, despite the fact, as he tells us, that it was summer and there was no water on the sandbanks.

So Uni received one charge after another, performing each and every one in an exemplary fashion. Clearly, we see in Uni one of the most successful aged administrators of the Old Kingdom.

Our third man, Rediu-Khnum of the Eleventh Dynasty, occupied a more modest position, although the tone of his autobiography would perhaps suggest otherwise. The text is written on a large rectangular stela, 152 by 62 centimetres, originally erected in his tomb at Dendera, and now in the Cairo Museum. At the bottom Rediu-Khnum himself is depicted, seated before a huge amount of offerings, with his pet dog under his seat and the small figure of the butler under the food.

All this is not exceptional, and neither is the text of twenty-three lines, although it differs completely from the factual, well-worded biography of Uni.

Beginning with the traditional offering formula, Redi-Khnum continues with a string of high-flown epithets in which he describes himself as, for example:

> ...... efficient in performance at every task,
> dignified, open-handed, pleasant mannered,
> white-robed, handsome, godly to behold ......

Such phrases do not really tell us anything about the man himself. As in most autobiographies of the Middle Kingdom, the text is more naive than we can appreciate. Confined within the funerary context – the stela stood in a tomb – it uses shameless *clichés*, stressing the code of moral behaviour instead of describing an individual life.

Yet, within this context, we can elicit some hard facts. Redi-Khnum states that he was:

> His lady's confidant whom she favours,
> whom she placed in the great estate ......
> I have spent a long time of years under my mistress,
> the Royal Ornament Nefrukayet ......
> foremost noblewoman of this land,
> foremost nobility of Upper Egypt,
> being a king's daughter and a king's beloved wife,
> and having inherited from all her mothers.

Who was this royal lady whom Redi-Khnum served? Very probably she is to be identified as the wife of Wahankh Antef II and the mother of Antef III, both rulers of the Eleventh Dynasty. In other texts she is referred to by the abbreviation Nefru. That she was a mighty personality in those days appears evident from the following lines:

> She resettled Upper Egypt, the van of men,
> from Elephantine to the Antaiopolite nome,
> (that is, the tenth Upper Egyptian nome),
> with women together with managers and officials
> from the entire land.

Rediu-Khnum passed "a long time, a span of many years" in the service of his mistress, so that it can be suggested that he was elderly when he erected the stela. Of course, he was "without there being any fault of mine, for my competence was great". In real life he was placed at the head of the Queen's estate at Dendera, a cattle farm she had inherited from her mother, and which Rediu-Khnum claims was "the greatest estate of Upper Egypt". Even if we take this with a pinch of salt, it is clear that Rediu-Khnum was a competent administrator in the period shortly before the reunification of the country under Montuhotep II Nebheptre (see pp. 212 and 246). It may be noted in passing that the plethora of modern studies on women in Ancient Egypt have as yet neglected the queen of this text, although she clearly seems worthy of some attention!

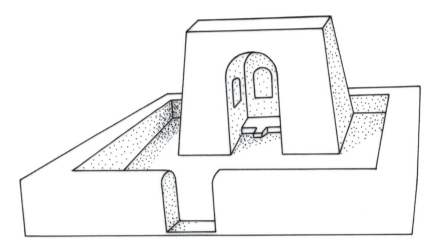

Fig. 104 Diagram of a reconstructed chapel. Abydos, Middle Kingdom

Rather more eminent than this local official is our next subject, who was called Ikhernofret. He was the owner of a chapel at Abydos in which not only the main stela which we will discuss was erected, but also, as was usual in Abydene tomb-chapels, the stelae of a number of his colleagues and subordinates. The chapel itself has long been destroyed, but we present here a possible reconstruction of such structures (fig. 104). Its elements have been dispersed over several Egyptological collections all over the world. That they originally belonged together is proved by the mention of Ikhernofret's name and titles on most of them. One even states explicitly that it was made for this particular tomb-chapel.

The stelae are mostly undated, but one of them is from year 1 of Amenemhat III, while the main one bears the names and titles of Sesostris III. Most revealing is a sentence at the bottom of a third one, now in Geneva, which states that the chamberlain Sisetyt, the son of the owner, went with Ikhernofret to the festival of Osiris, on order of Pharaoh Sesostris III, "when he threw down the vile Kush in regnal year 19". From other sources we know that Sesostris indeed campaigned that year in Nubia. So it is clear when the events described below exactly took place.

The round-topped limestone stela, measuring 100 by 65 centimetres and including a raised border, is now in Berlin (fig. 105). Since the text is one of the very few that informs us about the Osiris festival at Abydos, generally known as the Osiris mysteries, it has been the subject of several studies, although much still remains obscure. It begins with the king's command to the Overseer of the Treasury Ikhernofret – probably using the actual words of Pharaoh's letter – to go to Abydos

Fig. 105 Limestone stela of Ikhernofret framed by a raised border. From the tomb-chapel of Ikhernofret at Abydos, Twelfth Dynasty

and make monuments for Osiris Khentamenti (that is, "Foremost of the Westerners", the local name of this deity), and to adorn his sacred image with the fine gold which Sesostris had recently brought back from his victorious campaigns in Nubia.

The king gave this commission to Ikhernofret because, as the letter states, he trusted him, for he had grown up as a foster-son of the king. At twenty-six years old he had been made a "Companion", a favoured courtier in the inner circle. "Now" – that is, evidently years later, which implies that he was not young any more – he is sent to perform this significant task.

He served Osiris, in accordance with his Majesty's command, as a "beloved son", a function derived from the family cult in which the eldest son acted as priest for his deceased parent. He renewed the palanquin in which the god would be carried around during the procession, with gold, silver, lapis lazuli, bronze, and costly wood. He also embellished the cult statue and clothed it in its regalia, and rearranged the priestly service in the temple.

Thus for the first part of the text, which is followed by a report on the processions. Unfortunately, since we do not know what exactly happened and as the Egyptian words are not always clear, there needs remains a great deal of guesswork. First, as a prelude, there was a procession of Wepwawet ("Way-Opener"), a local jackal deity who was identified with Horus, for he is said "to rescue his father". It seems that a fight took place, either symbolic or actual, for Ikhernofret says: "I repulsed the attackers of the *neshmet*-barque (on which the Osiris statue was carried) and I felled the foes of Osiris". Evidently, the (deceased) god-king also took part in the ceremonial journey.

This was followed by the "Great Procession", which was actually the funeral cortège of the god. His boat is said to have sailed, but whether it indeed went over water is uncertain since the journey ended in Peqer, that is Umm el-Qa'ab (see p. 244), in the desert West of Abydos, and that could not be reached over water. Once again there is reference to a "great combat" in which all the enemies of Osiris fell. Then, what may be a rite connected with the burial and resurrection of the god is alluded to, but only vaguely since this was a secret mystery. At the end, the *neshmet*-barque was brought back, to the accompaniment of cheers, to "his palace". Ikhernofret followed the god to his house, that is, the Abydos Temple, where he came to rest.

This fascinating text has made Ikhernofret's name famous in the annals of Egyptology, even though we only partially understand what really occurred. Whatever he did in his function as Overseer of the Treasury – he does not tell us one thing about it – this particular commission was evidently the culmination point in the career of this aged administrator.

Proceeding to the Eighteenth Dynasty, we could mention a large number of elder statesmen, several of whom have already found a place in one of the preceding chapters. There are, for instance, Senenmut, the *éminence grise* of Hatshepsut (see p. 213), and Amenhotep, son of Hapu, the favourite of King Amenhotep III (see pp. 197 and p. 210), or also Amenemhat, the High Priest of Amun, who was the son of a simple artisan and remained an ordinary priest, until at the age of fifty-four he suddenly rose to this elevated position (see p. 210). Finally, there is Ay, the distinguished statesman of the Amarna Period, who ended up as Pharaoh after the untimely death of Tutankhamun (see p. 218). All these aged administrators are well-known, and sufficient has been said of them above and also in the literature in general.

Instead, we prefer to present here a less famous personality, namely the military officer Tjanuni. His Theban tomb (TT 74) is situated near the summit of the hill called Sheikh Abd el-Qurna. Its construction was begun under Amenhotep II, as some bricks and seals discovered here suggest, but the decoration of its walls dates, according to its style, from the reign of his son and successor Tuthmosis IV. As is usually the case with tombs from this period, it was never completed, only the entrance and the transversal hall having been painted.

Tjanuni was evidently of humble descent; his parents are nowhere mentioned. He may have owed his career in part to his wife Mutiri, a chantress of Thoth and, hence, probably from Hermopolis, who was a lady-in-waiting at the court. But Tjanuni himself was doubtless a competent administrator. Some information concerning his life is recorded on a stela in the tomb, which is, however, unfortunately rather lacunary.

He first followed Tuthmosis III on his campaigns into Syro-Palestine, from where, he states, "he brought back the princes of Djahi (Northern Palestine) as captives to Egypt, having conquered their towns and cut down their trees". Tjanuni continues: "It was I who recorded the victories which he (the king) made in all foreign counties – putting (it) in writing as it happened". That means that he was the author, or at least one of the authors, of the famous Annals of Tuthmosis III which are inscribed on the walls of the Karnak Temple.

Tjanuni carries on by stating that he "followed the Good God, the King of Upper and Lower Egypt, Aäkheperure (Amenhotep II)", whose confidant he claims to have been. That may not be a pure *cliché*. He records various court titles among his epithets, and seems in these years to have married his wife who belonged to the court, and in whose tomb-shaft in TT 74 wine-jars were found inscribed with the name of Amenhotep II.

Under the succeeding Pharaoh, Tuthmosis IV, Tjanuni is said to have "noted down for him numerous soldiers". Several wall scenes depict the manner in which he supervised the inscription of the troops and the registration of the recruits, "causing that everyone in the entire army knew his duties". Another scene portrays an even more extensive inspection, of "soldiers, priests, servants of the king, all artisans of the land in its entirety", as well as of cattle, poultry, and small cattle. This is a task which slightly exceeds what one would expect from a military officer.

From various titles in the tomb the rise of Tjanuni through the hierarchical system is clear, although we do not hear at what precise moment he was every time promoted. He started out as a simple scribe, later becoming a royal scribe, that is, a low-level administrator. He climbed up to the position of "scribe of the recruits", one of the higher ranks in the army. It was in this capacity that he supervised the inspections that are depicted. Under Tuthmosis IV he ended his career as a general. Then the king gave him "a fine old age" and finally made for him a burial appropriate to a man of his status.

That Tjanuni was old when he died is certain. The bringing in of the captives from Djahi mentioned above probably occurred in year 29 of Tuthmosis III, while he lived well into the reign of Tuthmosis IV. If he was approximately twenty years old when he started out, he must have been at least seventy by the end of his career, possibly even over eighty. A front-line soldier he never had been – he nowhere records deeds of gallantry – but an efficient executive he remained until the end, when, according to his autobiography, "he noted down for the king his numerous soldiers". So we should rightly reckon Tjanuni, despite his military career, among the ranks of the aged administrators.

From the Nineteenth Dynasty we will first discuss the Viceroy of Kush (Nubia) called Setau. Although we do not know exactly how old he became, it is likely, in view of the large number of his monuments and their wide geographical distribution, that he lived into ripe old age. The earliest date that we have for him is year 38 of Ramesses II, which occurs on stelae from Wadi es-Sebua and Abu Simbel. The autobiographical text which he placed on another stela at Wadi es-Sebua is dated to year 44. Since on the earlier ones he is already recorded as viceroy, one of the top positions in the state, he was certainly not young any more. So he must have been of approximately the same age as his king's reign.

One higher date that is attested for him occurs on a rock stela erected on the East Bank at Tonqala, North of Qasr Ibrim. Unfortunately, this date is badly damaged. Originally it was read as "year 63", but it could equally well be 39, 47, or 55. Whatever, there is no reason to suppose that this was the last year of Setau. He probably remained in office into his fifties, if not into his sixties, and may well have lived somewhat longer.

Setau is perhaps the most prolific private builder of the New Kingdom, particularly in his province of Nubia which he, in the words of one scholar, "cluttered with monuments". He constructed two temples, at Wadi es-Sebua and Gerf Hussein, and restored two others, at Amada and Ellesiya. All these sites are situated in Lower Nubia, the hub of Egyptian territory South of Aswan. Setau also founded two private chapels in this region, at Faras and Qasr Ibrim, which were devoted to the worship of his sovereign. To these can be added numerous stelae, statues, and rock inscriptions, totalling in all at least seventy-seven monuments. Clearly, this implies a timespan of at least fifteen to twenty years for the tenure of his office as viceroy.

Yet, it is not only in Nubia that he left signs of his building activity. There are traces of a gateway that he erected at Memphis, and of a chapel, now lost, at Abydos. But the best known of his Egyptian monuments is another small chapel, measuring only 6 by 5 metres, which he constructed at el-Kab, out in the desert and well away from the town. It is known locally as el-Hammam, and was devoted to Thoth, Horus, and to Nekhbet, the vulture goddess of el-Kab. As was usual in that period, it also housed a cult statue of Ramesses II, Setau's master. There was a reason why he built a sanctuary at this site, which was situated outside his province –

only just outside, in fact, for in those days the first two nomes of Upper Egypt down to Hierakonpolis, directly opposite el-Kab, also fell under the jurisdiction of the viceroy. The explanation is that Setau's wife Nefertmut very probably originated from this town. At least she was a chantress of Nekhbet. Setau himself may have come from Thebes, where he was also buried. His tomb (TT 289) has not yet been published.

Setau tells us something about his career on one of the stelae he erected in the Temple of Wadi es-Sebua. He was educated at the court, and grew up in the palace. At a rather early age, perhaps in his twenties, he was already appointed chief of the vizier's secretariat, a post in which he looked after the divine offerings and the granaries of Amun, which belonged under the authority of the vizier. Then he was promoted to the function of Chief Steward of Amun which gave him independent power; in this position he also acted as Overseer of Amun's Treasury and Festival Leader of the god. It is from these years that a stela housed in the British Museum must date, for the title viceroy is there still absent.

The next step was his appointment as Viceroy of Kush and Superintendent of the Gold Lands. In this function he was not only responsible for law and order in the large tracts of land in the South under Egypt's dominion, but also particularly for the sending of tribute to the capital, above all gold, but also valuable commodities from Central Africa. In this capacity Setau mentions a military action in which he captured a local chief together with his entire family and dispatched them to Egypt. One of his officers records, on another stela at Wadi es-Sebua, that people from the "lands of Tjemhu", West of the Nile, who seem to have been Libyans, were transported to work on the construction of the temple.

As stated above, that is the activity for which Setau is best known, in particular the building of the temple at Wadi es-Sebua and later that of Gerf Hussein. Both are of a hemispeos type, that is, partly cut into the rock. The former was dedicated to Re-Harakhte, and was embellished with a parallel row of lion-headed sphinxes along the middle passage, which occasioned its name (es-Sebua = "the lions"). The Gerf Hussein sanctuary was dedicated to Ptah and to Ramesses II himself. In contrast to the former it was poorly constructed and is now submerged under the waters of Lake Nasser, whereas the other temple has been moved and rebuilt on a spot two kilometres North of its original site.

Probably Setau resided as viceroy in Buhen, as opposed to the traditional capital of the province at Aniba, for in Buhen a large number of his monuments have been discovered: a statue and fragments of several stelae. One better preserved stela, now in the British Museum, shows Setau kneeling before the goddess Renenutet, represented as a cobra. As the deity of fertility she symbolizes the produce of Nubia which Setau sent to Egypt. For, whatever his prolific building activities, this was the main duty of a viceroy.

Fig. 106 Khaemwaset: (a) upper part of a yellow limestone statuette ?of this prince. Unprovenanced, Nineteenth Dynasty; (b) black steatite headless shabti. ?From the tomb of Khaemwaset at Saqqara, Nineteenth Dynasty

A contemporary of Setau was Prince Khaemwaset, the fourth son of Ramesses II. He must have been born in about the same year as the Viceroy, at the very beginning of his father's reign, as the third child of Isinofre, the king's second official consort (see p. 251). His eldest half-brother was the crown-prince Amenhikopshef, and Khaemwaset also had a full brother Ramesses and a sister Bentanat. The third son, born from the king's first wife Nefertari, had died young, but Amenhikopshef remained for a considerable time, until about regnal year 40, the heir apparent to the throne. When he died, he was succeeded by Prince Ramesses, until at least year 52, and then Khaemwaset became crown-prince. The situation lasted only a few years, since in year 55 or soon afterwards he too died, to be succeeded by the thirteenth son Merenptah, also a child of Isinofre, who would eventually become king. The other, older brothers were not considered eligible for this position because their mothers were of lower rank.

Khaemwaset may have been the crown-prince only a few years, but he was certainly for a long time one of the leading authorities in the state. His main function was that of High Priest of Ptah at Memphis. This was to him not a sinecure, as it could so easily have been for a son of the Pharaoh, but a position that he really held, from about his twenty-fifth year onwards. A military man like his elder brothers he seems never to have been, but as High Priest of Ptah he represented his father in the area, particularly when the ageing monarch became less active (see p. 252).

Khaemwaset was actually called on his monuments *sem* and "Great Chief of the Artisans", two titles of the High Priest. The latter indicates that he directed the so-called "gold-house", the workshop where the statues of valuable materials were made. In the representations he is usually shown with the youth-lock, the braided plait at one side of the head (fig. 106a), and clad in a leopard skin. This is the ancestral dress for a prince when he fulfils the duty of "opening the mouth" for his father's mummy. In that capacity he was called *sem*, and from the old ritual both the garment and the title of the Ptah-priest were derived.

Prince Khaemwaset is primarily known for three reasons. Firstly, he announced the first five *sed*-festivals of his father, for which he travelled through Upper Egypt (see p. 252). Very probably he also played a prominent rôle in the ceremonies themselves. Then, he rebuilt the Ptah Temple at Memphis, and erected a temple for the Apis bulls at the Serapeum at Saqqara. He also placed colossi of Ramesses II in front of the former. One of these was standing in Ramses Square in Cairo, in front of the main railway station, while another is still lying, in a special building, close to its original site. On the former he is depicted in relief near the legs, his sister Bentanat being shown at the other side.

At the Serapeum he buried, as was the duty of the High Priest of Ptah, the Apis bulls. The first one, which died in year 30, was the last bull to receive its own isolated tomb. Then Khaemwaset constructed for the succeeding sacred animals what are known as the Lesser Vaults – the large galleries that can at present be visited date from the Twenty-Second Dynasty. In the smaller galleries remains which are supposed to belong to his own tomb have been discovered (fig. 106b), so that we may conclude that the prince was buried in the vicinity.

Elsewhere Khaemwaset also placed statues in the temples. A famous example is that in breccia from Abydos, which shows him standing with sacred staffs in both arms, that on the left side surmounted by the enigmatic symbol of Abydos. This sculpture is now one of the treasures of the British Museum.

Finally, Khaemwaset is also famous because he was a scholar, the earliest archaeologist whom we know of. He was interested in the builders of the many pyramids and tombs at Giza and Saqqara, and left on them inscriptions stating that he had restored them. This will not mean more than that he made minor restorations, but the main purpose was to keep the ancient names alive.

A striking proof of this facet of his personality was discovered at Memphis. It is a fragmentary statue of Kawab, the eldest son of Pharaoh Khufu (see p. 153), which bears an inscription from the Nineteenth Dynasty. This relates how it was found by Khaemwaset in Kawab's tomb at Giza, evidently still intact, and brought to the Ptah Temple. Possibly it was not the only one.

From such scientific activities Khaemwaset received his later fame as a magician, in which capacity he is the leading character in the Demotic *Story of Setne*. The events told here bear little relation to the historical High Priest, but that the latter was one of the great administrators of his time is certain.

Let us now descend from the lofty realms of a Prince and a Viceroy to look at an executive in the community of workmen at Deir el-Medina (see p. 145 and *passim*). He was called Qenhikhopshef, and his title was "scribe (that is, administrator) of the necropolis". In that capacity he supervised the delivery of provisions to the men and their families as well as the work in the Royal Tomb itself.

Qenhikhopshef occurs for the first time in an ostracon from year 40 of Ramesses II, but he could have been appointed a decade earlier. His appalling handwriting is very conspicuous and as such can be easily recognized. Its characteristics can be seen in another ostracon dated to year 31, so that he may well have functioned from approximately year 30. He remained in office until year 6 of Seti II, sixty years later. If he was about twenty when he was nominated, he was therefore approximately eighty years old when he died.

He was the son of a workman, but in his youth he was adopted by a childless couple, the necropolis scribe Ramose and his wife (see p. 222). On the pass above the Valley of the Kings, along a path from Deir el-Medina to the Royal Tombs, a group of stone huts can still be seen in which the workmen passed the night. The most spacious of these belonged to Qenhikhopshef. On a stone seat discovered there a mention occurs of the scribe Ramose, followed by the words: "his son, who makes his name alive, the scribe Qenhikhopshef". Clearly, the latter honoured the name of his adoptive father in later years.

In other respects he seems not to have been such a decent person. In the papyrus in which the crimes of Paneb are enumerated (see p. 222) there is a record that this chief workman bribed him, and in an ostracon formerly in the Gardiner collection and now in the Ashmolean Museum, we read that the workman Rahotep shaved Qenhikhophef's hair, "and gave him 15 cubits of cloth and 9 fathoms of yarn, after he had concealed his (Rahotep's) crimes". Bribery was certainly not considered a serious offence in those days, but our scribe seems rather to have overdone it.

Ramose, his adoptive parent, was obviously comfortably off: he built no less than three tombs at Deir el-Medina (TT 7, 212, and 250), and he erected several stelae and statues. This wealth Qenhikhopshef will have inherited, and he seems to have invested part of it in a library, some of the papyri of which were still in the possession of future generations of the family.

One of these papyri bears three different texts. When he acquired it, the document was covered on the recto by a "Dream-Book", a list of subjects that can appear in dreams, each accompanied by a statement concerning its quality (good or bad) and an interpretation. A few examples will suffice to make clear what is meant by this:

towing a boat:	good; his landing happily at home.
threshing grain upon the threshing floor:	good; the giving of life to him in his house.

or:

looking into a deep well:	bad; his being put in prison.
removing the nails of his fingers:	bad; removal of the work of his hands.

These examples are more or less rational, but others remain mysterious:

the gods making tears cease for him:	bad; it means fighting.
eating hot meat:	bad; it means his not being found innocent.

The second text, which Qenhikhopshef himself wrote on the blank verso of this papyrus, is a copy of a poem on the Battle of Qadesh, which he could find inscribed on the walls of several temples in the neighbourhood. He must have noted it down many years after the event, in the time of Merenptah. This text is proof of his great interest in history, which is also aptly demonstrated by an ostracon containing the names of twelve Pharaohs of the Eighteenth and Nineteenth Dynasties, with on the other side those of Montuhotep II Nebhepetre and Horemhab. The execrable handwriting is again unmistakably that of our scribe. Similar lists of royal names occur on his offering table in Marseilles, and on another papyrus which bears a ritual of Amenhotep I, who as patron of Deir el-Medina had a chapel in the vicinity.

The third text of the Dream-Book papyrus is a letter written by Qenhikhopshef to the Vizier of Merenptah, Panehsy, concerning the affairs of the workmen's community. Other such letters, of an earlier date, are known from ostraca. They are either drafts or copies, for the originals were of course sent away. They prove that the sender, although merely a local administrator, stayed in close contact with one of the heads of government. The reason is that the vizier had responsibility for the supervision of Pharaoh's tomb and of its workmen; he was Qenhikhopshef's immediate boss.

From our scribe's hand is also a prophylactic charm on a sheet of papyrus, now in the British Museum. The spell is directed against a demon called Sehaqeq who appears to be threatening him. Qenhikhopshef identifies himself with an obscure deity in an attempt to ward off the evil power. He indicates that the incantation should be recited over a stem of flax, which would then be used as an arrow, the sheet of papyrus being folded and attached to it.

*Fig. 107 Limestone headrest decorated with fabulous creatures. From the tomb of
Qenhikhopshef at Deir el-Medina, Nineteenth Dynasty*

To the same magical sphere belongs an elaborate limestone headrest which once formed part of the funeral equipment of Qenhikhopshef's tomb (fig. 107). The burial place itself, certainly somewhere in the Valley of Deir el-Medina, has long been destroyed, but some elements from it survive. The headrest, which is less than ten centimetres in height, is on one side decorated with Bes figures. The other side, illustrated here, shows left a griffin with a lotus flower on its head, and right a lioness devouring a snake. Both creatures are armed with knives. They are reminiscent of the designs on ivory apotropaeic wands that play a rôle in pregnancy magic. An inscription on the headrest, now partly illegible, contains the words "good sleeping in the West, the Land of Righteousness" and the name of the owner, which shows that the object was not used in daily life.

Whether Qenhikhopshef married in his youth we do not know. He nowhere mentions the name of a wife or a child. In his old age, however, he found happiness with a very young bride, barely old enough to be his granddaughter. She was called Naunakhte (see p. 229). Soon she would become a widow, inheriting part of his property, including his beloved library. Clearly she was fond of the old man, for when she remarried she named her first son after him.

So we can see that Qenhikhopshef was a distinct personality with varying traits: prone to be seduced by bribery, believing in magical forces, but also devoted to the child-wife of his latter days. We can best picture him as an old man sitting on his seat cut out of the rock above the tomb of Merenptah, from where he could supervise the activities of his workmen. An inscription there perpetuates his name and titles. Sadly, however, the seat is in recent years no longer visible, being covered by an extensive mound of rubble. Nevertheless, the picture can live on in the imagination.

Finally, we present a long-lived celebrity who flourished at the end of Egypt's independent rule. This is Udjahorresnet ("Horus of Resnet is prosperous", Resnet being a chapel in the Temple of Neith at Sais), who became chief physician under the first Persian rulers of the so-called Twenty-Seventh Dynasty. Most of what we know about him derives from his green basalt, naophorous statue that originally stood in Sais and is now in the Vatican Museum (fig. 108). It is almost completely covered in texts, and dates from the very beginning of the reign of King Darius, *circa* 520 B.C.

Udjahorresnet began his career, according to his biographical account, under Pharaoh Amasis, the last great ruler of the Twenty-Sixth Dynasty. He then occupied the position of Commander of the Fleet. Hence, he will already have been 'middle-aged'; what he did earlier he does not tell us. His father, Peftuaneith, was a priest of Neith at Sais, and in view of the later career of Udjahorresnet it is evident that he received a scholarly and priestly education. Yet, he may have been from a family with a military tradition, the combination not being exceptional in those days.

Udjahorresnet remained a fleet commander during the short reign of Psammetichus III. Then, in 525 B.C., the Persians conquered Egypt. The biography laconically states that: "The Great King of all foreign lands, Cambyses, came to Egypt". Not a word is uttered concerning any defence against the invaders, as one would expect from an admiral, nor about the misery that is wont to accompany such a conquest. In two separate, short inscriptions on the statue, however, in which the author sets forth how admirably he cared for the people in his city as well as for his own family, he speaks of the days "when the cataclysm befell his nome (of Sais), in the midst of the very great cataclysm which happened in the entire land". This certainly refers to the events which are suppressed in the main story.

That text deals predominantly with the period of Persian rule. First we are told that Cambyses appointed our former military officer to be his chief physician, and induced him to live at the court as a Companion and Director of the Palace. As the king's favourite he made himself useful by composing Cambyses' Egyptian royal titulary and names.

Fig. 108 Green basalt naophorous statue of Udjahorresnet. H. 69 cm. Head and hands modern. From Sais, Twenty-Seventh Dynasty

271

All this may surprise us. The Greek "Father of History" Herodotus, writing in *circa* 450 B.C., and following him other classical authors, tell us that Cambyses behaved in Egypt as a monster of depravity. This culminated in his slaughter of the sacred Apis bull. That story dates, however, from later years when, after a short period of freedom, the Egyptians were again shackled under an alien yoke. Also we must ask the question as to whether it was Cambyses' action against the revenues of the temples which had stirred up such bitter feelings in priestly circles. From Udjahorresnet's record we gain the impression of an attempt by Cambyses to reconcile the Egyptians to his régime, by assimilating his activities to the traditional model of Egyptian kingship. That appears evident from what follows. Hence, Udjahorresnet was not the collaborator he has sometimes been accused of being, an abject Quisling who betrayed his own people, but rather a wise statesman who fully supported his sovereign in his policy of reconciliation.

He told the king, he relates on his statue, about the greatness of Sais and the Temple of Neith and pleaded with him to remove the foreigners who had settled in the complex. Indeed, the alien ruler commanded that they be expelled and, after their houses had been demolished and their belongings carried off, the temple was cleansed. The divine offerings were restored, festivals and processions again installed, and the priesthood reorganized. All this took place under Udjahorresnet's supervision, as he records in another text on the statue. Then he entreated Cambyses to come himself to Sais, as a final act of reconciliation. This the Persian did, prostrating himself before Neith, and offering to her, as well as venerating the other deities in the temple, particularly the local form of Osiris.

The biography then jumps to the reign of the next Persian ruler Darius. It appears that Udjahorresnet had gone to Persia, presumably as a doctor; whether he did this voluntarily or not in unclear. Darius now ordered him to return to Egypt, to restore the office of the House of Life at Sais. This is the scriptorium in which the sacred books were copied and studied, and where new ones were composed. Some of them deal not with religious matters but with what we would call science: astronomy, medicine, and so on. The study had its practical implications, for one of Darius' reasons for the restoration was that "he knew the usefulness of this craft for causing the sick to live and in order to cause to endure the names of all the gods, their temples, their offerings, and the conduct of their festivals for ever". Our physician was enabled to provide the renewed institution with students "who were the sons of well-born men, no low-born among them, and he placed scholars in charge of them to teach them".

So much for this statue. We possess some further evidence concerning Udjahorresnet, but it is all rather vague. In the early Nineteenth Century A.D., one of Jean-François Champollion's travelling companions, Ippolito Rosellini, glimpsed a statue somewhere in Cairo. He copied parts of its inscriptions, only being interested in those in which a cartouche occurred. It seems to have been a sculpture much alike that in the Vatican, of a similar size and relating the same facts. At least, the self-same kings and identical phrases were recorded on it. Unfortunately, no trace of it has ever subsequently been discovered.

In 1956 there came to light at Memphis the torso of a statue bearing a most interesting text. It was made 177 years after the death of Udjahorresnet, when a statue of him had been found decaying. Therefore, this new one was fashioned. This teaches us that Udjahorresnet was a celebrated character long after his death.

In the late 1980's, the Czech expedition excavating at Abusir located a tomb which turned out to belong to our physician. It was built at a lonely spot in the desert, at some distance South of the Abusir pyramids; later on it attracted other burials in the area. The discovery contained a riddle, for it appears that the inner sarcophagus, although it was sealed, had never been used for the mummy.

We must now leave the reader of this long chapter with the enigma that, as with so much funerary archaeology, we are, until now, not much wiser about Udjahorresnet himself, who was doubtless one of the last great aged administrators of Egyptian history.

POSTSCRIPT
A Centenarian Egyptologist

In A.D. 1963 an Egyptologist was to beat the record of Ramesses II and equal the alleged age of Pepi II by reaching a century. Dr (Miss) Margaret Murray (1863-1963) is the only professional Egyptologist to have done so, although it is a discipline which clearly attracts longevity as women such as Gertrude Caton-Thompson and Elizabeth Riefstahl have lived into their late nineties. In order to add one man, mention can be made of the American archaeologist Dows Dunham who died at the age of ninety-three.

In 1959 Margaret Murray had the unnerving experience of reading that she was dead! She at once wrote a witty and well-formulated rejoinder to the national newspaper in question, and the faded yellow clipping still survives in her personal file in the archives of the Petrie Museum. Printed under the heading "Very Much Alive", it deserves to be quoted in full:

> Sir – Miss Stevie Smith in her review headed 'In Defence of Witches' (February 15), refers to 'the late Dr. Margaret Murray'. I was not aware till then that I was dead. Perhaps she or some of your readers can inform me when and where I died, for the event appears to have slipped from my memory.

The comment of the abashed editor appears below: "Miss Stevie Smith asks us to add her apologies to our own".

Here is not the place to discuss Margaret Murray's long career, information on which can be found in the literature cited in the bibliography at the end of this book. Instead our concentration will be on her activities as a nonagenarian. However, this may be a suitable point to quote verbatim the resolution passed by the Professorial Board at University College London (UCL) on the 11th June 1963, to record its thanks and appreciation to Margaret Murray, as this gives an excellent summary of her achievements:

> That on the occasion of Dr. Margaret Murray's 100th birthday, they wish to place on record their deep appreciation of the high honour which, through her renowned scholarship, she has brought to University College London, where she taught for so many years. Trained in her early Egyptological study by Sir Flinders Petrie, Dr. Murray became his 'right hand', and in relieving him of a great part of his teaching work in the College, she made possible the vast output of his work in the field; Sir Flinders Petrie was always first in acknowledging his debt to her. And there were others: scholars of international repute such as Wainwright, Brunton, Engelbach,

Starkey, Lankester Harding and Faulkner, who owed their early training at the College to Dr. Murray.

In her own research, she was just as successful as in her teaching. Books and articles, both scientific and popular, have come from her pen, not only on Egyptology, but in many other fields, such as her latest book, *The Genesis of Religion*, published in this year, the hundredth of her long life. In addition to this, Dr. Murray's excavations at the Osireion at Abydos, and her epigraphic work in the necropolis at Sakkara are recognized as monumental contributions to Egyptological research.

The Professorial Board desires to express to Dr. Murray its thanks for all she has done for the College, not only during the long period of her service on its academic staff but also for her valuable association with its Department of Egyptology, in which her interest still continues long after her official retirement.

An illuminator was commissioned to prepare this resolution for presentation to Dr. Murray at her hundredth birthday celebration luncheon held at UCL on the 15th July 1963 (see fig. 111). Elegantly inscribed on vellum, in black, red, blue, and burnished gold, the citation now resides in the College Library.

As indicated in the resolution, Margaret Murray was still busily writing in her hundredth year. In fact, despite being badly crippled by arthritis, two books were published in 1963, the second of which was her autobiography *My First Hundred Years* (first announced under the original title *A Century in View*). One wonders if there have been any other centenarians with such a prolific output?

Indeed, following her official retirement from UCL in 1935 at the age of seventy-two, she had refused to "go to that uncomfortable and flat resting place" – the shelf – and had set out to actively pursue her literary career. She then published six more books, including *The Splendour of Egypt*, a permanent bestseller which appeared on her eighty-sixth birthday – "A fact of which I think I may be proud".

Her enormous output in the fields of both Egyptology and folklore amounted to getting on for a hundred and fifty books and articles. She herself kept no record of her published works for, when one was finished, she at once proceeded with the next. Not surprisingly, this caused considerable difficulties to her 1961 bibliographer, who could by no means be certain that he had managed to track down all her articles, and wisely decided to omit her reviews as being too difficult to trace.

When she was ninety-seven Margaret Murray had written an article for the prestigious archaeological periodical *Antiquity* entitled "First Steps in Archaeology". In his editorial of this issue Dr. Glyn Daniel stated that they had "immediately commissioned her to write another article for the June 1963 number of *Antiquity*". "Centenary" was duly delivered without any further reminder or urging, to the delight of the editor who could only lament: "If only our younger contributors would be so faithful and forthcoming!"

Margaret Murray was always poor. Until 1922 her salary was only £200 per annum, and despite bearing the brunt of the teaching load in Petrie's absence, she had been forced to undertake much outside lecturing in order to literally double her income. In 1931 her devoted students had clubbed together to pay for her gown when she was awarded her honorary doctorate (fig. 109). Naturally, she then retired on an inadequate pension which compelled her to continue to conduct numerous evening classes well into her eighties. Many of her pupils were themselves elderly ladies; she was once asked why she spent so much time with such students. She had so much to do in terms of research and publishing, whereas they, by contrast, were never going to be Egyptologists and were not even particularly interested. The witty retort was: "Ah, my dear, the important thing is: when I've got them here, they can't get into mischief".

Fig. 109 Margaret Murray, aged sixty-eight, wearing her doctoral robes of 1931

Her encouragement of all pupils, even the miscellaneous crowd of women of a certain age, was noteworthy, as was her endless patience. Countless generations of students remember the very welcoming and friendly atmosphere of one or other of her London 'bed-sits', where they would gather cosily around the fire and listen to her entertaining stories of witchcraft or excavations. For over sixty years she was, as she termed it, a "paying-guest" in one of such establishments in the environs of UCL. In 1960, aged ninety-seven she had to vacate the house in 16 Endsleigh Street where she had resided since the forties and find somewhere else to live for six months. She fully admitted that this was not easy as people did not want the responsibility of a person of her age.

Fig. 110 Margaret Murray, aged ninety-seven, on the steps of the portico at University College London, 1960

Margaret Murray loved children. In her late eighties she became a great favourite with the son of one of her *protégés*, who regarded her as an extra grandmother. She would give him little trinkets – bits of lapis lazuli, a Roman lamp, some beads from Egypt – and each time tell him a little about them. He in turn would put them religiously in his treasure box.

She remained an unforgettable figure to those who were at the College in the 1950's and early 1960's (fig. 110). Many people remember to this day the picture of the tiny four foot ten (*circa.* 1.47 metres) frame of this former suffragette alongside the towering six foot two (almost 1.90 metres) figure of Professor W.B. Emery, who was at that time the incumbent of the Edwards Chair of Egyptology. The stories surrounding her at this time are legendary; two will have to suffice here.

Professor Emery visited her in University College Hospital after an emergency appendicitis operation performed when she was in her nineties. He found her ensconced in her own private room, already sitting up in bed and typing furiously. That morning, she informed him, the French police had visited her, seeking her advice on a case of witchcraft in their country. Indeed, she had become a celebrated, albeit highly controversial authority on the subject, her *The Witch-Cult in Western Europe* (1921) being described as "revolutionary" and "epoch-making".

The second anecdote concerns another visit to her by Emery, accompanied by his secretary, which took place in May 1962 when she was nearly ninety-nine. Just as they were leaving she remarked: "You know I've got an incurable disease?" Thinking that something very serious had developed, they were understandably relieved when she continued: "Yes, old age".

Whatever, Margaret Murray's mind continued to remain as clear and active as ever throughout her nineties. At all times she took a lively interest in College affairs in general and of the Egyptology Department in particular. Until the age of ninety-four when the many stairs began to defeat her, she appeared regularly in the Department, occasionally invading a language class, and invariably wanting to see a particular object in the museum.

The Petrie Museum archives contain a series of letters from the 1960's exchanged between Margaret Murray and Professor Emery, or, in his absence on excavation, his secretary Miss Cynthia Cox. They show her delight in her particular fields of research to be undimmed, and as such it is a joy which is infectious as one shares her excited zest for discovery. She is mainly writing about her "bit of research on the Hierakonpolis finds, with what are, to me, surprising results". (She regarded this excavation as one of the three to have revolutionized Egyptology at the turn of the century). In one letter she tells Emery: "I have now identified the serpopard, and am on the trail of the seraph (the hawk-headed winged leopard)".

At the end of 1961 she was admitted to the Queen Victoria Hospital at Welwyn in Hertfordshire, following an acute attack of arthritis. She was to stay here for the remainder of her life. In 1962 she writes to Emery: "I do appreciate the feeling that I can keep in touch with Egyptologists and know the advances that are being made, and I hope that before long I also may make a small contribution, and be again one of the splendid band of researchers. I wish for all of you good luck in your research and the fun of 'finding out'".

Her final two letters, dating from February and September 1963, show her dream to have come true. Her characteristic large, round hand has now sadly deteriorated to a shaky scrawl, but she is still desperate for information. The last letter is indeed remarkable and deserves to be quoted in full:

> Dear Professor Emery,
> I am writing to ask some help on my Hierakonpolis work. It is about the temple. Is the revetment of any real importance for the early buildings, and are there any buildings, except the Painted Tomb, of the date of Scorpion? What date is the revetment that bulks so largely in Green's plans and letterpress?
> Also, would you agree that Aha as Menes is a combination of Scorpion and Narmer? ... (The next sentence is illegible) ... Also there are I think three *serekhs*, each of which has a large hieroglyph associated with it. All these might well be titles of the <u>functions</u> of different important offices held by one man. I claim these three *serekhs* all belong to one man, Mena-Nar, the Founder of the 'United Kingdom'.
> There are other bits of evidence to support this theory which you have already suggested for Mena-Aha, but not I think with sufficiently strong evidence. I therefore want to give the credit of the suggestion to the right quarter.

Emery's long handwritten draft reply is appended. He tells her of an Archaic inscription of a scorpion noted in Nubia during his last campaign. "During the coming season I intend to make tracings and rubbings and I think we will find something very interesting indeed. I will keep you informed. Definite evidence of Scorpion in Nubia would indeed be a sensation". Alas, Margaret Murray would never know the outcome, as she died two months after this letter was written.

One further missive is found among the series. Dated to January 1962 it is a reply to Cynthia Cox who had forwarded a letter from someone who "evidently wants to become an active member of a local coven". Margaret Murray replies in characteristic fashion. "What asses there are in the world! I have replied to that idiot, whose letter you forwarded, with a snorter!"

"We shall certainly run the flag to the top of the mast to mark what must be a unique occasion in the annals of the College". This took place on Monday 15th July 1963, two days after Margaret Murray's birthday, when the centenarian was brought by her doctor to UCL for the celebration buffet luncheon. Margaret Murray's preparations had involved a consultation with the Queen's hat designer, who had visited her at the Hospital with a selection from his range. She arrived for her party wearing a very fetching toque (fig. 111). Surrounded by thirty of her friends and pupils, she managed, despite her deafness and the confines of a wheelchair, to talk to many people, fully remembering everyone. At the appropriate moment the College Chef ceremoniously carried in the cake which had been designed by Margaret Drower, who was later to become Petrie's definitive biographer and is now a nonagenarian herself. Decorated in marzipan were her initials "M.A.M." together with the appropriate hieroglyphs for "life, prosperity, and health".

Fig. 111 Margaret Murray reading her citation at her hundredth birthday celebration at University College London, July 1963

After receiving her citation, the centenarian made a short speech of acknowledgement and departed from UCL for the last time. Despite her doctor Charles Dansie writing on the 19th July that "Dr. Murray has had a few quiet days and is now getting down to the second century in her usual fashion", this was not to be. Exactly four months after her birthday – on the 13th November 1963 – this indefatigable character, who still took the greatest interest in everything, finally died.

It will come as no surprise that Margaret Murray had left strict instructions as to the nature of her funeral. Throughout her life she had held an abiding horror of high churches. Her funeral therefore was to be "of the plainest kind, without any Romish or High Church extravagances. No wreaths or flowers to be given in remembrance of me". At the end of the service she requested "some <u>cheerful</u> hymn and a gay and lively recessional voluntary".

In her hundredth year Margaret Murray followed the discoveries of the space age with as much zest as she had given to the invention of the bicycle. As she herself said: "I have lived though one of the most momentous periods of that miracle of world-history, the advance of Man". Indeed, she had witnessed the growth of archaeology practically from its beginnings. When she was born in 1863 the acceptance of the antiquity of humankind and the publication of Darwin's *The Origin of Species* was only four years old.

The last tribute will be left to her physician quoted above who shortly before her death wrote: "To have known Dr. Murray is in itself the best reward for looking after her – she has added greatly to the fullness of our lives in the past two years".

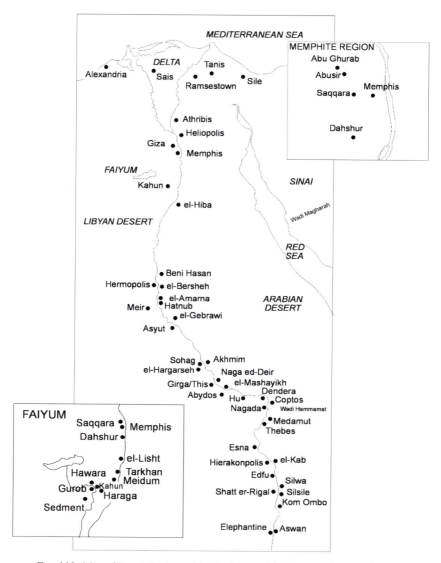

*Fig. 112 Map of Egypt, the Memphite Region and the Fayium, showing the sites
mentioned in the text and the captions*

Key to map of Thebes:

1. Valley of the Kings;
2. Deir el-Bahri;
3. Sheikh Abd el-Qurna;
4. Deir el-Medina;
5. Qurnet Murai;
6. Medinet Habu;
7. Malkata;
8. Colossi of Memmon;
9. Ramesseum;
10. Valley of the Queens.

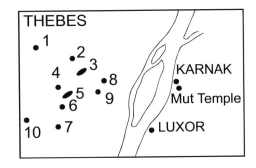

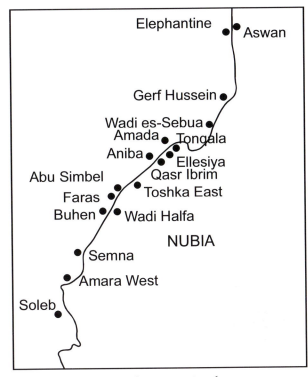

*Fig. 113 Detailed map of Thebes and Nubia, showing the sites mentioned
in the text and the captions*

283

List of Museums
(mostly mentioned in the text under toponyms)

Baltimore	:	Walters Art Gallery.
Berlin	:	Ägyptisches Museum und Papyrussammlung, Staatliche Museen zu Berlin.
Bologna	:	Museo Civico Archeologico.
Bolton	:	Bolton Museum and Art Gallery.
Boston	:	Museum of Fine Arts.
Brussels	:	Musées Royaux d'Art et d'Histoire.
Cairo	:	Egyptian Museum / Musée Egyptien.
Cambridge	:	Fitzwilliam Museum.
Chicago	:	Field Museum of Natural History.
	:	Oriental Institute Museum, University of Chicago.
Geneva	:	Musées d'Art et d'Histoire.
Glasgow	:	Hunterian Museum, University of Glasgow.
Hanover	:	Kestner Museum.
Hildesheim	:	Roemer- und Pelizaeus-Museum.
Kansas City	:	Nelson-Atkins Museum of Art.
Leiden	:	Rijksmuseum van Oudheden.
London	:	British Museum.
	:	Petrie Museum of Egyptian Archaeology, University College London.
Liverpool	:	University Archaeology Museum, School of Archaeology, University of Liverpool.
Luxor	:	Luxor Museum of Egyptian Art.
Manchester	:	Manchester Museum, University of Manchester.
Marseilles	:	Musée d'Archéologie Méditerranéenne.
Moscow	:	Pushkin State Museum of Fine Arts.
Munich	:	Staatliches Museum Ägyptischer Kunst.
New York	:	Metropolitan Museum of Art.
Oxford	:	Ashmolean Museum.
Paris	:	Musée du Louvre.
Philadelphia	:	University of Pennsylvania Museum of Archaeology and Anthropology.
Rome	:	Museo Gregoriano Egizio (Vatican).
Stockholm	:	Medelhavsmuseet.
Toulouse	:	Musée Georges Labit.
Tubingen	:	Ägyptische Sammlung der Universität Tübingen.
Turin	:	Museo Egizio.

Select Bibliography

I – GENERAL

Feucht, Erika, *Das Kind im Alten Ägypten. Die Stellung des Kindes in Familie und Gesellschaft nach altägyptischen Texten und Darstellungen,* Frankfurt/New York, 1995.

Review of this work by Janssen, Jac. J., *Journal of Egyptian Archaeology* 83 (1997), 228-231.

Helck, W. and Otto, E. (eds.), *Lexikon der Ägyptologie,* 6 vols., Wiesbaden, 1972-1986.

Janssen, Jac. J. and Janssen, Rosalind M., A Cylindrical Amulet Case: Recent Investigations, in: *Gegengabe.* Festschrift für Emma Brunner-Traut. Herausgegeben von Ingrid Gamer-Wallert und Wolfgang Helck, Tübingen, 1992, 157-165.

Lichtheim, Miriam, *Ancient Egyptian Literature,* 3 vols., Berkeley, 1973-1980.

Robins, Gay, *Women in Ancient Egypt,* London, 1993.

Robins, Gay, Women and Children in Peril. Pregnancy, Birth and Infant Mortality in Ancient Egypt, *KMT* 5 (4) Winter 1994-95, 24-35.

Théodoridès, Aristide, L'enfant dans les institutions pharaoniques, in: *L'Enfant dans les civilisations orientales. Het Kind in de oosterse beschavingen.* Onder leiding van/sous la direction de A. Théodoridès, P. Naster, J. Ries, Leuven, 1980 (= Acta Orientalia Belgica, 2), 89-102.

II – SPECIAL SUBJECTS

(in the order of the chapters)

CHAPTER 1

Baines, John, Egyptian Twins, *Orientalia* 54 (1985), 461-482.

Brunner-Traut, Emma, Gravidenflasche. Das Salben des Mutterleibes, in: *Archäologie und Altes Testament.* (= Festschrift Kurt Galling). Herausgegeben von A. Kuschke und E. Kutsch, Tübingen, 1970, 35-48.

Brunner-Traut, Emma, Die Wochenlaube, *Mitteilungen des Instituts für Orientforschung* 3 (1955), 11-30.

Bulté, Jeanne, Talismans égyptiens d'heureuse maternité. "Faïence" bleu vert à pois foncées, Paris, 1991.

Cole, Dorothea, Obstetrics for Women in Ancient Egypt, *Discussions in Egyptology* 5 (1986), 27-33.

Erman, Adolf, *Zaubersprüche für Mutter und Kind. Aus dem Papyrus 3027 des Berliner Museums* = Abh. Kon. Preuss. Akad. der Wiss. zu Berlin, Phil.-hist. Klasse 1901, 1-52; reprinted in: Adolf Erman, *Akademieschriften,* Leipzig, 1986, I, 455-504.

Pinch, Geraldine, Childbirth and Female Figurines at Deir el-Medina and el-'Amarna, *Orientalia* 52 (1983), 405-414.

Wenger, Josef, A Decorated Birth-brick from Abydos, *Egyptian Archaeology* 21 (Autumn 2002), 3-4.

CHAPTER 2

Brunner-Traut, Emma, Das Muttermilchkrüglein. Ammen mit Stillumhang und Mondamulett, *Die Welt des Orients* 5 (1969-1970), 145-164.

Maruéjol, Florence, La nourrice: un thème iconographique, *Annales du Service des Antiquités de l'Égypte* 69 (1983), 311-319.

Roehrig, Catharine Hersey, *The Eighteenth Dynasty Titles Royal Nurse (*mn't nswt*), Royal Tutor (*mn' nswt*), and Foster Brother/Sister of the Lord of the Two Lands (*sn/snt mn' n nb t3wy*),* Dissertation University of California at Berkeley, 1990.

CHAPTER 3

Vogelsang-Eastwood, Gillian M., *Tutankhamun's Wardrobe. Garments from the Tomb of Tutankhamun*, Rotterdam, 1999.

CHAPTER 4

David, A. Rosalie, Toys and Games in the Manchester Museum Collection, in: *Glimpses of Ancient Egypt. Studies in Honour of H.W. Fairman.* Edited by John Ruffle, G.A. Gaballa and Kenneth A. Kitchen, Warminster, 1979, 12-15.

Tooley, Angela M.J., Child's Toy or Ritual Object?, *Göttinger Miszellen* 123 (1991), 101-111.

Janssen, Rosalind M., Rectification: a case of moveable arms, *Göttinger Miszellen* 126 (1992), 83-86.

CHAPTER 5

Decker, Wolfgang, *Sport und Spiel im Alten Ägypten*, München, 1987.

Touny, A.D. and Wenig, Steffen, *Der Sport im Alten Ägypten*, Leipzig, 1969.

CHAPTER 6

Brunner, Hellmut, *Altägyptische Erziehung*, Wiesbaden, 1957.

Fischer-Elfert, Hans-Werner, Der Schreiber als Lehrer in der frühen ägyptischen Hochkultur, in: *Schreiber, Magister, Lehrer. Zur Geschichte und Funktion eines Berufsstandes.* Herausgegeben von Johann Georg Prinz von Hohenzollern und Max Liedtke, Bad Heilbrunn, 1989, 60-70.

Foster, John L., Some Comments on Khety's Instruction for Little Pepy on his Way to School (Satire on the Trades), in: *Gold of Praise: Studies on Ancient Egypt in Honor of Edward F. Wente.* Edited by Emily Teeter and John A. Larson, Chicago, 1999, 121-129.

Williams, Ronald J., Scribal Training in Ancient Egypt, *Journal of the American Oriental Society* 92 (1972), 214-221.

La scuola nell' antico Egitto, Museo Egizio di Torino, 1997.

CHAPTER 7

Bailey, Emoke, Circumcision in Ancient Egypt, *Bulletin of the Australian Centre for Egyptology* 7 (1996), 15-28.

Grunert, Stefan, Nicht nur sauber, sondern rein. Rituelle Reinigungsanweisungen aus dem Grab des Anchmahor in Saqqara, *Studien zur altägyptischen Kultur* 30 (2002), 137-151.

Jonckheere, Fr., La circoncision des anciens Égyptiens, *Centaurus* 1 (1951), 212-234.

Montserrat, Dominic, Mallocouria and Therapeuteria: Rituals of Transition in a Mixed Society?, *Bulletin of the American Society of Papyrologists* 28 (1991), 43-49.

Spiegelman, Mark, The Circumcision Scene in the Tomb of Ankhmahor: the First Record of Egyptian Surgery?, *Bulletin of the Australian Centre for Egyptology* 8 (1997), 91-100.

Wit, Constant de, La circoncision chez les anciens Égyptiens, *Zeitschrift für ägyptische Sprache und Altertumskunde* 99 (1972), 41-48.

CHAPTER 8

Feucht, Erika, Gattenwahl, Ehe und Nachkommenschaft im alten Ägypten, in: *Geschlechtsreife und Legitimation zur Zeugung.* Herausgegeben von E.W. Müller, Freiburg/München, 1985, 55-84.

CHAPTER 9

Schmitz, Bettina, *Untersuchungen zum Titel* s3-njśwt *"Königssohn"* (= Habelts Dissertationsdrucke. Reihe Ägyptologie, Heft 2), Bonn, 1976.

CHAPTER 10

Feucht, Erika, The *ḥrdw n k3p* Reconsidered, in: *Pharaonic Egypt. The Bible and Christianity.* Edited by Sarah Israelit-Groll, Jerusalem, 1985, 38-47.

CHAPTER 11

Meskell, Lynn, *Archaeologies of Social Life*, Oxford, 1999.

Meskell, Lynn, *Private Life in New Kingdom Egypt*, Princeton and Oxford, 2002.

Meskell, Lynn, *Object Worlds in Ancient Egypt. Material Biographies, Past and Present*, Oxford and New York, 2004.

INTRODUCTION – Gerontology

Bond, J., Coleman, P. and Peace, S. (eds.), *Ageing in Society*, London, 1997.

Jamieson, A. and Victor, C. (eds.), *Researching Ageing and Later Life*, Buckingham, 2002.

Tinker, Anthea, *Elderly People in Modern Society*, London, 1997.

Victor, Christina, *Old Age in Modern Society*, London 1994.

CHAPTER 12

Omlin, Jos. A., *Der Papyrus 55001 und seine satirisch-erotische Zeichnungen und Inschriften*, Turin, 1973.

Ryder, Arthur W., *The Panchatantra. Translation from the Sanskrit*, Chicago and London, 1972.

CHAPTER 13

Riefstahl, Elizabeth, An Egyptian Portrait of an Old Man, *Journal of Near Eastern Studies* 10 (1951), 65-73.

Ward, William A., Neferhotep and his Friends, *Journal of Egyptian Archaeology* 63 (1977), 63-66.

CHAPTER 14

Aufderheide, Arthur C., *The Scientific Study of Mummies*, Cambridge, 2003.

Cockburn, A., Cockburn, E. and Reyman, T.A. (eds.), *Mummies, Disease and Ancient Cultures*, Cambridge, 1998.

Ikram, S. and Dodson, A., *The Mummy in Ancient Egypt. Equipping the Dead for Eternity*, London, 1998.

Podzorski, Patricia V., *Their Bones Shall Not Perish. An Examination of Predynastic Human Skeletal Remains from Naga-ed-Dêr in Egypt*, New Malden, 1990.

Taylor, John H., *Unwrapping a Mummy. The Life, Death and Embalming of Horemkenesi*, London, The British Museum, 1995.

CHAPTER 15

Demarée, Robert J., *The Ꜣẖ-iḳr n Rꜥ-Stelae. On Ancestor Worship in Ancient Egypt*, Leiden, 1983.

James, T.G.H., *The Hekanakhte Papers and Other Early Middle Kingdom Documents*, New York, 1962.

Sweeney, Deborah, Women Growing Older in Deir el-Medina, in: Dorn, A. and Hofmann, T. (eds.), *Living and Writing in Deir el-Medine. Socio-historical Embodiment of Deir el-Medine Texts* (= Aegyptiaca Helvetica), Basel, 2006, 135-153.

Whale, Sheila, *The Family in the Eighteenth Dynasty of Egypt*, Sydney, 1989.

CHAPTER 16

Gardiner, Alan H. and Sethe, Kurt, *Egyptian Letters to the Dead. Mainly from the Old and Middle Kingdom*, London, 1928.

Keith-Bennett, Jean L., Anthropoic Busts II. Not from Deir el Medineh Alone. *Bulletin of the Egyptological Seminar* 3 (1981), 43-71.

Schneider, Hans D., *Een Brief voor Anchiry. Scenes uit een Egyptisch huwelijk*, Zutphen, n.d.

CHAPTER 17

Janssen, J.M.A., On the Ideal Lifetime of the Egyptians, *Oudheidkundige Mededelingen uit het Rijksmuseum van Oudheden te Leiden* 31 (1950), 33-43.

CHAPTER 18

Blumenthal, Elke, Ptahhotep und der 'Stab des Alters', in: Osing, J. and Dreyer, G. (eds.),
Form und Mass (= Festschrift Gerhard Fecht), Wiesbaden 1987, 84-97.

Hassan, Ali, Stöcke und Stäbe im Pharaonischen Ägypten bis zum Ende des Neuen Reiches,
Munich/Berlin, 1976.

Shehab el-Din, Tahia, The Title 'Staff of Old Age', Discussions in Egyptology 37 (1997), 59-
64.

CHAPTER 19

Blumenthal, Elke, Die 'Gottesväter' des Alten und Mittleren Reiches, Zeitschrift für
ägyptische Sprache und Altertumskunde 114 (1987), 10-35.

Brunner, Hellmut, Der 'Gottesvater' als Erzieher des Kronprinzen, Zeitschrift für ägyptische
Sprache und Altertumskunde 86 (1961), 90-100.

Habachi, Labib, God's Fathers and the Role They Played in the History of the First
Intermediate Period, Annales du Service des Antiquités de l'Égypte 55 (1958), 167-190.

Kees, Hermann, 'Gottesväter' als Priesterklasse, Zeitschrift für ägyptische Sprache und
Altertumskunde 86 (1961), 115-125.

CHAPTER 20

Gardiner, Alan H., Adoption Extraordinary, Journal of Egyptian Archaeology 26 (1940), 23-
29.

Kanawati, Naguib, Polygamy in the Old Kingdom?, Studien zur altägyptischen Kultur 4
(1976), 149-160.

Simpson, William Kelly, Polygamy in Egypt in the Middle Kingdom, Journal of Egyptian
Archaeology 60 (1974), 100-105.

Stol, M. and Vleeming, S.P. (eds.), The Care of the Elderly in the Ancient Near East, Leiden
1998.

[Chapter by Andrea McDowell: Legal Aspects of Care of the Elderly in Egypt to the End of
the New Kingdom]

CHAPTER 21

Janssen, Rosalind, Growing old disgracefully at Deir el-Medina, Ancient Egypt 5 (3)
(December/January 2004/2005), 38-44.

Janssen, Rosalind, The Old Women of Deir el-Medina, Buried History = Journal of the
Australian Institute of Archaeology 42 (2006), 3-10.

CHAPTER 22

Blackman, Aylward M., The Stela of Nebipusenwosret: British Museum No. 101, Journal of
Egyptian Archaeology 21 (1935), 1-9.

Gohary, Jocelyn, Akhenaten's Sed-Festival at Karnak, London, 1992.

Hornung, Erik und Staehelin, Elisabeth et al., Studien zum Sedfest (= Aegyptiaca Helveltica I),

Geneva, 1974.

Kaiser, Werner, Die kleine Hebseddarstellung im Sonnentempel des Neuserre, *Beiträge zur ägyptischen Bauforschung und Altertumskunde* 12 (= Festschrift Herbert Ricke), Wiesbaden, 1971.

Simpson, William K., The Sed Festival in Regnal Year 30 of Amenemhet III and the Periodicity of the Festival in Dynasty XII, *Journal of the American Research Center in Egypt* 2 (1963), 59-63.

Spalinger, Anthony, Dated Texts of the Old Kingdom, *Studien zur altägyptischen Kultur* 21 (1994), 275-319.

Toivari-Viitala, Jaana, *Women at Deir el-Medina. A Study of the Status and Roles of the Female Inhabitants in the Workmen's Community During the Ramesside Period*, Leiden, 2001.

[Chapter 5: Elderly Women: Aspects of Old Age, Illness and Death]

Uphill, Eric P., The Egyptian Sed-Festival Rites, *Journal of Near Eastern Studies* 24 (1965), 365-383.

CHAPTER 23

Brack, Annelies und Artur, *Das Grab des Tjanuni. Theban Nr. 74*, Mainz am Rhein, 1977.

Gomaà, Farouk, *Chaemwese. Sohn Ramses' II. und Hoherpriester von Memphis*, Wiesbaden, 1973.

Habachi, Labib, Setau the Famous Viceroy of Ramses II and his Career, in: *Sixteen Studies on Lower Nubia*, Cairo, 1981, 121-138.

Lichtheim, Miriam, *Ancient Egyptian Autobiographies*, Freiburg/Göttingen, 1988.

Lloyd, Alan B., The Inscription of Udjahorresnet. A Collaborator's Testament, *Journal of Egyptian Archaeology* 68 (1982), 166-180.

Posener, G., *La première domination perse en Égypte*, Cairo, 1936.

Simpson, William Kelly, *The Terrace of the Great God at Abydos: The Offering Chapels of Dynasties 12 and 13*, New Haven and Philadelphia, 1974.

POSTSCRIPT

Janssen, Rosalind M., *The First Hundred Years. Egyptology at University College London 1892-1992*, London, 1992.

Murray, Margaret, *My First Hundred Years*, London, 1963.

List of Tombs at Thebes

The following abbreviations occur in the text, and precede the official number assigned to a particular tomb in the Theban necropolis by the Antiquities Service. The numbering follows no topographical order.

TT	=	Theban Tomb (private)
KV	=	(tomb in the) Valley of the Kings
QV	=	(tomb in the) Valley of the Queens

TT		TT	
1	Sennedjem	93	Kenamun
3	Pashedu	95	Mery
4	Ken	96	Sennefer
7	Ramose	97	Amenemhat
11	Dhuti	100	Rekhmire
29	Amenemope	107	Nefersekheru
34	Montuemhat	109	Min
38	Djeserkareseneb	131	Useramun
39	Puyemre	155	Antef
40	Huy (Amenhotep)	162	Kenamun
45	Dhout/Dhutemhab	192	Kheruef
49	Neferhotep	212	Ramose
50	Neferhotep	216	Neferhotep
52	Nakht	217	Ipuy
55	Ramose	224	Ahmose-Humai
60	Senet	226	Heqareshu
61	Useramun	250	Ramose
64	Heqaerneheh	252	Senimen
69	Menna	260	User
74	Tjanuni	289	Setau
78	Haremhab	290	Irinefer
79	Menkheperresonb	343	Benia-Paheqamen
81	Ineni	335	Nakhtamun
82	Amenemhat	359	Anherkhew the
85	Amenemhab-Mahu		Younger
87	Nakhtmin	367	Paser
88	Pekhsukher		
90	Nebamun		

KV		QV	
42	Sennefer?	46	Imhotep
46	Yuya and Thuyu		
48	Amenemope		

Index

Page numbers in italic refer to illustrations

Wadi Hammamat, 163, 244
Wadi Magharah, 244
Wadi Shatt er-Rigal, 204, *212*, 212, 246
Wadzmose (Prince), 99, *102*, 105
Wepwawet (god), 234, 261
Wepwawet-aa (priest), 225
Wilbour Papyrus, 182
William III (King), 216

Winlock (Herbert), 174
Yuya (KV 46) (commander of the chariotry), 107, 217, 250

Zeus, 1

The Authors

Rosalind Janssen is Senior Honorary Research Fellow, UCL Collections, University College London. She was previously Lecturer in Egyptology and before that a curator at the Petrie Museum of Egyptian Archaeology, UCL. She now teaches Egyptology for Birkbeck, the WEA, and the University of Reading. The holder of an MSc in Gerontology from the University of London, she also lectures on the sociology of ageing at Birkbeck. Her MA in Lifelong Learning and a PGCE in Adult and Community Education have recently resulted in a post as Visiting Lecturer at the City Lit. She has published widely, particularly in the fields of Pharaonic textiles and dress (*Egyptian Textiles* [1986]), and the history of Egyptology.

Jac. Janssen is Emeritus Professor of Egyptology at the University of Leiden (The Netherlands). He is a specialist in the social and economic aspects of New Kingdom Egypt, especially in relation to the workmen's community at Deir el-Medina. He has written many books and articles on the subject, including his famous *Commodity Prices from the Ramesside Period* (1975), a publication referred to in Holland as "the price Bible". His latest investigations have resulted in a book entitled *Donkeys at Deir el-Medîna* (2005). He has also published various hieratic papyri in the British Museum, including his *Grain Transport in the Ramesside Period* (2004).